MANUAL OF ETHNOGRAPHY

MANUAL OF ETHNOGRAPHY

Marcel Mauss

Translated by
Dominique Lussier

Edited and introduced by
N.J. Allen

Durkheim Press/Berghahn Books
New York • Oxford

148842978

First published in 2007 by

in association with
Berghahn Books the Durkheim Press

www.berghahnbooks.com

©2007 Durkheim Press

Translated from the French: *Manuel D'Ethnographie*
Published by: Editions Payot & Rivages
© 1967, Editions Payot
© 2002, Editions Payot & Rivages

Ouvrage paru avec le concours du centre national du livre du ministère de la culture et de la communication.

This book was published with the assistance of the Centre National du Livre of the French Ministry of Culture and Communication.

Library of Congress Cataloging-in-Publication Data

A C.I.P. catalogue record for this book is available from
the Library of Congress

British Library Cataloguing in Publication Data

A catalogue record for this book is available from the British Library
Printed in the United States on acid-free paper

978-1-84545-321-3 (hardback)

Contents

Preface and Acknowledgements

Several years ago Bill Pickering of the British Centre for Durkheimian Studies in Oxford became convinced that Mauss's *Manuel d'ethnologie* should be translated into English. The reasons will be apparent from the Introduction to this book. The project for such a translation has taken longer to realise than was originally expected, owing to financial and contractual difficulties.

Although the resulting book has been very much a group effort, I was asked to be responsible for the production of the final text. In that capacity I should like to thank most warmly the translator, Dominique Lussier, who, after completing his doctorate at the Institute of Social and Cultural Anthropology, undertook the formidable task of wrestling with the long and difficult text.

My thanks are also extended to others, some of whom are not closely associated with the Centre: Jeremy Coote, Paul Dresch, Josep Llobera, Anne de Sales, Nathan Schlanger, Susan Shelton; however, responsibility for defects lies with the editor.

N.J.A.

Abbreviations and Conventions Used in Notes

AAA	American Anthropological Association
AMNH	American Museum of Natural History
Am. Anth.	*American Anthropologist*
AS	*Année sociologique*
ARBAE	Annual Reports of the Bureau of American Ethnology (Washington)
EPHE	École Pratique des Hautes Études
FMNH	Federal Museum of Natural History
HERE	*Hastings Encyclopaedia of Religion and Ethics*, Edinburgh, 1908–1926
IAE	*Internationales Archiv für Ethnographie*, Leiden.
JAI, JRAI	*Journal of the (Royal) Anthropological Institute*
Jesup	publication associated with the Jesup North Pacific Expedition 1897–1903
JSA	*Journal de la Société des Américanistes*
Mem.	Memoir(s)
RHR	*Revue de l'histoire des religions*
SAJS	*South African Journal of Science*
Smiths. Inst.	Smithsonian Institution
trans.	translated into French from English (if no other source language is given)
U.	University
USNM	United States National Museum
Z. (f.)	*Zeitschrift (für)*

Numerals following an oblique (/) indicate number, part or fascicle; those following a colon indicate pages. For technical reasons the bibliographies that in the French are appended to the end of some (but not all) chapters are here presented as endnotes at the end of the chapter.

Introduction

N.J. Allen

Marcel Mauss (1872–1950) was the leading social anthropologist in Paris between the world wars, and his *Manuel d'ethnographie*, dating from that period, is the longest of all his texts. Despite having had four editions in France,[1] the *Manual* has hitherto been unavailable in English and is seldom cited in the Anglophone literature. This contrasts with his essays, longer and shorter, many of which have long enjoyed the status of classics within anthropology, and some of which (notably *The Gift*) have even transcended disciplinary boundaries.[2] It is easy to think of reasons why the *Manual* has been neglected; for a start, its title might suggest that it is no more than a textbook for ethnographers. However, to see the book in that light would be to misunderstand its place in Mauss's life and oeuvre.

Mauss's apprenticeship into academic life had been supervised by his austere and self-disciplined uncle, Emile Durkheim, who was then (the 1890s) engaged in conceptualising and institutionalising his vision of the discipline of *sociologie* – the science of social facts or social phenomena. Uncle and nephew collaborated closely, both in their own writing and in building up a circle of contributors to their new yearbook, the *Année sociologique*. It was here that Mauss published, not only some substantial and seminal research papers, but also more than 450 reviews of books or articles. The steady development of *sociologie* was rudely interrupted by the Great War, during which many of the younger 'Durkheimians' were killed, and Durkheim himself died.

After demobilisation, Mauss took on the task of carrying forward his uncle's vision. With this in mind he revived a proposal he had made in 1913 and helped to found the Institute of Ethnology at the University of Paris (December 1925).[3] The new science needed facts, lots of them, accurate and well organised, from as many societies as possible, and especially from premodern societies. Those who could or might contribute to collecting them needed advice on how to go about it, and each year Mauss delivered a course of more than thirty lectures entitled 'Instructions in descriptive ethnography, intended for travellers, administrators and missionaries'. These lectures form the basis of the *Manual*.

When he lectured, Mauss had some notes in front of him but spoke without reading from them, relying heavily on his encyclopedic memory. By 1935 he had in mind to write up the lectures for publication, but in view of his work habits, his failing health, and the circumstances of the German occupation (Mauss was Jewish), one doubts that he would have done so. Fortunately, however, one of his students, Denise Paulme (later a distinguished Africanist), took shorthand notes of the lectures and produced a typescript, which in a letter of 1943 Mauss claimed to be 'tidying up'. Since Paulme records that particular sections of the course were specially elaborated in successive years (technology and aesthetics in 1935–36, jural phenomena and finally religion in the next two years), presumably she had to synthesise notes taken from different courses; but this is not clear to me – nor is the process by which the bibliography was compiled.[4] What we can be sure of is that if Mauss had written the *Manual* rather than speaking it, the text would not have been as we now have it, and in particular it would have included the final chapters mentioned in the Plan for the Study of a Society (Chapter 2). Like a number of Mauss's works, the *Manual* remains unfinished: the lecture series were not completed by the end of the academic year.[5]

The *Manual* does not fall readily under any recognised genre. Is it a textbook? Writing a textbook usually implies summarising a body of established knowledge belonging to a recognised academic discipline – an uncreative activity perhaps, even a commercial one, somewhat set apart from research. Or is it, as Paulme suggests, a questionnaire, like the others listed at the end of Chapter 1? But despite points of contact with both these genres, it is better seen in more personal terms: it is the culmination of a life's work.

The *Manual* does not cover all of Mauss's interests – his audience heard nothing of his research on the nation or on Bolshevism, let alone of his moderate left-wing political activism (cooperative societies, journalism, etc.). But it starts off from the foundational Durkheimian vision of a science of social facts (Chapter 1), and draws in most of Mauss's other papers and those of his Durkheimian friends and colleagues. Obviously too, it draws in, massively, the factual knowledge he acquired as a reviewer. It may be less obvious, though it is stated in the first sentence, that the *Manual* aims to teach not only how to observe social facts but also how to classify them – a long-standing preoccupation that originated in part with the question of how to organise the *Année sociologique*. However, the retrospective and summational aspect should not be overemphasised. The life's work of a successful academic has to point forward, and the lectures were intended to stimulate and inspire the next generation. Some of the students found them too difficult – the richness of content dizzying, the connections of thought elusive – but the courses were well attended (89 students in 1928–29, 145 five years later), and Mauss the man was regarded by many with unusual affection and admiration; and among the admirers many went on to make major contributions. Mauss was deeply conscious of scholarship as a collective and cooperative undertaking.

The charismatic impact of the original lectures is inevitably diminished by passage through print, and modern anthropologists, while acknowledging Mauss's erudition and historical significance, will wonder about the relevance of the text today. So much has changed – in the postcolonial world, in anthropology and the culture of academe, and in the situation of fieldworkers with their laptops and internet access. On his first page Mauss claims to be limiting himself to the societies found in the French colonies 'and others of the same stage'; but the world of bounded tribal societies and colonies has more or less vanished. Nevertheless, certain questions remain and will remain, whether or not one has any interest in undertaking ethnography.

One perennial question is: what is a society? Chapter 3 opens with a formal definition, but the implicit answer is more revealing. A society is an entity that exhibits the types of social phenomena treated in the chapters that follow (supplemented by those that should have followed). Mauss's classification of social phenomena may or may not be accepted, but it is carefully thought out, proceeding from more material to less material and more conceptual; it aspires to be complete, and is well supplied with definitions. Moreover, Mauss regretted the abandonment of the unitary Durkheimian conception of *sociologie*, which was in the process of splitting into a sociology that ignored tribal populations and a social anthropology that (at that time) emphasised them.[6] He himself had started out helping his uncle with the statistics for his book on suicide in Europe, and the split between the disciplines made no sense to him – in practice, the *Manual* often ignores it. In any case, we were all once tribals, and no serious student of the social dimension of humanity can ignore them.

Another enduring question concerns the range or variety of societies that humanity has created and experienced. From this point of view, Mauss's period was a good one in which to be working. The scrappy and amateurish quality of much nineteenth-century ethnography was giving way to more professional work, but the quantity of literature was still such that a person of Mauss's intellectual ability was able to gain familiarity with a good proportion of it.[7] The *Manual* refers occasionally to colonialism (probably less than would now seem appropriate), but the corrosive effects of globalisation on the linguistic and cultural diversity of the world were still relatively limited. Since Mauss's day ethnographic literature has naturally become not only more voluminous, but also in general more sophisticated (for instance, in its emphatic recognition of the inevitable element of subjectivity that is involved), but it is debatable whether it has brought to light significant dimensions of cultural difference that escaped Mauss's attention. In telling his students what to look for, Mauss was at the same time telling us how rich and how varied 'simple' societies really are.

Above all, however, Mauss is demonstrating to us how he thinks about social facts: he is exhibiting an adventurous and well-supplied anthropological curiosity at work. Although his range of insights cannot be reduced to a single formula, the central preoccupation is perhaps with categories and classifications[8]– not, for instance, with causes, individual motives or adaptive advantage. Members of society think things and do things, and we need to know what sort of things these are. Thus, at some time and place, people swim in a particular way or adopt a particular posture while awake but resting. Mauss was pleased when he understood that these were techniques – ones that used not tools or machines but the body itself – and should be classified alongside other techniques. Similarly, the fortifications of Marrakesh are simply 'a huge piece of sun-dried pottery' (p. 34). But the taxonomic aspect of Mauss's curiosity should not be oversimplified, as if every ethnographic observation belonged under a single heading. The essence of a fieldworker's task may lie in weighing up how much religious value is superimposed on a technical act (p. 160).

It may seem odd, at least within the contemporary Anglophone world, that instruction for ethnographic fieldwork should be given by someone who, though he often drew on personal observations of the life around him, never carried out anything resembling sustained fieldwork. But it is not clear that a writer of ethnography is necessarily better equipped to write a manual than is a reader of ethnography. If Mauss had done fieldwork, no doubt he would have given more space to the epistemological and methodological problems of extracting 'facts' from ethnographic experiences. On the other hand, he would have had less time to assimilate the fieldwork done by others and would have risked overemphasising the idiosyncrasies of one particular region. In principle, as Mauss shows, anthropologists can think themselves into a variety of geographically remote cultures just as historians can into temporally remote ones. Indeed he constantly passes from the one to the other and back again – here is another disciplinary divide that he treated as insignificant. One should remember that his first teaching job was as a Sanskritist, giving courses on early Indian religions including Vedanta and Yoga.

This brings up another reason why the *Manual* has not been translated sooner, namely the demands it makes on both reader and translator. Some of the difficulties arise from its original orality, which has had various effects – among them the stylistic awkwardness of passages in ordinary prose alternating with list-like nouns or noun phrases. Another is represented by occasional mishearings or misunderstandings, e.g. the meaningless *cinécisme* in place of *synécisme* (p. 22). But difficulties also arise from the density of the thought (there are passages where the argument is far from easy, for instance in the chapter on aesthetics), and from Mauss's polymathy. These problems come on top of ordinary translation problems such as semantic mismatches between French and English (e.g. *juridique* – legal or jural, *oral* – oral or verbal), and what if anything to do about male-biased language or outdated ethnonyms. Where it seems appropriate, I have addressed such problems by inserting glosses or footnotes in square brackets, but it is a matter of judgment how far to go along that path.[9] Overall, the text remains something of a challenge.

The *Manual* can be read in many ways – as a textbook, a questionnaire, an epitome of the anthropological understanding of one of the best minds to have studied the subject. It is also, of course, a historical document reflecting the state of knowledge sixty-five years ago: I leave it to readers, including students, to reflect on the gap between then and now. Finally, however, the *Manual* is a classic, a contribution to thought about human society and one that continues to provoke and inspire. The careful reader will find many little gems. For instance, one to savour is: 'The fieldworker should make a practice of systematically rupturing all the divisions that I am expounding here from a didactic point of view' (p. 181).

N.J.A.

References

Allen, N.J. 2000. *Categories and Classifications: Maussian Reflections on the Social*. Oxford: Berghahn.
Cohen, M. 1947–48. Review of M. Mauss, Manuel d'ethnographie. *Bulletin de la société de linguistique de Paris* 44: (comptes rendus) 14–15.
Evans-Pritchard, E. 1954. Introduction to M. Mauss, *The Gift* (trans. I. Cunnison), London: Cohen and West.
Fournier, M. 1994. *Marcel Mauss*, Paris: Fayard. (Abridged English trans.: *Marcel Mauss: a Biography*. Princeton U. Press.)
Fournier, M. and J.C. Marcel (eds) 2004. 'Présences de Marcel Mauss'. *Sociologie et sociétés* 36/2.
James, W. and N.J. Allen (eds) 1998. *Marcel Mauss: a Centenary Tribute*. Oxford: Berghahn.
Mauss, M. 2003. *On Prayer*. New York, Oxford: Durkheim Press/Berghahn.
——— 2005. *The Nature of Sociology, Two Essays*. New York, Oxford: Durkheim Press/Berghahn.
——— 2006. *Techniques, Technology and Civilisation*, ed. and intro. N. Schlanger. Oxford: Berghahn.
Mergy, J. (ed.) 2004. Mauss et les durkheimiens: textes inédits. AS 54/1.
Métais, P. 1947. Review of M. Mauss, Manuel d'ethnographie. *J. de la Société des Océanistes* 3/3: 155–156.
Tarot, C. 1999. *De Durkheim à Mauss: l'invention du symbolique: sociologie et sciences de religion*. Paris: La Découverte/MAUSS.
——— 2003. *Sociologie et anthropologie de Marcel Mauss*.

Notes

1. 1947 (211 pp.): 1967 and 1989 (264 pp.): 2002 (362 pp., the text used by the translator). An electronic version can be found at http://classiques.uqac.ca/classiques/mauss_marcel/manuel_ethnographie/manuel_ethnographie.html; the 1926 date given on its coverpage is erroneous.
2. The bibliography relating to Mauss is selectively reviewed in James and Allen (1998: 248–251). Recent English translations are Mauss (2003), (2005), and (2006). Cf. also Tarot (1999) and (2003), Mergy (2004) and Fournier and Marcel (2004).
3. The following remarks are based on the biography by Fournier (1994: see esp. pp. 502–512, 548, 596–606, 724, 749), and the prefatory material by Paulme in the printed French editions of the *Manual*.
4. Notes made by three other students have been preserved but apparently have never been used. The bibliography was attributed to Paulme by Cohen (1947–48), but presumably she was helped by Mauss.

5. The likely content of the missing chapters is suggested by Mauss's articles cited in Chapter 2, note 2. Moreover, some of the existing content might have been revised. During the period 1942–44, influenced by Leenhardt and Granet, Mauss was still rethinking the relationship between mana and totemism, and the nature of clans (Métais 1947).

6. The fact that the secondary literature on Mauss has been dominated by non-anthropologists has contributed to the relative neglect of the *Manual*.

7. I have not found in Mauss's work any reference to Russian-language ethnography (despite the implication of Evans-Pritchard 1954: viii). Of the bibliographic entries in the *Manual* some 30% are in French, 45% in English, 20% in German, 2% in Dutch, plus the occasional rarity (one in Spanish, a few in Latin). Exact figures would have little meaning, but the total number of references is of the order of 650. The book that is cited most often is *Gens de la grande terre*, by M. Leenhardt, co-founder of the Institute of Ethnology.

8. Allen (2000) elaborates on this point and tries to develop some of Mauss's lesser-known insights.

9. I have called attention to factual errors that I noticed, but have not searched for them; and similarly, I have made some improvements in the bibliography, but without checking every item. I have retained Mauss's paragraphing, judging it to be deliberate and meaningful.

1

Preliminary Remarks

The course of lectures published here mainly seeks to address practical questions; it is meant to teach how to *observe* and classify social phenomena.

One might see in these lectures simply an accumulation of useless details. But in fact, each of the details mentioned here presupposes a whole world of studies. Thus biometry, seeking to establish the curve of age distribution, presupposes statistics and probability theory; the study of colours requires, together with some knowledge of physics, familiarity with the Chevreul and Broca scales. What may appear to be futile detail is in fact a digest of principles.

The field of study here is limited to societies inhabiting the French colonies and to societies of the same level – which seems to exclude all the so-called *primitive* societies.[1]

Within these limits, we shall provide the instructions that are necessary to compile in scientific fashion the archives of these more or less archaic societies.

The purpose of ethnology as a science is the observation of societies; its aim is the knowledge of social facts. It creates a record of those facts and, when appropriate, establishes their statistical pattern; it publishes documents offering the greatest possible certainty. The ethnographer must strive for exactness and thoroughness; he or she must have a sense of the facts and of the relations between them, a sense of proportions and articulations.

Intuition plays no part whatever in the science of ethnology, which is a science of facts and statistics. Sociology and descriptive ethnology require one to be at once an archivist, a historian, a statistician ... as well as a novelist able to evoke the life of a whole society. It is not that intuition on the one hand, and theory on the other, are useless here. But their use must be restricted; one must know their value and their dangers.

The true role of theory is to inspire research aimed at testing its claims. Science has its fashions, which change, but which make it possible to understand the facts. Theory possesses a 'heuristic' value, a value as prompting discovery. The false *a prioris* of the Vienna School have served to produce a rich harvest of facts.

The young ethnographer embarking upon fieldwork must be aware of what he or she knows already, in order to bring to light what is not yet known.

Social facts are first of all historical; they therefore cannot be reversed and cannot be rejected – for example, the flight of an army (How many soldiers? What have they done? The role of the leaders, of the men, etc.). Furthermore, a social phenomenon is simultaneously a phenomenon of facts and ideals, of rules. In the Sèvres factory, nine vases out of ten are discarded; elsewhere, ten pieces out of ten are retained. In this latter case, there is no longer any difference between the fact and the norm.

Statistics enable us to reach a degree of certainty that the discipline of history has never yet known. We don't know the number of slaves in Rome, but we know how many there are in Timbuktu.

Let me add that ethnography is not a historical science in the true sense, in that the facts do not present themselves in chronological order. Ethnology nonetheless includes a historical component, which will consist in establishing the history of human settlement: Negro race, yellow race, etc. Currently, ethnology is only in a position to reconstruct such history within narrow limits; but our science has no future unless we keep to a method that is reliable and prudent.

In fact, comparative ethnography will be valuable only if it is based on comparison between facts, not between cultures. Only the criterion of the archaeological fact, embedded in the strata of the soil, will give a value to criteria that are cultural, linguistic, etc. For instance, the existence of the panpipe everywhere around the Pacific (cultural criterion) only allows one to affirm the existence of a community of civilisation in that it is backed up by discoveries of ceramics (archaeological criterion). It then becomes legitimate to state that the whole periphery of the Pacific, like the whole periphery of the Mediterranean, has participated in a single civilisation.

Difficulties of Ethnographic Investigation

Subjective difficulties. The danger of superficial observation. Do not 'believe'. Do not believe you know because you have seen, and do not make moral judgements. Do not be astonished. Do not lose your temper. Try to live in, and as a member of, the indigenous society. Choose your evidence carefully. Be wary of *lingue franche*, pidgin French, English, etc. (disadvantages of the use of words like fetish, tom-tom, etc.). Many specific terms remain untranslatable. If you must have recourse to interpreters, use the philological method as much as possible, and have the phrase itself written down without using a conventional system. A good example is provided by the work of Callaway on the Amazulu.[2] This method produces raw documents that can be worked over at leisure in a study.

There remain the *material* difficulties, to be overcome in the following ways:

1) By calling on informants who are well aware of the topic and have a good memory of events; these can be found among legal or religious officials, priests, fetish owners, heralds, and the like.
2) By collecting and cataloguing objects. In a great many cases, objects are proof of social facts. A catalogue of charms is one of the best methods to draw up a catalogue of rites.

Principles of Observation

Objectivity is the goal in the written account as well as in observation. Say what you know, all that you know and only what you know. Avoid hypotheses, whether historical or of any other kind, which are useless and often dangerous.

A good method of working is the philological method, which consists in first of all gathering tales, collecting the variants (an example is the first edition of Grimm's fairy tales); then the traditions specific to each village, each clan and each family. The task is often enormous and very complex. Note the studies already carried out, those which remain uncompleted, and all the difficulties concerning the individuals involved.

Exhaustiveness. No detail can be neglected (for example: while studying the preparation of a magic potion, note the conditions under which each magic herb is picked). Not only must everything be described, but this must be followed by in-depth analysis, which will reveal the quality of the observer and his or her sociological insight. Study lexicography, the relations between noun classes and objects, jural phenomena, heraldic animals, etc. To the list of ritual prohibitions add examples of casuistic decisions concerning these prohibitions.

In the account of the observations one strives for clarity and sobriety. Plans, diagrams and statistics may with advantage replace several pages of text. For kinship, present family trees, together with the kinship terms. Write at length only while producing evidence; bring in multiple testimonies, and do not be afraid either of telling anecdotes or explaining in detail the trouble taken in order to make observations. Every fact mentioned must always be localised (give the name of the village, family and individual observed) and dated. Give all the circumstances surrounding the observation, unless the observer has spent a long period in the area.[3]

Notes

1. Only the Australian aborigines and the inhabitants of Tierra del Fuego should be counted as genuine primitives. The Negroes are at the same stage as the one at which Tacitus observed the Germans. People living in the forests of Cameroon and Congo have a bow which is said to be most primitive; in fact, it is not a tool, but a machine, one presupposing a stage that is already quite advanced. The Moï of Annam [in Central Vietnam] are archaic and proto-historic. The whole of Northern Asia has a great civilisation, Eskimoid and Mongoloid.

2. Callaway, H., *The Religious System of the Amazulu*, London and Cape Town, 1870.
3. **General Presentations**. Bastian, A. *Die Culturländer des alten Amerika*, Berlin, 1878–89, 3 vols. Boas, F., *Handbook of American Indian Languages* ... Washington, 1911–12; *The Mind of Primitive Man*, New York, 1911. Buschan, G., *Illustrierte Völkerkunde* ... Stuttgart, 1922–26. (Vol. 1: *Amerika, Afrika*; vol. 2: *Australien und Ozeanien*; vol. 3: *Europa*). Deniker, J., *Les races et les peuples de la terre*, 2nd ed, Paris, 1926 (retains its value). Goldenweiser, A.A., *Early Civilisation, an Introduction to Anthropology*, New York, 1922 (a good book). Graebner, F., *Methode der Ethnologie*, Heidelberg, 1910; 'Ethnologie' in G. von Schwalbe and E. Fischer (eds), *Anthropologie*, Leipzig, 1923. Haddon, A.C., *Les races humaines et leur répartition géographique*, revised and corrected by the author, trans. A. van Gennep, Paris, 1927. Kroeber, A.L., *Anthropology*, New York and London, 1923. Lowie, R.H., *Traité de sociologie primitive*, trans., Paris, 1935; *Manuel d'anthropologie culturelle*, trans., Paris, 1936. Marett, R.R. *Anthropology*, London, 1914. Montandon, G., *L'Ologénèse culturelle*, Paris, 1928 (a book to be used with caution). Powell, J.W., 'Sociology, or the Science of Institutions', *Am. Anth.* 1, 1899: 475–509, 695–745. Preuss, K.Th., *Lehrbuch der Völkerkunde*, Stuttgart, 1937. Ratzel, F., *Völkerkunde*, Leipzig, 1885–1890 ('inimitable', but lacks references and seldom indicates sources). Schurtz, H., *Völkerkunde*, Leipzig, Vienna, 1903. Thurnwald, R., *Die menschliche Gesellschaft in ihren ethno-soziologischen Grundlagen*, 3 vols., Berlin and Leipzig, 1931 (the three volumes are fairly accurate, tabulating material for each group of a civilisation; good ideas, in difficult German). Tylor, E.B., 'Anthropology' in 14th edition of *Encyclopaedia Britannica*. Separate edition: *Primitive Culture*, London, 1921. Vierkandt, A., *Handwörterbuch der Soziologie*, Stuttgart, 1931. Waitz, T., *Anthropologie der Naturvölker*, Leipzig, 1877. Wundt, W. *Völkerpsychologie*, Leipzig, 1900–09. Wissler, C., *Man and Culture*, London and New York, 1923.

Questionnaires. Foucart, G. *Questionnaire préliminaire d'ethnologie africaine*, Société de Géographie, Cairo, 1919. Keller, A.G., *Queries in Ethnography*, New York, London and Bombay, 1903. Labouret, H., *Plan de monographie régionale*, Outre-Mer, Paris, 1st term, 1932: 52–89. Luschan, H. von, *Anleitung für ethnographische Beobachtungen und Sammlungen in Afrika und Oceanien*, 3rd ed., Berlin, 1904. Mauss, M., 'Fragment d'un plan de sociologie descriptive...' [Chapter 2, n. 2]. *Notes and Queries of the Royal Anthropological Institute of London*, 5th ed., 1929. Powell, J.W., *Questionnaire*, ARBAE 20 (1898–99), 1903 [erroneous; if the intended reference is to pp.xxix–cxcvii of the *Report of the Director*, it belongs above under **General Presentations**]. *Questionnaire de l'École Française d'Extrême-Orient*, text by M. Mauss, explanation by Colonel Bonifacy. Read, C.H., *Questionnaire ethnographique pour le Congo*, British Museum, London, 1904.

2

Methods of Observation

The method of extensive fieldwork, consisting in seeing as many people as possible within a given area and time, was widely practised at the period when all that mattered was to collect as fast as possible the largest possible number of objects that were likely to disappear, and to stock the museums that had just been created.

The extensive method in many cases makes it possible to identify a location where a more intensive study can be carried out later; qualified travellers can, in the course of a large-scale survey, decide which tribes are to be selected for a return visit. The great danger of such a method lies in its superficiality. The ethnographer is only passing through, and the objects have often been assembled prior to his or her arrival. Another danger, for example, is the use of inadequate linguistic criteria; the drawing of a good linguistic map, necessary as it is, is dependent on the progress that needs to be made in the study of every non-European language.

Undertaking extensive ethnography is necessary, but do not think it is sufficient. The professional ethnographer will certainly prefer to practise the intensive method.

Intensive ethnography consists in the detailed observation of a tribe; the observation should be as complete and as thorough as possible, omitting nothing. A professional ethnographer working really well can, by himself, in the space of three or four years, carry out the more or less exhaustive study of a tribe. The study of the Zuñi alone, to which Cushing and also the Stevensons gave their lives, consists of seven quarto volumes from the Bureau of American Ethnology. This work, which is extraordinarily dense, is still not enough.[1]

The instructions in the present book are intended for administrators or colonists who lack professional training. Instructions of the 'working knowledge' type, they should make it possible to carry out work intermediate between an extensive and intensive study of a target population – a study which respects the proportions of the various social phenomena.

Ethnographic studies too often look like caricatures. A student with an interest in museography will effectively neglect everything apart from material culture. Another, specialising in religious studies, will only notice cults, shrines and magic. A third will only observe social organisation, and will only talk of clans and totems. And yet another will only look for economic phenomena.

Above all the observer must respect the proportions of the various social phenomena.[2]

Table 2.1 Plan for the study of a society

I. Social morphology	Demography
	Demography
	Human geography
	Technomorphology
II. [Social] Physiology	Techniques
	Aesthetics
	Economics
	Law
	Religion
	Sciences
III. General phenomena	Language
	National phenomena
	International phenomena
	Collective ethology

I. *Social morphology.* Every society is first of all composed of an aggregate. The study of the society as human aggregate and of its distribution across territory constitutes what is called social morphology, which includes *demography* and *human geography*, the importance of which seems to be fundamental. Human geography is supplemented by *Technomorphology*.

II. *Social physiology* studies phenomena in themselves and in their movements – no longer as the material aggregate on its physical substrate. Under this heading, according to their degree of materiality, I include *techniques*, that is to say all the productive arts and crafts without exception: war is the art of destroying; it is an industry or a technique. Techniques culminate in *sciences*; there is no 'primitive' society completely lacking in sciences. *Aesthetics* still remains quite material, even when it seems very much a matter of the ideal. Three-dimensional esthetics differs little from techniques. Progressively less material, yet governed by collective representations – very clear ones – *economics* offers, by way of disengagement from materiality, the currency that is found all across America and Africa. Above economics and ruling over it is *law*, which consists of jural and moral phenomena. Higher still are *religion* and *science*, the latter recurring at this level.

III. *General phenomena.* After *language* come morphological phenomena (for example, society in general), *national phenomena* (permeability of the tribe), and then *international phenomena*:[3] nomadism presupposes that a society can go and pasture its sheep in territory that does not belong to it, or can take them across foreign tribes, which in turn implies international peace, often over considerable distances. Civilisation is an international phenomenon. The study of civilisational phenomena comprises the study of the internationalisation of certain customs and certain tools. Finally come general phenomena proper, or *collective ethology*, the study of national character or national political psychology and their relations with psychological phenomena and biological phenomena (for example, the relation between cleanliness and mortality – or non-mortality).

The present book contains a certain number of museographic instructions in the context of social morphology on the one hand, and technique and esthetics on the other. The inventory of economic, legal and religious objects will complete the plan of a museographic study, which is contained implicitly in these pages. The museography of a society consists in establishing its material archives: museums are archives.

Methods of Observation

Ideally, an expedition should not set out without its geologist, botanist and ethnographers. This would reduce general expenses. On the other hand, a biological anthropologist can show himself to be a sociologist, and anyone can be a first-rate museographer. So, set out *as a group*.

One will often find local people who are very well informed about the indigenous society: missionaries, settlers, non-commissioned officers, not necessarily French, who generally live in far closer contact with the natives than do the high-class French. This is how the Roman Empire was formed, thanks to centurions living with Gauls.

The first working method is to start a *fieldwork diary*, in which the work done during the day should be written up each evening: cards filled out and objects collected should be entered in this diary, which will become an easily consultable catalogue.

The fieldworker should draw up an *inventory* as progress is made in assembling the collection. In addition, each object collected should have its detailed *descriptive card*, in duplicate. Fieldwork diary, inventory and cards are the first components of the study.

For many travellers, the essence of the ethnographic work will consist in assembling and organising collections of objects. This is part of museography, which includes also the methods of conserving and exhibiting these objects. All studies of diffusion pointing towards civilisational strata are still usually classified under museography.

As a branch of descriptive ethnography, museography records the products of a civilisation – all its products, in all their forms. Creating collections of objects is important both practically and theoretically. Practically: collections are central to knowledge of a country's economy; more than any other type of study, technology can put us on the track of industries. Show the ingenuity of invention, and the type of ingenuity you observe. The theoretical importance comes from the presence of instruments typical of a particular type of civilisation. Museum collections remain the only means for writing [their] history.

The collector should attempt to construct logical series, assembling if possible all the varieties of a single object in terms of size, form, etc., without being afraid of duplicates or triplicates. Localisation is absolutely mandatory; without it, the object cannot find a place in any museum. Identify the area over which the collected object is in use.

Each object should be labelled with a number, written in ink, referring to an inventory and to a descriptive card providing information on the use and manufacture of the object. The descriptive card should be accompanied by several annexes, in particular a photographic annexe and, if possible, a film annexe. A drawing should be attached whenever it is necessary to show how the object is manipulated, or the associated movements of hand or foot (for example: for a bow and arrow, it is important to determine the method of shooting in terms of the position of arms and fingers at various moments; likewise, a loom is incomprehensible without documentation of how it works). Furthermore, one should note with utmost precision the period of use, since certain objects have a seasonal existence (one does not use secateurs in winter). Moreover, an object may be used only by men, or only by women. Finally, one should try to explain objects whose value is not only technical, but religious or magical; such and such a decoration may correspond to a mark of ownership, or a trademark, etc.

The drawing of distribution maps should be undertaken only towards the end of the investigation, preferably on a return trip, when it is felt that everything has been seen. It is the culmination of a study and not a method in itself. But the fieldworker can set himself a similar objective in the course of his work, for instance if he visits successively two fractions of a single society.[4] To achieve such a goal presupposes that one has observed all of the tribe's objects. Thus Professor Maunier, using statistics, has been able to establish that the canon for the Kabyle roof is Greek rather than Latin.[5]

The inventory method, used for building up collections of objects, is itself only one of the means of material observation used in the study of social morphology.

Methods of observation are divided into material methods of recording and observing objects on the one hand, and moral methods of observing and recording on the other. The distinction is rather arbitrary, since social life includes neither purely material elements nor purely moral elements. Music – the art of the ideal and impalpable – also acts upon people in a most physical way.

Material methods of observation include the following:

Morphological and Cartographic Method

The first point in the study of a society is to know who one is talking about. To this end, produce a thorough mapping of the society under scrutiny, which is often a difficult task: a society always occupies a given territory, which is not the territory of the neighbouring society. Note carefully all the locations where you have witnessed the presence of individuals belonging to the group being studied, with the number of locations and the number of inhabitants living in each, and all this for the different moments of the year. No good sociological enquiry can cover less than one year. The mapping of a society is the mapping of its content. It is not enough to know that a particular tribe numbers two or three thousand; each individual of the three thousand must be located. For this purpose the method to use is census-taking in relation to a map: make an inventory of the people in each place, the number of houses in each village, the number of huts and granaries; map these granaries and houses. An extended family in the Sudan is generally a joint family, living around a courtyard; a clan lives in one ward of a settlement. In this way one can see high-level social structures appearing immediately in material form. If possible, use aerial photography.

Geographic and demographic statistics are indispensable and form the foundation of any work. The dwelling of each extended family and of each of the clans constituting the society can thus be discriminated. At this point one can draw up the inventory of each house and each sanctuary, from foundations to rooftop. This was how M. Leenhardt discovered the totem in the rooftop of the Kanak hut.

The inventory should be complete, with exact localisation by age, sex and class. The inventory method includes the precise mapping of each place where objects are gathered: plans of houses and, where relevant, plans of storeys. The material recording thus obtained will form the essential basis of all other work.

For this recording of material culture, one should again employ the photographic method and the phonographic method.

Photographic Method

All objects must be photographed, preferably without arranging them artificially. Telephotography will make it possible to capture significant *ensembles*. Do not use the same equipment in warm countries and in cold countries, nor the same films; and in principle, develop the films as soon as possible.

One can never take too many photographs, provided they are all supplied with a commentary and precise localisation: time, place, distance. These data should appear both on the film and in the diary.

Motion pictures will allow photographing life. Do not forget stereo vision. Dramatic performances have been filmed in Liberia, and the transhumance of entire tribes in the Algerian Aurès.

Phonographic recording and motion picture recording with sound allow us to observe the moral world as it enters into the purely material world. So let us now move on to the problem of moral recording.

Phonographic Method

Phonograph recording and motion pictures with sound. One should record not only the human voice, but also all the music, noting the tapping of feet and clapping of hands. For each recording transcribe the texts, and if possible, provide a translation together with a commentary. It is not enough to record; one must be able to reproduce.

Philological Method

This method presupposes knowledge of the indigenous language. A full compilation should be made of all the texts heard, including the most commonplace, which are never the least important. Transcribe all the indigenous words in the indigenous language, separating the words – which is very difficult. One should notate the music; when dealing with tonal languages, notate the tones just as you would any other phonetic sign.

Try to find indigenous anthologies, and informants capable of giving a sustained tradition. A good way to learn the native language is to turn to the bibles already published in countries where Christian missionaries are active. For each text give as many commentaries as possible by local people – not by yourself. Leenhardt's books provide excellent examples.[6]

In principle, philological recording should be verbatim, the French word appearing under the native word; no violation of the native syntax, and no elegant flourishes in your translation: the most direct rendering, unintelligible though it may seem. To this line-by-line translation attach a text in French that gives the gist of the original. Any word that is added should appear in square brackets; mark the line number of the native text in the French text. Ensure complete alignment of the texts.

Record versification, indicating longs and shorts, stressed and unstressed.

Besides Leenhardt's books, Thalbitzer's[7] studies on Greenland and Malinowski's on the Trobriands[8] are very good examples of this type of publication.

Sociological Method

This method consists above all in the history of the society. A good model of the type of work to follow is Montagne's book on the Berbers.[9]

One can write the detailed history of a tribe going back at least three or four generations, that is to say a hundred to a hundred and fifty years. To this end, question the old people, whose memory is usually perfectly precise. One will find extreme precision in geographic localisation.[10]

A society is always made up of sub-groups: tribes, clans and phratries. Each of these groups must be studied in its own right; military organisation should not be forgotten. All this is recorded in the memory of those concerned. One should therefore study family histories. A better method is the genealogical method, which consists in compiling genealogies for all the individuals in the census. The names of relatives and affines should be immediately apparent. Individual histories will intersect; one will know that at one particular time and not at another, this individual called that one his brother.

The autobiographical method, which consists in asking a number of natives to provide their biographies, as used by Radin, gave excellent results.[11] The data obtained in this way should be cross-classified with the help of statistics. Thus the genealogies obtained by Thurnwald in the Solomon Islands show in the figures for deaths more than 8 per cent due to violence.[12] Finally, but only as a final step, one should turn to cross-questioning.

The simultaneous use of these various methods will make it possible to end up not only with the determination of the demographic aggregates, but also with the determination of the place of individuals within these aggregates. This knowledge at the level of the individual is of considerable use.

The ethnographer working in an extensive manner will hardly be able to use these methods. At best, he or she will be able to establish rapport with a few settlers or administrators, who will collaborate with him at a distance and will spot some interesting facts. The advantage of an expedition including several members shows up here quite clearly. The cross-checking that is always mandatory will be easily carried out by three or four colleagues working on different periods of tribal life.

In order to be precise, an observation must be complete: where, by whom, when, how, and why such and such a thing is done or has been done. It is a matter of reproducing the native life, not of stringing together impressions; a matter of constructing sequences of data, not just arrays of facts.[13]

Notes

1. Cushing, F.H., *Outlines of Zuñi Creation Myths*, ARBAE 13 (1891–92), 1896: 321–447; *A Study of Pueblo Pottery as Illustrative of Zuñi Culture Growth*, ARBAE 4 (1882–83), 1886: 467–521; *Zuñi Fetishes*, ARBAE 2 (1880–81), 1883. Stevenson, M.C., *Ethnobotany of the Zuñi Indians*, ARBAE 30 (1908–09), 1915; *The Religious Life of the Zuñi Child: the Sia*, ARBAE 11 (1889–90), 1894; *The Zuñi Indians: their Mythology, Fraternities and Ceremonies*, ARBAE 23 (1901–02), 1904.
2. See Mauss, M., 'Divisions et proportions des divisions de la sociologie', *AS*, n.s., 2, 1924–25: 98–173, and 'Fragment d'un plan de sociologie générale et descriptive: classification et méthodes d'observation des phénomènes généraux de la vie sociale dans les sociétés de type archaïque (phénomènes généraux spécifiques de la vie intérieure de la société)', *Annales sociologiques*, série A/1, 1934: 1–56. See also Brown, A.R., 'The Methods of Ethnology and Social Anthropology', *SAJS* 20: 127–247; and Thurnwald, R., 'Probleme der Völkerpsychologie und Soziologie', *Z. f. Völkerpsychologie und Soziologie* 1925/1: 1–20.
3. [Mauss's adjective *national* means 'pertaining to the society', not 'pertaining to the nation state'.]
4. For an example see Soustelle, J., 'La culture matérielle des Lacandon', *JSA*, 1937.
5. Maunier, R., *La construction collective de la maison en Kabylie*, Paris, Institut d'Ethnologie, 1926.

6. Leenhardt, M., *Notes d'ethnologie néo-calédonienne*, Paris, Institut d'Ethnologie, 1930; *Documents néo-calédoniens*, Paris, Institut d'Ethnologie, 1932; *Vocabulaire et grammaire de la langue houailou*, Paris, Institut d'Ethnologie, 1935; *Gens de la grande terre*, Paris, Gallimard, 1935.

7. Thalbitzer, W., *Légendes et chants esquimaux du Groenland*, trans. from Danish, Paris, Leroux, 1929; see also *The Ammassalik Eskimo: Contributions to the Ethnology of the East Greenland Natives*, Copenhagen, 1923. In two parts; 2nd part, nos 1 and 2. Thuren, H., *On the Eskimo Music*. Thalbitzer, W. and Thuren, H., *Melodies from East Greenland*, no. 3. Thalbitzer, W., *Language and Folklore*.

8. Malinowski, B., notably *Coral Gardens and their Magic*, London, 1935.

9. Montagne, R., *Village et kasbas berbères*, Paris, Alcan, 1930.

10. Study of the Ashanti constitution in Rattray, R.S., *Ashanti Law and Constitution*, Oxford, 1929.

11. See Radin, P., *The Winnebago Tribe*, ARBAE 37 (1915–16), 1923.

12. Thurnwald, R., 'Adventures of a Tribe in New Guinea (The Tjímundo)', in *Essays presented to C. G. Seligman*, London, 1934: 345–360.

13. **Examples of fieldwork methods**. Brown, A.R., *The Andaman Islanders*, London, 1922. *Census of India*: tables and reports. One volume per State; one volume on India as a whole, 1903. Firth, R.W., *Primitive Economics of the New Zealand Maori*, London, 1929; *We, the Tikopia*, London, 1936. Hunter, M., *Reaction to Conquest* Oxford, 1936 (on South Africa). Junod, H.A., *Moeurs et coutumes des Bantous*, Paris, 1936. Malinowski, B., *Argonauts of the Western Pacific*, London, 1922; *La vie sexuelle des sauvages du Nord-Ouest de la Mélanésie*, trans., Paris, 1933. Mills, J.P., *The Lhota Nagas*, London, 1922. Rivers, W.H.R., *The Todas*, London, 1906. Seligman, C.G. and Seligman B.Z., *The Veddas*, 1911. Skeat, W.W. and Blagden, E.O., *Pagan Races of the Malay Peninsula*, 2 vols, London, 1906.

See also, on North America, all the Reports of the Smithsonian Institution of Washington: Reports of the Secretary; Annual Reports of the Bureau of American Ethnology to the secretary of [the same]; Bureau of American Ethnology Bulletins.

3

Social Morphology

By society is meant a *social group, usually named both by itself and by others, whether large or small, but always large enough to include secondary groups – two being the minimum, normally living in a particular place, having its own specific language, constitution and, often, tradition.*

The most notable difficulty, which has to be decided more or less arbitrarily at first, then worked through in the course of the investigation, is the determination of the social group under study. In fact, one should not rely on the name the natives give themselves, a name that most often means 'man', 'noble', etc., or is borrowed from some linguistic idiosyncrasy; in contrast, the names given by outsiders often express contempt. There are two means by which to define the group: settlement area and language.

1) *Settlement area.* The territory shared by a relatively large group of people, who are believed to be united by social bonds, normally indicates a society. However, this criterion is often insufficient – whole countries such as the Sudan are made up of peoples who have been amalgamated since the 12th century. In Dahomey, central royal power, by imposing the payment of tribute, has achieved a unification which is solely political, leaving the subject tribes almost totally autonomous. Elsewhere, the decline of the societies surviving in the interior is sufficiently clear for the territorial criterion to be satisfactory.
2) *Language* is an excellent criterion, but a most delicate one. Delimiting a dialect or a language is very difficult unless one possesses a remarkable gift for philology. In Black Africa, research is complicated by the existence of common roots at the origin of very large groups. Seeking the aid of linguists is therefore advisable.

The use of both these means can provide sufficient delimitation. They can be supplemented by information drawn from jural phenomena, from the spread of central power, from national cults, from frontiers, as well as by information drawn from external signs: dress, hair-style, tattoos, etc. A description of all these signs should be given at the beginning of the text.

The difficulty in determining social groups is explained by the non-existence of the nation in primitive societies. The nation only exists in part of modern Europe, and even here sociology shows that the degree of internal unification is relative. In practice, the ethnographer only observes interactions between groups or temporary groupings, spanning the whole range from infinity to nil. One should thus not picture a Sudanese or Bantu society according to the European type, localised in time and space, with war and peace excluding perfect integration.

In practice, it is advisable to take a population group inside a given society, and within it a limited number of localities obviously sharing a common organisation. The observer with a taste for studying the whole will attach a strict catalogue, place by place, of the phenomena studied.

Once a *map of frontiers* has been drawn, the fieldworker should seek to construct a *statistical map*, location by location, of the society under study. All the locations, whether temporary or permanent, of the various local groups should be indicated on a large-scale plan. Some societies actually have a dual or even a triple morphology. On the map, the eye will immediately take in towns and villages; isolated camps, temporary camps and even temporary villages; and finally, total dispersion, whether temporary or permanent. As is well known, a major difference exists in France between agglomerated villages and dispersed villages. Similarly, all Kabylian villages are agglomerated – they are indeed small towns. Arab villages, in contrast, are often dispersed. Furthermore, peoples can be found who may live alternately in groups and dispersed (phenomena of dual morphology), and again, entire tribes who may be constantly on the move: such is the case with the Dioula in West Africa, and also in part with the Mauritanians. Lastly, pastoral peoples move over long distances as the pastures become depleted. Nomadism can be observed on the spot.

In many cases, the notion of instability can be replaced by the notion of a fixed route: even the Gypsies have their itineraries. One should therefore record for each group, not only its location at a given moment, but the whole area it covers in the course of its journeys, which are often lengthy. The Peul in West Africa, the Masai in East Africa, and generally all pastoral peoples living side by side with non-pastoral peoples, will be serfs and peasants in one place, while elsewhere they form the dominant class.

To the map of each village should be attached:

- *A map of the agricultural land used for grazing and transhumance.* The map should show everything relating to the fauna, flora and mineralogy, and more generally, everything that conditions social life, including human things: cultivated land, pastures, hunting grounds, game tracks, fishing spots. Note the seasons for hunting, fishing, gathering, and the variation of the locations according to the seasons;

- A *geological map*, which will make it possible to fix the number of square kilometres available for a given population to inhabit;
- A *map of dwelling places*: huts, tents, caves, boats ...

The house-by-house study yields the demography of the society under scrutiny: large parts of the social structure are immediately apparent.

The study of a group of tents will always yield results that are interesting in relation to studies of the family. The plan itself should be accompanied by statistics organised by houses, or by canoes (for instance, among the Maori).

Thus, as soon as it is undertaken, such a study no longer appears merely as a cartographic exercise, but already as a detailed study.

Then comes the study of technomorphology, that is to say of all the relations between technology and environment, between environment and techniques. The geographical basis of social life should be observed as a function of techniques: sea, mountain, river, lagoon ...

Is it on account of special needs that people adapt to a particular terrain in a particular way, and very often seek it out? Or, conversely, is it because people find themselves on a certain terrain that they have adapted to it? The two questions arise together. I am convinced that the population factor and the technical factor for a given people determine everything, *given the environment*. Given the environment, a change in techniques can completely change the adaptation to the terrain. One example is the iron-mining industry in Lorraine, which was made possible not by the presence of iron pyrites, but by the discovery of methods allowing the mining of this ore. For centuries, charcoal was used for processing iron since people did not know the technique of blast furnaces, which make it possible to use coke as fuel. Elsewhere, the long-distance journeys of the Eskimos would be impossible without the *umiak* (a large boat propelled with paddles).

All of this requires (though without enabling us to predict it beforehand) dual or triple morphologies, something that cannot be predicted beforehand. The Eskimos have a dual morphology.[1] The inhabitants of the Rhine Valley in Switzerland have a triple morphology: vinyards and fields in the valley, fields on the mountainside, extensive pastures on the heights – these make them at once horticulturalists and pastoralists, with total migration of the whole village in summer and, throughout the year, partial migrations of men who go and look after their vines.

Once the population agglomerations, their density, and their relations with the environment have been defined, one should study the relations between agglomerations. These relations are inscribed on the soil, and depend directly on techniques. They are first of all the communication routes (use maps and aerial photographs) on which the intensity of traffic as well as the length of journeys should be measured. A river can be a total barrier when it is in spate, while being on the contrary an excellent trade route, superior to any land route, when the water level is low. The sea is not an obstacle: all forms of water provide waterways or seaways, and have done so from remotest times.

Note the location of the various agglomerations that have succeeded each other in the region since the appearance of metals; neolithic sites in particular show sophisticated toolkits: clearing undergrowth with a stone axe and otherwise than by using fire is a major problem when creating lines of communication.

The cartographic study of the society is now completed – a study that is at once static and dynamic, human and non-human.

Variations across time remain to be studied. A society lives and dies; its age can be measured – a major principle, first stated by Durkheim, and still too often neglected. A society can die because all its members die – for instance, the Tasmanians; it can also be pulverised at a given time – for instance, the Lobi of West Africa – and reconstitute itself on different foundations; or else it can fuse with other societies so as to form a synecism.[2] Rome is a synecism of several towns: Alpine, Latin, Etruscan and Greek. Jerusalem, the city of Semitic purity, once sheltered ancient Canaanites, Israelites and Hittites. The description of Carthage in [Flaubert's novel] *Salammbô* is defective on this point.

Population movements will need to be studied in historical perspective, as the history of migrations, which often cover long distances (for instance, the Polynesian migrations). In some cases, the search for a better world can impel a whole population to migrate.

Study in detail the processes of emigration and immigration – that filtering of one society into another. It raises the whole immense colonial problem, and the problem of manpower as well.

So much for movements at the ground level: they are governed by war, peace, population, technomorphology and natural phenomena, in particular biosociological ones. The dominant factor in the population history of Africa is the presence of the tsetse fly, and the arrival of the pachyderms which bring the fly with them. Natural equilibria, both of plants and animals, epidemics, and epizootics relate to the final questions to be asked on this topic.

Finally, a statistical and demographic investigation in the strict sense will complete the study of social morphology. One should draw up statistics at the level of the house, but now taking time into account; at the level of the family (note absentees), and at the levels of clan and tribe (when the society includes several tribes). Thereby one will measure fecundity, birth rate according to sex, and morbidity and mortality, carefully distinguishing deaths by accident or violence from natural deaths.

For everything concerning morphology and adaptation to the terrain, one should use the country's geological map as a starting point, which will immediately settle the problem of water. It is usually said that the presence of a water source is indispensable for a settlement. But what is a water source? A place where water comes to the surface naturally? Not necessarily. The best well-diggers in the world are those from southern Algeria and southern Tunisia, who construct real underground tanks, fed by pipes which are also underground. Similarly, the techniques of terrace cultivation, especially irrigation, can greatly improve crop yields. The Pygmies, those so-called 'primitives', have terraced fields in the Philippines. This issue of the adaptation of the terrain and of the life of a society on its terrain – this life so full of movement – is of capital interest. Every society lives in an environment larger than itself and certain fundamental elements of social life can normally be explained by the presence of another society living on the frontier of the society in question. Even among the Australian Aborigines, even among the Tasmanians, there are 'us' and the others. Therefore, avoid individual explanations: the foreign observer will never know what is the cause of a phenomenon; his or her task is limited to recording the phenomenon in question.

In all of this, the relations between the most material phenomena and the most spiritual ones are constantly in play: an example is the admirable work of Hoernlé on the category of water among the Nama Hottentots-turned-Bushmen.[3]

One never knows where a social phenomenon will lead: a society may pack up and depart as a whole, having heard rumours of a better world elsewhere. So, never forget the moral while studying the material, and vice versa.[4]

Notes

1. Mauss, M.. 'Essai sur les variations saisonnières des sociétés Eskimo'. *AS* 9, 1904–05.
2. [*Cinécisme* in the French is a mistake for *synécisme*.]
3. Hoernlé, R.F.A.. 'The Expression of the Social Value of Water among the Nama of South West Africa'. *SAJS*, 1923: 514–526.
4. **Social morphology.** Vidal de la Blache, P. and Gallois, L. (eds). *Géographie universelle*. Paris, 15 vols. Gourou, P., *L'homme et la terre en Extrême-Orient*, Paris, 1940. Mauss, M., 'Les civilisations: éléments et formes'. *Centre international de synthèse*, première semaine. 2nd fasc., Paris, 1930: 81–106. Ratzel, F., *Politische Geographie*, Munich and Leipzig, 1897 (analysis by P. Vidal de la Blache, 'La géographie politique', *Annales de géographie*, 1898: 97–111); *Raum und Zeit in Geographie und Geologie*, Leipzig, 1907: *Anthropogeographie*, 1. Stuttgart, 1899; 'Le sol, la société et l'état', *AS* 3, 1898–99: 1–14. Simmel, G. 'Über räumliche Projectionen soziales Formen', *Z. f. Sozialwissenschaft*, 1903. Sion, J., 'Note sur la notion de civilisation agraire', *AS*, ser. E/2, 1937: 71–78. Vidal de la Blache, P., *Tableau de la géographie de la France*, in Lavisse, E., *Histoire de la France depuis les origines jusqu'à la Révolution*, 1/1, Paris, 1903. All the studies of Albert Demangeon in the *Annales de Géographie*. The works that have appeared in the collection 'Le Paysan et la Terre' (Gallimard).

4

Technology

The history of technology – of the study of techniques – is a recent one: the studies launched by the Encyclopaedists were not pursued by their successors. The Pitt Rivers Museum in Oxford, the Horniman Museum in a London suburb, and the Cologne museum offer excellent examples of the history of techniques.

Techniques are to be defined as *traditional actions combined in order to produce a mechanical, physical, or chemical effect, these actions being recognised to have that effect.*

It will sometimes be difficult to distinguish techniques from:
1) the arts and fine arts, since aesthetic activity and technical activity are on a par as regards creativity. In the plastic arts, no differentiation can be established other than the one that exists in the belief system of the artist;
2) religious efficacy. The difference lies entirely in how the native conceives of the efficacy. It is therefore necessary to estimate the respective proportions of technique and magical efficacy in the native's mind (e.g. poisoned arrows).

The combination of techniques constitutes industries and crafts. Techniques, industries and crafts, taken together, constitute the technological system of a society, which is essential to it. A correct observation of this system will have to respect the different proportions of its constituents.

Absolute precision is indispensable in the observation of techniques. The most insignificant tool should be named and located: by whom is it used, where was it found, how is it used and for what purpose, does it have a general purpose or a special one (e.g. the use of a knife)? It should be photographed as it is used, together with the object on which it is used, or with its end product; the photographs will show the various stages of production. The industrial system to which the object belongs should be identified; the study of a single tool normally implies the study of the craft as a whole.

Finally, the position of crafts in relation to one another conditions the state of society. The mistake of Karl Marx is that he believed the economy to condition technology: the converse is true.

Investigation and collection will always go hand in hand. Duplicates are essential, since, for instance, the same fabric must be studied from several angles: weaving, spinning, embroidering, ornament, etc.

Investigation and classification can take various approaches. Starting from a logical viewpoint leads to the setting up of series, the study of types, and the study of style. The technological viewpoint will lead for instance to the study of the axe, but not to the study of all weapons indiscriminately. Lastly, the perspective of industry and craft will make possible a living description of the society: describing a dinner service will include the history of its manufacture and of the conditions under which it is used.

Techniques of the Body[1]

Some techniques involve only the presence of the human body, but the actions they bring about are nonetheless traditional ones, tried and tested. The sum of bodily habits (*habitus du corps*) is a technique that is taught, and whose evolution has not yet come to an end. The technique of swimming improves day by day.

Body techniques should be studied with the aid of photography and if possible with slow-motion cinema. The study of body techniques should be divided, according to age, into techniques dealing with:
- *childbirth* (position during delivery, handling of the child at birth, cutting of the umbilical cord, attention given to the mother, etc.);
- *breast-feeding* (posture of the breast-feeder, how the child is held).
- Weaning is an important moment, which often signals the definitive physical separation of mother and child.
- The study of *techniques among children* will include the study of the cradle, then of the whole of a child's life: education of sight and hearing, elimination of certain postures, imposition (or not) of ambidexterity, the study of the use of the left hand; finally, the deformations the child will undergo (deformation of the skull, scarifications, extraction of teeth, circumcision or excision, etc.).

Among adults, the following techniques should be studied in succession:
- *rest while awake*: standing, on one leg, lying down, on a bench in front of a table ...
- *rest while asleep*: standing; lying down on a bench; use of the pillow; of the head rest (apparently localised between 15° and 30° of latitude); use of the hammock.
- The study of *bodily movements* should include *movements of the whole body*: do people crawl, do they walk on all fours? The gait will vary according to whether clothes are sewn or draped.
- Breath and *breathing* differ while running, dancing or performing magic; the rhythm of breathing should be noted, together with the associated stretching of arms and legs.

- *Running* will cover movements of the feet and arms, and the endurance of the runners. Study *dance*; and *jumping*: long jump, high jump, pole vault, etc. How does one take off? How does one climb [a tree]: with a belt, with spikes, or gripping with arms and legs? ...
- *Swimming* is entirely determined by tradition. How do people start off, how do they dive? Do they swim using a board, or a beam?[2] Swimming races on a turtle's back are held all over the Pacific.
- How do people carry out *movements requiring force*? How do they push, pull, lift, and throw?
- Note the *use of fingers and toes*; conjuring tricks and legerdemain (using the armpit, the cheek ...).
- *Gymnastics* and *acrobatics* can be the object of detailed study.
- In relation to the care of the body, note whether washing is done with or without soap (what is soap made of?). What are the procedures for excreting: how do people spit, urinate and defecate? The study of perfumes and cosmetics, with the collection of catalogued samples, should not be left out.
- The division of life according to the *timetable* followed by the natives will yield interesting results: some societies stay up late at night while others do not. Full moon nights are almost always festive nights.
- Finally, *reproductive behaviour* should be studied, including the complications caused by deliberate mutilations,[3] and noting the presence or absence of sodomy, lesbianism and bestiality.

General Techniques with General Uses

Techniques, strictly speaking, are generally characterised by the presence of an instrument. 'Instrument' here includes all categories of instrument. The basic classification in this matter remains that of Reuleaux,[4] who divides instruments as follows:

- *Tools.* The tool, which is usually conflated with the instrument, is always simple, consisting of a single piece of matter. Examples of tools are the cold chisel, wedge, lever.
- *Instruments.* An instrument consists of a combination of tools. An example is the axe, which in addition to the metal head includes a handle serving as lever; a knife fitted with a handle is an instrument, in contrast to a chisel; an arrow is an instrument.
- *Machines.* A machine consists of a combination of instruments. For example, the bow comprises the wood of the bow, the string, and the arrow.
  Starting from the Palaeolithic Age, humanity can easily be divided up according to the eras implied by this classification. Thus the Tasmanians did not know of axes, which were possessed by the Australians. This does not mean that the Tasmanians had remained entirely at the Chellean stage: they are Aurignacians, but without knowledge of the axe: their biface was hand held.[5]

Table 4.1 Classification of Techniques

	physico-chemical (fire)	
General techniques with a general use	mechanical	tool
		instrument
		machine
Special techniques with a general use, or General industries with special uses[6]	basketry	
	pottery	
	rope manufacture and esparto goods	
	glues and resins	
	dyes and decoration	
Specialised industries with special uses[7]	consumption (cooking, drinks)	
	simple acquisition (gathering, hunting, fishing)	
	production	stockbreeding
		agriculture
		mineral industries
	protection and comfort	dwelling
		clothing
	transport and navigation	
	pure techniques. Science (medicine)	

The transition from tools to instruments, from the Lower Palaeolithic (Chellean and Acheulean periods) to the following eras, corresponds to one of the most significant upheavals to have rocked humanity.

The third era of humanity is the era of the machine, a combination of instruments. A bow, a trap, a boat with oars, such as the Eskimo *umiak*, are all machines. The Upper Palaeolithic is the great age of development of machines.

Finally, the sum total of techniques implied by the use of various machines converging towards the same goal constitutes an industry or craft: hunting implies bows, traps and nets; fishing implies a boat and fishing tackle.

Some industries can reach an extraordinary level of complexity, e.g. the pharmacopoeia, or certain agricultural techniques: the use of poison is a sign of the perfecting of techniques, just as the preparation of manioc involves several processes to remove the poison.

Mechanical Techniques

General principles of observation. Any object must be studied (a) in itself; (b) in relation to its users; and (c) in relation to the whole of the system under scrutiny. The mode of manufacture will be the subject of extensive investigation: is the raw material local or not? Some calcites were transported over considerable distances; the search for flint deposits is typical of the entire Palaeolithic and Neolithic eras; several Australian tribes travel six hundred kilometres to fetch ochre. The same questions need to be asked if the object is made of softwood, or of hardwood. Sometimes, too, the tool is imported ready-made. Study the different stages of manufacture, from the raw material to the end product. Then study similarly the mode of use and the production of each tool.

Tools

In the history of the beginnings of humanity no examples are known of humans who are wholly devoid of tools. *Sinanthropus* himself is found in association with a certain pre-Mousterian toolkit, linked with Chellean and pre-Chellean toolkits. Humankind enters history already equipped: as soon as humans appear, tools are there.

The main tools are classified as follows:

- *Weight and impact tools*. One example is a club. The stick with a star-shaped stone typical of Polynesia is an instrument; and the Australian spear, cast with the aid of a thrower, is a machine. A Chellean pick is sometimes a tool of weight and impact, sometimes a point.
- *Friction tools*: grattoir, scraper.
- *Piercing tools*: knife, brace, etc.

Instruments

The hammer is an instrument, and so is the axe. Since an instrument is a combination of two or several elements, each element should be studied separately, then in their relations.

Instruments can be distinguished as solid combinations (e.g. a knife fitted with a handle) and separable combinations (e.g. the mortar and pestle). A mill in fact consists of two mill-wheels; an anvil on its own is but half an instrument. These elements need first to be isolated, so that subsequently they can be brought together. A nail, a tenon, a mortise, a dowel are tools, but they form parts of instruments.

When the parts are not separate, the fundamental question is how to assemble them: this is where the greatest strength is needed but the least is found. Some assemblages can be made entirely of ropes and creepers: such is the case with Malayans when they are putting together structures; similarly, rope by itself is used by our carpenters for temporary scaffolding. Glues and resins are an important way of joining things: glue is used throughout Central Australia. The Moroccan region is very poor as regards junctions; the only methods known are glue and flour-and-water, and there are no good-quality joins in the woodwork. In Morocco, there are some poor-quality swing-ploughs built with a dowel and that is all. Such observations of detail can serve to characterise a whole civilisation.

The classification of instruments is more or less the same as that of tools, since the useful part of the instrument is a tool.

- *Crushing and pounding instruments*. For instance, the axe (haft, head and junction). There are many ways of fitting the handle of an axe: the main one consists of a curved haft, strongly bound to the head with strings, but other forms are far more complicated: the junction involving a slit haft or an elastic one. The adze is far better represented across the world than the axe proper: the entire Pacific region knows only the adze. A peak seems to have been reached with the Indian axe, which can be found in identical form, made in one piece, in Upper Dahomey (an observation by Graebner).

- *Scissors and pliers.* The history of scissors is displayed at the Deutsches Museum of Nuremberg.
- *Instruments that resist forces.* Anvil, mortar and pestle, dowels and tenons. Glues and resins (see below).
- The file or grater can be a simple tool; or else it can be an instrument with complicated shapes; normally, the file is used on top of another file.

Machines

Together with the spear thrower, one of the most primitive machines – if the expression be allowed – is apparently the trap.[8] Elephant traps in India wholly defy imagination; the Eskimo traps, in which the fur of the animal must not be damaged, are extraordinary. The use of traps, with their interplay between springs, resetting devices, weights and balance implies the knowledge of a certain amount of mechanics; the knowledge remains unformulated, but exists nonetheless.

The bow is probably older than the trap. There are many ways in which the wood and string of a bow can be assembled; they can serve as the basis for a classification.

The simplest form of sling, namely the bolas, is in itself already very complex.

Moreover, a particular set of machines can on its own provide the basis for an industry, e.g. navigation. The boat, equipped with oars or paddles plied by humans, is a machine. Similarly, all scaffoldings are items of machinery. An important question here is that of devices used for lifting. Once a construction is set up, mechanics stop being dynamic and become static.

Sometimes, very complicated machines have developed where detailed work is required. The time element is irrelevant in the making of such machines, which were required for executing very delicate operations of fitting or threading, e.g. working with the brace drill to make coins; or the pump drill throughout the Pacific, especially among the Maoris.

Finally, all the general industries with a general use should be studied according to their raw materials: techniques using stone, wood (including paper), leather, bone, horn ... noting the relative importance of the various techniques in social life. Take account not only of what goes with what, but also of what is missing. It is hardly possible any longer to find in the French countryside a peasant who knows how to mend a metal vessel; villagers simply wait for Gypsies to pass through. A study of cultural areas, carried out only on the basis of arbitrary decisions and failing to take into account what is absent as well as what is present, is an incomplete and poor study.

Fire[9]

Fire is a significant means of protection; it not only produces heat, but also keeps off wild animals. For a very long period of time, fire must in the main have been conserved. So one should first of all study *methods for conserving fire*: firebrands made of twisted straw, torches, fire-covers. Fishermen in Concarneau [Finistère] still carry with them their fire horn, a cattle horn closed at one end and containing some smouldering fern or sawdust; the fisherman blows on the embers to light his pipe.

Location of the fire. The hearth is located sometimes in the doorway, sometimes in the middle of the house. In Tierra del Fuego the natives group their shelters around a shared fire. Chimneys appear only very late, since smoke is not generally felt to be unpleasant.

The study of the *methods of obtaining* fire is of considerable interest, since the discovery of these methods coincides with the appearance of the first machines. Fire can be obtained by friction, compression or percussion.

By *friction*, by systematically rubbing a piece of hardwood (male) in the groove of another piece of softwood (female). The friction can be carried out in various ways: *drilling, sawing, ploughing. Drilling* can be simple, with two cylindrical sticks sometimes handled by two people. The Indians produce fire by this method in less than twenty seconds. Drilling was the method used in India by the Brahmins to rekindle the sacred fire; in Rome it was the only means by which the fire of the Vestal Virgins could be lit. A refinement of drilling with two sticks is drilling with a *string*, practised in Madagascar and among the Eskimos; a string is wound and unwound in turn around the male stick. In the bow drill of the Eskimos a bowstring is wrapped around the male stick; the operator makes the bow move backwards and forwards horizontally, while holding the male stick in place with the aid of a bone cap held between his teeth. And lastly, the pump drill is know by the American Indians. In *sawing* – a method characteristic of Malaysia – the two sticks, male and female, are placed at right angles to each other; the rigid saw is often half a bamboo, while the flexible saw is a creeper. Finally, in *ploughing* – the only method known to the Polynesians – the male part is rubbed backwards and forwards along a groove in the female part.

Fire can also be obtained by *compression*, on the principle of the pneumatic lighter, whereby a piston supplied with tinder is driven violently inside a cylinder, and taken out immediately it catches fire. Europe discovered the pneumatic lighter at the start of the nineteenth century, but it was used much earlier in Indochina and Indonesia. Finally, *percussion* is known to peoples as miserable as the Ona of South America who strike two pieces of iron pyrites one against the other. Of course, the use of matches is very recent.

Study of the methods of obtaining fire should be followed up with study of the various kinds of tinder (willow catkin, birch moss, floss cotton, etc.).

The various *uses* of fire should then be observed. *Methods of heating*: red-hot stones thrown into a container of cold water; heating on shards; ovens (there are various types of oven; the oven is universally known to mankind, at least in the guise of the countryside oven). *Methods of lighting*: brazier, torches, lamps (made of stone, shell, pottery, iron ...). Fire can also be used to split stone; and to soften wood or to harden it. Finally, it plays a part in techniques of pottery and metallurgy.

Myths of the origin of fire.[10] In many societies, the blacksmith appears as the culture hero.

Forge and blacksmith. Blacksmiths, human beings who alongside the secret of fire possess the secret of the transformation of metals, are very often sorcerers and magicians; hence they stand apart in society. Throughout Black Africa, the blacksmith belongs to a distinct caste and is despised, but nevertheless he fulfils the role of a peacemaker. A collection of the various tools of the blacksmith (crucible, bellows, nozzles, etc.) should be supplemented with samples of crude ore, preserved in grease paper, with their exact location; ingots collected at the various stages of casting; and finally, the products of the forge (agricultural implements, arms, jewellery, etc.).

Each one of the diverse operations of modelling, wiredrawing, beating, tempering, soldering, patinating, burnishing, damascening, and niello work can provide scope for thorough inquiry. Distinctions will be made, where necessary, between bronze, copper, brass, tin and zinc ware. Study the technology of precious metals: according to Elliot Smith and Perry, gold is found wherever traces exist of a megalithic industry.

The researcher should carefully gather all the myths concerning the different metals and their alloys (consider their influence on alchemy and metaphysics), as well as the traditional formulae of the blacksmiths.

Finally, the study of metallurgy should lead on to the study of industries using substitute materials – industries of wood and paper, stone, pottery, techniques using bone, horn ...

Instruments may be brought to a very high level of perfection. Among the best blacksmiths in the world are the Gold and other Siberian tribes. German metallurgy was far superior to Roman.

Special Techniques with General Uses or General Industries with Special Uses

Here, with the notion of division of labour, the notion of *métier* or craft specialisation begins to emerge: the French peasant is a general handyman, but craft specialisms exist.

As soon as there is a general technique with special uses there is division of labour: to operate instruments requires a skill that is not necessarily distributed evenly throughout society.

Generally, the division of labour is by sex or age. Naturally it is also by locality, depending on the presence of materials: a village of potters normally settles near a deposit of clay.[11]

The whole range of techniques is not distributed evenly across humanity: the finest basketwork comes from the Far East and America; the best hollow ware is found among the Annamites. Each art must be studied in itself, without considering whether or not it is primitive; the end products do not necessarily vary according to the quality of technology: thus the delicate fabrics of Morocco are made on primitive looms.

Whatever the technique under scrutiny, *all* its products should be collected, and *all* stages in the making of the machine should be studied.

Basketry[12]

The pinnacles of basketry are not reached in Europe, and certainly not in France, where the best basket-makers are Gypsies. The finest basketwork in the world is found in the Far East and Central America, most especially among the Pueblo Indians. Excavations conducted among the cliff dwellers of Central America have yielded curious results: the finest basketry in the world is that found in the deepest archaeological layers.

The study of all basketwork should begin with the raw materials (give both the local and scientific names) and with all its forms, as well as the passage from one form to another. Collect samples of the different stages.

For the principles of description one can use the instructions contained in the *Handbook of American Indians*.[13] There is a good classification in *Notes and Queries on Anthropology*, pp. 245 ff.

Basketwork is made up of two series of elements which are repeatedly brought into contact. In *woven* basketry the two elements are intertwined as they are on a loom; but the materials used by the basket maker are relatively rigid and wide, for instance, leaves of the coconut palm or pandanus, or rods of willow or acacia. A second type, *coiled basketry*, is in fact sewn: on a frame of rods or grasses corresponding to the warp the craftsman makes stitches, using a bone or metal awl. Coiled basketry without a frame cannot be distinguished from a net.

Each one of these main types is subdivided into many categories; we shall list only a few forms of woven basketry. When each thread (or weft) crosses the standards (or warp) regularly, the result is *check work*; standards and threads are indistinguishable once the product is completed. When the weft elements cross at regular intervals more than one warp element, the technique is called *twilled work*; it lends itself to decorative combinations. *Wickerwork* differs from check work in that its warp is rigid. Lastly, in *twined work* two or several thread elements twine around the rigid standards.

Generally, production is entirely by hand, almost without the aid of instruments; it requires considerable dexterity. The movements of the hands should be described, photographed and recorded with a motion camera, but, above all, make sketches. Samples of each type of basketwork should be taken at the three or four main stages of production.

All forms are derivations from elementary forms. The primitive form of the net is the thread, then come the various forms of braiding; plaiting or matting with three or four threads is a superior type of braiding.

The bottom of the basket often is the most difficult part. Is the basket conical or does it have a base? The bottom of a basket can be single, double or triple. Round baskets often have a square bottom made of four triangles joined edge to edge. Study the relationships between the geometrical shapes. From time immemorial a good number of the theorems in plane and solid geometry have been solved by women basket-makers who have no need to formulate them consciously – basketry is often women's work.

After the bottom of the basket, one should study the upsett: how are the risers joined to the base? What of the fastener and, where present, the cover? At each stage provide the ideology of the object; give the description in indigenous terms, including where appropriate the symbolism and mythology of each stage. Lastly, study the decoration. The decoration comes from the presence of elements with different colours; the resulting effects can be striking.

One should then classify the various types of basketry.

Basket: all varieties of baskets, for each and every use: simple or double baskets; baskets with a handle; with or without supporting strings. The edge of the basket should be studied carefully. *The winnowing fan. Matting* plays an important role in some civilisations: the whole of the Pacific region has mats, and the whole of the East has carpets; the tale of the flying carpet exists wherever the mat is known. Finally, *waterproofed* basketwork, in which liquids are stored, serves as a transition towards pottery.

Basketry can also serve a variety of purposes: as sheaths of swords and even as armour in Micronesia, in part of northern Asia and in North-West America. The *hafting* of the great stone axes of Micronesia is made of basketry. Basketry is also used to fashion plaits of hair, head-bands, bracelets and rings, as well as ropes.

Consider the links between basketry and other crafts, especially pottery.

Next comes the question of *fabrics made of fibre*. Roofs made of thatch or of plaited palm fronds or the like can up to a point be regarded as basketry. The observations of Cushing in a short work entitled *Manual Concepts* – observations which deal above all with basketry as the foundation of geometry, have had a decisive role in the study of this topic.

Pottery[14]

Pottery appears to be less primitive than basketry, from which it may partly derive: in a great many cases, the mould of the pot is a piece of basketwork smeared with damp clay and left to dry under the sun in order to make it waterproof. Originally, pottery must have been a substitute on the one hand for basketry, and on the other hand for containers made of stone – the latter necessarily being very heavy.

From an archaeological standpoint pottery is the sign of the Neolithic, or at any rate of very advanced Upper Palaeolithic. Completely lacking in Australia and in Tierra del Fuego, pottery remains very poor in all the Pygmy countries. At present, there is no pottery in Polynesia proper; however, traces of its prior existence can be found in the region. It was probably abandoned partly owing to the influence of oven cooking, a mode of food preparation requiring no fireproof containers. In fact, one of the main purposes of pottery is to create containers for cooking food; waterproofed basketwork in some cases, hollow ware in other cases can substitute for pottery in a region lacking clay soil, even among peoples whose industries are in other respects advanced. One can still find some very primitive societies producing admirable pottery, for instance the Pima of South America with their huge amphorae.[15] Among the most beautiful pottery known is that of the Toukala of Morocco, made with a wheel identical to that of Djerba in Tunisia, which is one of the most primitive known to humanity.

Pottery can be tested by the sound it makes.

The distribution of pottery is easily explained by deposits of clay. Trade in pottery exists almost everywhere, and over fairly long distances.

The investigation of pottery should start with an inventory of domestic and religious objects. A stroll in the market can yield unexpected results. Where does the pot come from? Who made it? Can the husband sell the vessel produced by his wife? See Malinowski's description of pottery markets in the Trobriand Islands.[16]

Production. Who makes the pots? Generally, there is specialisation by locality and gender. Very often the potter is a woman (as among the Kabyle).

Gather samples of earth; to keep the clay moist, wrap it up in damp rags and sticking plaster. Give the indigenous and the scientific name for the clay; where it came from; how it is prepared, and any admixtures. There are clay mines. The whole of South America possesses a myth about kaolin.

In studying the various types of pottery one should first consider pieces simply left to dry in the sun. Pisé is a form of pottery; the whole of Marrakesh's fortifications is but a huge piece of pottery dried in the sun. The extent of this use of sun-dried brick across the world is considerable. Whole granaries can be nothing but simple pieces of pottery. All the terraced houses in Africa, Peru and Mexico are pottery.

Then comes pottery that is fired, either in the open air or in an oven. Handmade pottery can be obtained by *slip casting, moulding,* or *pressing* the pottery body into moulds of fired clay. In each case the main difficulty is to move from the base to the edge, especially so when the object has a base with a particular shape.

In *casting* the craftsman uses an object such as a basket or gourd which he covers with clay, either on the inside or the outside; the mould may be made on purpose or not; it may be destroyed in the firing process or it may be reusable.

The artist moulding his pot starts with a single lump of clay to which he gives the desired shape either without using any instrument or using tools which are generally few and rather simple (mallet, bamboo knife, shell or piece of calabash used as smoother, etc.).

Finally, pressing is the most widespread method: the craftsman prepares slabs of clay that he curves before luting them together by applying pressure. Sometimes a single, long, spiralled slab will provide all the material for the whole pot. Traces of the processes of assembly are removed before firing. Very often, casting, moulding and pressing are used successively in producing a single pot.

The potter's *wheel* may originally have been a fixed support for the lump of clay which the craftsman pugged by making it turn between his fingers; this support (a flattish dish with notches on its edge) became a turning wheel and was fixed on a swivel (thus forming the 'whirler') prior to becoming the potter's wheel proper, simple or double, turned by hand or foot, either by the potter or an assistant.

Throughout the course of the whole process, whether the craftsman uses a wheel or not, one should study the work of the fingers and, if the wheel is used, the work of the feet; notice the return strings.

Drying can take place in the open air or inside the house, in the sun or in the shade. Firing will be carried out with an open-air fire, in a hole in the ground dug for that purpose, or with a true oven. Notice the nature and arrangement of the fuel, and the means used to increase or decrease the amount of air reaching the fire or the pots, so as to modify the degree of moisture, etc.

Decorating is done before or after firing, or both before and after. It can rest entirely on the choice of clay body and the firing conditions (e.g. adding coal dust); it can be the result of burnishing, with a smoother made out of wood, horn, bone or shell, or the result of glazing; it can be the result of impressing, whether with finger or fingernail, with string impressions from a rope (basketwork moulds explain the frequent occurrence of braids or checkwork as decorative motifs), with a piece of cloth or some other object, or with a stamp prepared in advance; it may result from an incision or an excision. Impressed or engraved decoration is sometimes heightened with the aid of white or coloured clays prior to firing or after it. Pottery can also be decorated by means of grooves, by ornaments applied on the surface; by applying a slip, that is a fine layer of white or coloured clay, or a glaze such as haematite, ochre, or graphite; by varnishing with a resin or glue after firing; by applying lead glaze or opaque enamel, with or without colouring; by painting with coloured clay or with the use of other colourants.

Use the philological method, asking for a description in local terms of the entire process of manufacture – including the knacks (*tours de mains*) – and of all the decoration.

Collecting. The classification of pottery is one of the most difficult sorts of classification. Pots could be grouped, using the inventory made locally, in relation to their use. A second classification could distinguish according to form, size and decoration. Here we meet the notion of typology that will recur in the context of art. Some forms are very rare, the most difficult to realise being naturally cubic shapes. Note the myth and ideology associated with every shape and decorative motif. Technical features offer yet another sort of classification: a whole portion of the first wave of Celts possesses beaked vases; vases with or without handles, or bases. The study of decoration can serve as yet another basis for classification.

A complete collection should include all sets, and for each one of them, all the samples showing variations in type. Mention the range of size within which the particular type evolves. For objects in high relief take an impression. Symbolism of decoration: links with sculpture and modelling. Sculpture is the moulding of a volume. Finally, study the relationships between pottery and other crafts.

There is nothing more uneven [in quality] than pottery, even in France; nothing, or almost nothing, is more variable. The *high points* of pottery are represented by the Central American complex, Peru and North-West America, where wooden vessels are at the confluence between basketry vessels and pottery. In Africa, some peoples possess a very sophisticated pottery technique and terracotta sculpture; others only know of coarse pottery, barely fired. Nothing is more traditional than pottery, which is at once art and industry, and is felt as one of the most essential plastic arts.

Pottery made with the potter's wheel is not necessarily superior to that made without it; it all depends on the artist. And the perfection of the wheel does not necessarily correspond directly to the perfection of the pottery.

Pottery normally goes with an ideology. The question of the tripods, to take but one example, can be very complicated. Almost all pots have symbolic values; even in our cafés, a glass for port is not the same shape as a glass for a half-pint.

Very often the pot has a soul, the pot is a person. Pots are kept in a specific place, and they can often constitute objects of considerable religious importance. The Japanese *reku* vary according to season. Urns used as coffins are found in India, Africa and South America. Finally, one should study the fate of each pot. What happens to shards?

Esparto Goods and Rope Making

There is not much difference between basketry and rope making or between basketry and esparto goods. In the latter case the work is carried out with the whole reed or the whole leaf (this is the case in Papua and Melanesia), but the art of plaiting remains the same. Underlying all fabrics one finds the notion of net and braid: a fabric is a net that has itself been netted. Esparto goods can be exemplified by the manufacture of wicker shoes, or by the making of fabric out of dried leaves. Esparto work will produce more or less the same objects as basketry – e.g. the sheath for a sword.

For everything to do with plaiting it is always necessary to study the fibre; the *strand*, in other words a composite of fibres; and the thread, which can be a composite of several strands. To analyse such composites, employ the tool used in drapery, the linen tester, and count the number of threads per decimetre or square decimetre. The study of fibre and thread should be followed by the study of techniques for plaiting, for the weave and for weaving.

Rope making differs from basketry in that it involves only the manufacture of the thread, i.e. the rope. There is the question of the twisting of the rope and its resistance to twisting; the casting off at the start and at the end. In the study of ropes the essential question is *knots*. One should unravel the interlacing of the various strands, noting the movements of fingers and hands that produce it. Knots are of considerable importance; the French can scarcely make a hundred knots while the Eskimos normally know at least two hundred.

Glues and Resins

Glues and resins can be studied here as well as in connection with tools and instruments (see above). Glue, resin, wax and varnish are instruments that resist forces.

There is no published synthesis covering this topic. Glues and resins are much used in Australia. The existence of substances of this kind allows us to understand hypothetically the use of a certain number of prehistoric tools, whose function would otherwise be inexplicable.

One of the most efficient types of glue is blood. Among the types of glue do not forget *waxes* (beeswax and others). Study the various uses of wax. Study the composition and modes of preservation of the *varnish* used in basketry, pottery, etc.

Weaponry[17]

Weaponry can be studied as forming a general industry with special uses – the same knife can be used for hunting, for war, for butchery; or else they can be studied according to their use: weapons of war, fishing weapons, hunting weapons. We can distinguish further between projectiles and impact weapons; and within the latter between crushing weapons and sharp weapons – cutting ones and piercing ones.

Whatever the weapon under scrutiny, the investigation should cover, in sequence, the name; the raw material and the various stages of manufacture; its use, handling, mode of action, its range, and effectiveness; who is entitled to use it (man or woman or both; is the weapon strictly personal or can it be lent to someone else, and if so to whom, etc.); finally, its ideology and its relations with religion and magic.

The inventory of the village's weapons carried out house by house and noting the name of the owner of each weapon will show the distribution of weaponry in the locality.

Table 4.2 Classification of Weaponry

Weight weaponry	club (of wood, stone, or metal) truncheon hammer biface hunting spear hoe
Offensive weaponry	axe knife and stiletto sword (scimitar, yataghan, kris) dagger
Projectiles	javelin, large and small sling bola lasso bow and arrow blowpipe
Protective armour	shield helmet armour
Parade armour	
Firearms	

Weight Weapons and Offensive Weapons

For each weapon one should note:
- Its name: the general name and the individual one, if it exists – as indeed it often does; it is of some importance to know that Roland's sword was called Durandal. Its myth.
- Its material: an axe can be made of iron, stone, jade or obsidian.
- Its shape: is it an axe proper, an adze, or a pickaxe?

The spear when held in the hand is a weight weapon; when thrown, it becomes a javelin. A removable head makes it a harpoon, which is thrown or held in hand and allowed to run out (whale hunting in the Torres Strait).

Offensive Weapons

In a sword, dagger or knife, the handle, guard and sheath need to be studied much as the weapon itself. Roman swords were in fact Celtic swords: the best blacksmiths in Rome were Celts.

Projectiles

The study of the *bow* should include several steps:
1. The bow itself, its components and its production. The composite bow[18] is widespread, from the Mongol world to Central America; a composite bow can be made of between three and seven different kinds of wood. The cross-section of the bow: ellipsoidal or shaped like a lens. The Pygmies of the

Philippines possess an enormous bow which is double in cross-section. The bow can present several different sections lengthwise.
2. The string and the way it is attached to the bow, whether fixed or movable. A very powerful bow requires a catch to which the string is attached when not in use. Study both the catch and the knot which fixes it in place.
3. The arrow (shaft, head, feathering, nock); is it poisoned (composition of the poison, its production, its effects, etc.)?
4. How is it shot? What is the posture of the archer, and the position of his fingers on the string?

One of the primitive forms of propulsion for projectiles is that provided by the spear-thrower, which is still in use in parts of Africa and America, and especially throughout Australia. The thrower is a small stick, about 50 centimetres long, with a hook; sometimes the hook is inserted in a cavity in the base of the spear ('male' thrower); sometimes the fluted stick ends with a concave butt on which the bottom of the spear rests ('female' thrower). A spear which, when cast by hand, has a range of twenty to thirty metres, can reach fifty to seventy metres when cast with a thrower. The thrower is often found at prehistoric sites.

Another primitive mode of throwing making use of a cord is throwing with a *sling*.

The *blowpipe* appears to be associated with the great equatorial forest. Its distribution is more or less that of the Pacific and American civilisations between latitudes 5° and 15°. The tube varies. It can be either simple one or double (as for elephant hunting among the Sakai of Malacca, where the animal must be hit in the eye), or else it can be made of several segments with different calibres. The inside of the tube is either smooth or grooved; the arrows are nearly always poisoned.

Protective Armour

Armour used for protection – armour, helmet, gauntlets, finger-guards, greaves – is also often used for parade.

The shield has a considerable history. The first shield was probably a simple stick enabling one to ward off blows from the enemy. Australia knows only of wooden shields, often very narrow. The Zulu of South Africa have an oblong leather shield, whose handle consists of a vertical stick. The leather disk of the shield moves on the axis of the stick; it turns at the slightest shock, thus deflecting the flight of the arrow. Study the history of shield handles.

A shield can be made of wood, skin, leather, metal or basketry. It can be round, oblong, oval or rectangular, or it can be a shoulder shield. The shield usually is a personal weapon that cannot be lent. In a society that is even moderately warlike, the shield's decoration can indicate the exact rank of its owner. The decoration of a shield usually corresponds to the coat of arms. The great Kwakiutl copper shields in North West America are true escutcheons. The entire ancient North America used to have *gorgets*, sometimes made of bronze.

The *helmet* is far less common than the shield and probably comes from the East. It is made of leather, basketry, or metal.

Total body armour exists in Micronesia (in basketwork) and in Africa (in basketwork, leather, coat of mail in Chad; parade armour in padded cotton as in Niger, hiding both horse and rider).

Parade Armoury

The finest weapons are for parades, for ostentation, e.g. the jade hatchet of New Caledonia. In some cases parade weapons can constitute a currency – one so precious as to be used only on the occasion of solemn ritual exchanges, e.g. shields in North West America. We know of two societies for whom the spear is truly the object of a cult: Rome and Black Africa.

Specialised Industries with Special Uses

The industries examined so far – fire, basketry, pottery, etc. – suggest the idea of a series of techniques, that is of skills and tools adding up to a trade. A pure technology [study of techniques], like that of Franz Reuleaux, has every right to limit itself to mechanical techniques – in fact, all other classifications only regroup elements already covered under mechanical techniques: a textile is nothing else but a system of resistance; the firing of a very fine enamel belongs among physico-chemical phenomena. This is a technology for engineers.

There is another approach to technology, that of the historian of civilisation. We have not only classified things in relation to the internal logic of mechanics, physics or chemistry; we have also grouped them according to the social contexts to which they correspond.

From this vantage point, an industry is defined as *an ensemble of techniques that combine towards the satisfaction of a need* – or more precisely towards the satisfaction of consumption. Needs are elastic in humankind, but it is the notion of consumption that allows us to define industries, i.e. systems of techniques appropriate for specific purposes, and the articulation of industries: thus hunting and fishing each form a system of general techniques with a general use, a system of general techniques with special uses, and a system of special techniques with special uses.

We shall now study techniques by classifying them according to the purpose they serve. From now on the technical aspects are no longer the only important ones, for the purpose in view determines even the technical aspects: fishing weapons differ from hunting weapons; and within fishing itself, trout fishing differs from gudgeon fishing.

Here we enter a field that does not belong to science alone, but one in which conscious practice is also involved. An inventor has a theoretical logic specific to himself; but it is this notion of the practical solution to a problem that is called the notion of the technician.

Under the word 'coordination' (*administration*) people too often conflate economics and technology. Of course, in order for several techniques to combine towards a single purpose, everything must be mutually adapted. So there exists a category corresponding to the coordination of movements: within a single individual all the techniques are coordinated one in relation to the others. But a person is not merely an economic agent – *homo economicus* – he is also a technician. French peasants spend a great part of their time on bricolage, in other words on technical activities. Some populations demonstrate an astonishing degree of industry, which is completely lacking among close neighbours who are characterised by complete mental laziness. The latter will not even adopt instruments that are ready to use; they will borrow nothing and imitate nothing, simply out of clumsiness or nonchalance.

Approached as above, the study of techniques immediately raises several questions: division of labour, according to time, place, society, gender ...; the question of consumption and its relations with production; and finally, the relation between techniques and techno-morphology, i.e. the question of the location of industries and the question of trade, often over long distances. Economic phenomena as a whole belong to this category, which the Germans call *wirtschaftliche Dimension*, but they belong only as superstructure, not as infrastructure.[19]

We shall classify special industries with special uses starting with what is most material and close to the human body:

- industries of consumption;
- industries of acquisition;
- industries of production;
- industries of protection and comfort;
- industries of transportation.

Industries of Consumption

Fieldworkers too often fail to study the consumption of food.[20] This kind of work requires sustained attention. It should in fact cover at least a year: the basic diet, consumed in normal quantities during some months of the year, can sometimes be reduced to famine portions, for instance during the hungry season in agricultural societies. Yet again, the fieldworker should turn to making an inventory. He or she should note food consumption in several families representative of the society under scrutiny (rich, average or poor families), for instance during the last week of each month: the quantity of food and the modes of preparing it; who ate what? Study the relations between the cycle of consumption and that of production.[21]

Consumption is nearly always confined to the domestic sphere, that is to the family. Even in Papua where meals are taken communally, it is the wives who prepare and bring the dishes; so although people take their meals together, the cooking is still a family matter.

Meals

One should study each meal of the day, drawing up a complete inventory, including drinks. Who is eating? With whom? It is exceptional for men and women to eat together. Where do people eat? Give the times for the meals.

Nature of the dishes. The ingredients and their collection. The food that is eaten may come from far away, thus giving rise to extensive trade: salt in Africa; spices; some tribes in Central Australia send military expeditions to find a condiment called *pituri* hundreds of miles away; the trade in maté; the spread of peyotl throughout Central America. On geophagy see the admirable work by Laufer.[22] As for cannibalism, distinguish between endocannibalism and exocannibalism: there are societies in Australia where it is customary to eat one's dead parents;[23] elsewhere, a victorious tribe will take slaves from among the peoples it has subdued and will eat them in the course of solemn ceremonies: this is still the norm among the Babinga in the Congo.

Order of dishes. This should be noted carefully. Such and such a morsel is normally reserved for such and such a member of the group.

Instruments of consumption. The fundamental instrument remains the hand. But which hand? And which finger? We can tell a Muslim easily by the fact that at a meal he strictly uses his right hand only, the use of the left hand for eating being prohibited. Forks are less common than knives; the first fork was probably one used by cannibals; the forks of man-eaters are often very artistic masterpieces (New Guinea forks). The spoon is used more frequently, yet it is not very widespread. Wooden plates are used across the whole of North West America. Note the use of a mat or a table, though the latter appears to be very rare.

Cooking

For any type of meat the mode of preparation should be studied from the moment the animal is killed until the moment the meat is eaten. One should proceed in similar fashion for each item of the meal: fish, cereals, green vegetables, etc.

Preparation of food. Study the mortar, the millstone, the mill, the methods of detoxification – e.g. of manioc. What kind of food is eaten raw, smoked or dried? For cooked food a distinction should be made between food that is boiled (the normal method of Chinese cooking, alongside frying), roasted (the oven is far more widespread than the spit), or fried. Note the substances used for cooking.

Preservation of food. Native people generally are much more far-sighted than is claimed. The Eskimos know quite well how to pass from one season to the next. Study their store-rooms and reserves buried in the ground. The Klamath of Oregon bury their seeds in the ground adding a few leaves from a plant whose scent keeps off bears. Pemmican; smoked, dried and salted fish. In the Marquesas Islands, the breadfruit was stored in wells ten metres deep and five metres in diameter, walled with banana and coconut palm leaves. Such reserves could last fifty years. Every type of polar 'sauerkraut'.

Ideology of Food

For each type of food study its relations with religion and magic, the connection with totemism, age and sex; and the relationship with the dead and the living.

Prohibitions can be seasonal: a Jew cannot eat leavened bread at Passover. Prohibitions attached to a war expedition. Mention any food taboos and prejudices, taking care not to confuse religious prohibitions with mere rules of prudence. Above all, never forget that the needs to be satisfied are in the first instance social (in Australia, the food prohibitions imposed on the uninitiated boy leave him with nothing but a famine diet).

Condiments

The study of condiments is of particular importance. Learn all about the salt trade (in Africa), the pepper trade, the spice trade; the various types of oil or grease. Animal butter, vegetable butter (shea butter). Societies can be classified easily into those who eat their butter fresh and those who prefer it rancid, the latter being far more numerous. Study yeasts, ferments, and sauces; and food that is left to go bad.

Drinks

The study undertaken for food needs to be repeated for drinks. Where, who, when, for whom, for what? Methods of drinking: with the hand, with a leaf, with a tube. Ideology attached to each type of drink, especially to fermented drinks.[24] The issues of purification, transport and preservation of the liquid. In the whole of Australia, big wooden plates are the only means known for transporting water. Transport is facilitated by the presence of gourds, calabashes and coconuts. Part of Australia lives by cutting the trunk of the gum tree.

The study of fermented drinks leads straight to religion. The issue of etiquette is most significant here: when does one drink, who drinks, etc. Millet beer; palm wine; rice alcool, maté, chicha. The vine seems to be of Indo-Chinese origin.

Finally, the study of *narcotics* and *intoxicants*. Everything that is chewed: tobacco, betel nut, chewing-gum. Hemp, from which a drink is produced in North West America, and which is causing devastation in the Arab world; opium; tobacco – was it not preceded by something else in America? Lastly, one should collect myths concerning fermented drinks, and concerning all psychotropic substances.

Industries of Acquisition

Simple acquisition (gathering, hunting, fishing) can be distinguished from production (stockbreeding, agriculture) in that it consists in the gathering of material things that will be used as they are, without further preparation. But the truth is that the distinction between acquisition and production is a secondary issue: the producer is never a creator, but only an administrator; humankind does not produce, it only manages production: to make a knife is not to create iron, but only to transform it through a succession of improvements. The Germans distinguish more aptly between *Sammler* and *Produzenter*.

From another point of view, we are accustomed to a division of humankind into three ages: beginning as hunter and fisherman, humans would have been stockbreeders prior to becoming sedentary at the stage of agriculture. Men of the Lower Palaeolithic would have been exclusively gatherers, hunters, and fishermen, that is direct exploiters. I am not entirely sure of this. It seems that the beginnings of agriculture appeared very early on.

In the final analysis all of this needs to be seen as a matter of relative proportions: hunting and fishing are often found side by side with nascent or occasional agriculture. There is not an opposition between herders and farmers but, more often, an exchange of produce. The individual Peul in West Africa can afford to confine himself to herding because he buys grain from his Black neighbours who are farmers.

Gathering

Simple collecting, or gathering (animal, vegetable), should be studied by making a collection of all the things the indigenous people gather, and by making a complete inventory of all that is gathered and all that is used. It is a serious mistake not to attach enough importance to natural production – on which human production rests.

The natives know very well what can be eaten, what can be drunk, and what is useful. They know the habits of insects and animals. A good study of gathering should go side by side with an investigation into ethnobotany and ethnozoology.

Gathering of animals. It is more widespread than is usually believed: dead quadrupeds, worms, caterpillars, snails, rats, bats, lizards, lice, and termites. Locust swarms. Gnat cakes in East Africa.

Gathering of plants. Europe's inventions in this regard are poor by comparison with those of America or Asia: 45 per cent of Africa's cultivated species are of American origin.[25] The Australians are familiar with 300 plants from which they eat the fruits, roots and tubers.

The exploitation of the forest should be studied first: how do people climb? How do they get through thickets? How do they dig the earth to find tubers? As early [in human history] as [the stage represented by] Australia, women dig the earth with a sharp stick in order to find wild yams. The Babinga pygmies in the Congo dig up wild yams using a very long probe, one end of which is equipped with wooden boards attached with a creeper. They prepare the earth with the other end, and then thrust the cone into the soil; the earth piles up on the cone, which is then removed with a stick.[26] Gathering is well developed among the American Indians, and forms an essential part of their diet. The Californian

Indians gather everything: groundnuts, berries, graminaceae, roots, bulbs, and especially acorns that they eat either boiled or roasted. East of the sierras, pine cones replace acorns; each tribe has its own pine zone, whose borders it should not cross. The Indians also dig up roots and tubers; the flour is eaten as a soup, as a stew, or as pancakes baked under ashes; while they are excellent basket makers, they have no knowledge of pottery. On the gathering of wild rice in the region of the Great Lakes, see the work of Jenks.[27] The Klamath Indians of Oregon pick the fruit of a nymphea called *woka*, in the marshes, from mid-August to the end of September; it is women who harvest these fruits, using canoes.

In Indochina, the search for camphor involves the use of a special language. The search for rare oils, and rare gums.

Beekeeping. One of the most advanced forms was practised in Ancient Mexico. Who undertakes it?

Then come seafood and shells from the coast. Study the heaps of shells ([Danish] *kiøkkenmødding* [now spelled *køk-*]), which form one of the most important elements for the study of the European Palaeolithic.

The equipment for gathering will include digging sticks, poles to knock down ripe fruits, sacks for gathering, back-baskets, etc.

Hunting[28]

Hunting has its starting point in gathering: a given social group has its own hunting ground, and even if it is nomadic it will not hunt beyond its limits. The native knows his ground: waterholes, plants, nature, number and habits of the animals; finding himself elsewhere, he will very often feel lost. Hunting can be divided into small or individual, and large or collective (buffalo or elephant hunt; hunting with dogs in Europe; hunting with fire in Africa).

Hunting can be studied in two main ways: according to the weapon used, or according to the game hunted (weapons, technique, time of the year, etc.). An individual does not simply 'go hunting'; he goes hare-hunting, and not hunting just any old hare, but this particular hare which he knows well. So we should classify according to the people who hunt, the game being hunted, and the instrument used for hunting it.

Trapping is called passive hunting, since the hunter remains passive once the trap has been set; but the trap is a mechanical device which functions as such. All human groups know how to dig pits in which game can be made to fall; the Pygmies are said to know of no trap that is more elaborate; the Australians only have hoopnets or dams for fishing; the use of traps for big game requires mechanical ideas that go beyond the range of their thinking. Some Asian fences for hunting elephants, who are thereby directed towards a pit, reach huge dimensions. The great chicanes of the Iroquois for caribou hunting spread over tens of kilometres. The great nets of New Caledonia are made from the hair of the flying fox.

Traps can be distinguished as follows:

- Traps which the animal can enter without injury, but from which it cannot escape (e.g., nets set horizontally or vertically; the lobster pot; hoopnets for fishing).
- Traps in which the animal is wounded and caught; these often include a bait that will lure the animal into triggering the trap mechanism (e.g. the mouse trap or elephant trap).
- Spring traps, where the spring can be triggered by traction (bird traps in Indochina) or by pressure (deer traps in Sumatra); the spring trap can also be set like a crossbow (rat traps in Madagascar).
- Birdlime traps, used in Hawaii to obtain the feathers of a bird, which is immediately released.
- Traps with a slip knot (parrot hunting among the Maori; squirrel hunting in Alaska; lark hunting in our own countryside; traps with radial sticks for hunting the antelope in Africa).

Whistle decoys allow the hunter to call game; they are often used in combination with a *disguise* that allows the hunter to come conveniently close to his prey. The Eskimos disguise themselves to hunt reindeer, the Bushmen to hunt ostriches (the hunter holds an ostrich head above his own head while imitating the bird's gait), and the Sudanese for hunting cranes. When hunting deer, the California Indians wear deer skins and fix antlers on their heads as they advance on all fours to windward of the game, pretending to graze; the Manchu Tartars behave similarly at the season of rut when stags look for each other in order to fight. The hunter imitates the game's call with the aid of a caller, and the deer runs forward presenting its chest to the hunter, who pierces it with his spear or sword.

The rules of hunting can vary depending on the type of game, the terrain, and the season.

The use of *dogs* in hunting; the pointer remains an auxiliary of secondary importance; only the hound can provide useful services.

The *ideology* of hunting, of the hunter, and of game. The hunter must know the names of the divinities associated with hunting and with the forest. He must be able to use incantations against the game and must know the meaning of omens. The whole of North America lives a life pervaded by the mythology of deer. An Australian hunter would not go hunting without holding a piece of quartz in his mouth.

The consumption of game generally has a ritual character and varies with the seasons.

The preservation of game, with its skull and bones. Do people break the bones and eat the marrow? Which parts can be roasted? Use of the remnants: fur, skin, guts ...

Animals that are half hunted and half domesticated (e.g. pheasants) lead us to the question of domestication and stockbreeding. Pigs are half wild in Indochina, Melanesia, Papua and Polynesia. Cattle pens. Goats were domesticated in pens.

Fishing[29]

Hunting and fishing haunt the mind; they occupy a great place in the preoccupations of the natives: the myth of the hunter and the myth of the fisherman are among the most important myths. Some of the usages and beliefs that get associated with totemism are in fact stories about hunting or fishing. The whole of Black Africa lives by the hunter; the whole of Melanesia conceives of its gods in the form of sharks. From another point of view, fishing develops earlier than hunting. It is evidenced throughout southeast Australia by the presence of large-scale constructions – whole rivers provided with barrages.

Fishing should be studied just like hunting, according to the weapons used and the species targeted. Thus the trident, which is used very widely, is nevertheless adapted for each type of fish. Nets and traps are designed with a view to a particular kind of fish.

Bare hand fishing is practised by Tierra del Fuego women with the aid of a seaweed stalk weighed down with a stone; squatting in her canoe, the woman uses the flesh of a shellfish as bait, lets the line sink, and seizes in her hand the fish that comes to take the bait. Bare hand fishing is also practised in West Africa in the season of low water, in riverside backwaters that are then cut off; the whole village then gives itself over to fishing that is truly miraculous.

Net fishing is generally poorly studied. For each net note should be made of its manufacture (thread, method of weaving, size of mesh, use of the shuttle), its mode of use and its setting. The net can be left in place, manipulated by hand, weighted, held up with floats, and can be used as draw net, drop net, casting net, trammel, etc.

Angling is done by hand or with a rod. Study all the elements of the fishing line: the line itself (a different thread is required for each fish); the hook, which can be composite (Polynesian hooks are among the finest); the bait and its fastening; floats and lead weights if present; sometimes, also, the decoy.

Angling and net fishing are relatively rare. Spear fishing is practised far more frequently. It is done with bow and arrow, with a gaff or with a harpoon. The harpoon appears quite suddenly in the Upper Palaeolithic. Some peoples are still unaware of such a weapon. How is the harpoon paid out? Spear fishing is generally practised from a fishing platform: standing on a kind of watch tower the harpooner pierces the bigger fish from fairly high above. The fishing platform is the same in part of Indochina, in Polynesia, in Papua and throughout South America.

Trap fishing is significant for the diversity and the number of the types of trap observed: dams (simple, with an inlet, or V-shaped), dykes, large chicanes; all kinds of nets, often huge; fixed traps, with or without bait; mechanical traps, etc.

Finally, *fishing by poisoning the water*, practised in many African waterways, implies some subsequent procedure to detoxify the fish.

It would be impossible to exaggerate the significance of pearl fishing and tripang fishing in the history of the relations between the Oriental worlds of India and China, and the whole of Insulindia [south-west Pacific], and even Polynesia.

When practised from boats rather than from the shore, the study of fishing naturally involves the study of fishing boats; consider the relation with navigation.

Study reserves and dams. Study the legal rules of fishing.[30]

Fishing rituals can be very important. Australia has some very complex rituals, notably for calling up the whales which natives claim to be able to drive ashore.

Relations between fishing and social organisation. Generally, tribes are internally divided between moieties of fishermen and non-fishermen, the fishermen living on the coast and carrying on exchange with the non-fishermen who live further inland. Thus some villages are peopled by fishermen alone: here is one of the first forms of division of labour. Fishing involves an element of regularity that makes it easily susceptible to calculated exploitation.

Fishing can also be seasonal and depend on fish migrations. This applies to salmon fishing, which plays a major part in the life of the inhabitants of North West America. Accordingly, among fisherfolk, the migrations lead to the phenomena of double morphology affecting the whole group. In this case, the fishing villages, built for a few months of the year, will nonetheless involve the installation of fishtanks, drying areas, and warehouses to process fish.

The permanent villages of fishermen are often built on piles to withstand floods or storms. Conversely, building on piles or stilts may have been practised initially for purposes of defence; but it would then have led the inhabitants to practise fishing (lake dwellings in Switzerland).

Preparation and storage of fish. It may be eaten fresh, dried, high, rotten, and smoked.

Use of associated products. Fish oil, roe, condiments made of rotten and crushed fish, bladders ...

Industries of Production

We have already seen that in fact there is no such thing as production by humans – only an administration of nature, an economy of nature: one breeds a pig, one does not create it. Humans are animals who live in symbiosis with certain animal and vegetable species. They must follow their plants and animals. This explains the vast extent of migrations by certain peoples such as the Huns or the Peul. However, while the industries of acquisition – gathering, hunting and fishing – correspond to direct exploitation, the industries we are about to study involve some alteration of nature, a difference that needs emphasis.

The study of a particular society necessarily includes study of the animals and plants of the society: the African elephant, half wild, was domesticated in

Antiquity; one does not know Dahomey without knowing the serpents that it worships. The stirrup was introduced to Europe in the eleventh century by the invasions of pastoral peoples from the East; previously, the horseman's weapon was inevitably the javelin, a projectile weapon, rather than the spear, a weight weapon. The entire history of Polynesian migrations is linked with the history of the plants and animals with which men and women set off in their ships and which they afterwards worshipped.

On the other hand, each animal, each plant has been worked on to an extraordinary degree. See the demonstration by Vavilov of the purely American origin of the two kinds of maize. We are only at the beginning of such creations.

The native has an acute awareness of the individuation of each animal and each plant: a Maori knows each sweet potato in his field and distinguishes it from all the others, just as a French gardener knows individually each one of his rosebushes. It is important that the observer acquire this idea of the individuation of each animal and each plant.[31]

Stockbreeding[32]

Stockbreeding scarcely appears until the Maglemosian, that is, the latest forms of the Palaeolithic. It arises suddenly together with pottery and brachycephalic humans. The latter brought to Europe pottery, stockbreeding and agriculture. Domestication may have appeared first on the slopes of the Himalayas. All domestic animals, or nearly all of them, come from this region. The definition of the domesticated animal is an anthropocentric one: humans have domesticated the dog, but it is the cat who has domesticated humans. Moreover, some animals are tamed without necessity, for pleasure (e.g. crickets in China). The important issue in domestication is reproduction: certain species that are unable to breed in captivity remain half wild (e.g. the elephant, pheasant, Melanesian pig).

The investigation of stockbreeding should be made via the individual study of each domesticated animal, taken individually: age, sex, name, photographs, life history of the animal, naming of its body parts.

The *ethnozoology* of each species will include the study of its habitat, its origin (theories about the souls of breeding animals), and selection. There is a textbook on equine science by a Hittite prince dating from the seventeenth century BC. An Arab tribe possesses the pedigrees of its horses and is as proud of these as it is of its own genealogy. Researches on hybrids are often quite remarkable. At the courts of China, the Pharaoh, and the Great Mogul everyone bred hybrids.

How are the animals fed? Fodder, grazing and migrations that result from the exhaustion of the grazing. Transhumance. Watering places.

How are the animals kept? Study of the pens. The kraal, an enclosure formed by huts built in a circle, with an open space in the middle where the animals are penned at night, is typical of the whole Bantu world. Study the shepherd and his relationship with the animals: the shepherd's call; his postures. Throughout

East Africa, the shepherd rests on one leg like a wading bird. Has he given an individual name to each of his animals? Presence or (more common) absence of cowsheds.

Rearing. Castration; labour; delivery. What knowledge do the natives have of selection? How is each animal treated according to its age?

Use of the animal. As a means of transportation (see below). Is it eaten? If so, under what circumstances, which parts, and who has a right to it? Butchering is nearly always a sacrifice among the pastoral peoples of East Africa. The animals are killed with a spear or with an arrow shot at point-blank range. Use of the blood. The consumption of hot blood often takes a ritual character. Are the bones broken or are they not? What becomes of them (links with the ideology)? Is the marrow eaten? What is done with the gut, and skin? The working of skins is one of the most ancient industries known, as is witnessed by the large Chellean scrapers. Recipes for cooking. Do people make butter, and how? Do they make cheese, and how?

Veterinary arts are highly elaborated among the Sakalavas [of Madagascar]. Notions of pathology concerning the origins of disease among animals; therapy; surgery; obstetrics. The study of veterinary magic.

Ornamentation and deformation of animals. Example: pigs' tusks twisted in a spiral in Melanesia, Papua and the whole of Indonesia. Working with horn in Madagascar and throughout the Indian Ocean. Property marks on animals: who owns the mark, myth of the mark?[33] Take an impression of all the deformations, of all the marks; when these impressions are classified according to their owners, families or clans often become apparent.

Ideology. Study all the ceremonies connected with the worship of animals. Mythological and scientific notions on the origin of animals, theories about the souls of breeding animals, trophies of sacrificed animals. A Malagasy village is an ossuary of cattle skulls.

Law and economics. Animals serve as currency throughout East Africa. They were once the first currency of the Indo-European world (*pecunia* comes from *pecus*). On the other hand, the deforestation in North Africa, with all the changes it entails in the economy, coincides with the introduction of sheep to the region.

Agriculture[34]

Agriculture comes under ethnobotany, as stockbreeding comes under ethnozoology. Agriculture is known throughout the Neolithic world. This technique is present in all the French colonies. Agriculture exists in nascent form among the tribes of northern central Australia. It is known to a good many Pygmies, notably those in the Philippines, and is apparently unknown today only to the inhabitants of Tierra del Fuego and the Arctic – the climate of these regions renders its practice impossible.

The theory that presents women as the sole inventors of agriculture seems to go too far. On the other hand it is useless to ask whether agriculture does or does not represent a higher stage of civilisation than that represented by stockbreeding. Some purely pastoral civilisations have been great civilisations (e.g. the Mongolian empire in the twelfth century). What matters rather is to know whether each breeder and each farmer is or is not of the highest standing within his technique.

Agricultural *implements* derive from the instruments used for gathering, and particularly from the digging stick, which started as a simple sharpened stick and evolved into a spade or hoe. Cultivation can be divided fairly easily into cultivation with the hoe, cultivation with the spade, and cultivation with the aid of primitive or evolved forms of plough. But the plough (and harrow) imply the use of domesticated animals, and hence the knowledge of stockbreeding. In many regions the plough has remained very primitive, a simple hoe that is dragged along. It is striking that the seeder, which is fairly widespread across the world, has been rediscovered in Europe only quite recently. Some prehistoric stone tools seem clearly to be primitive ploughshares.

The observer should distinguish as many types of agriculture as there are cultivated species. He or she should study each plant in all its parts, at all ages from seed to fruit, noting the indigenous terms. The products from each plant can be very numerous and very varied. Some of these products rank among the most important that we use today; shea butter, palm oil, etc., are not European inventions. The researcher should also trace the ideology that accompanies each plant – an important part of the study: the birth, life and death of the plant; its relation with vegetation, with Mother Earth, sky and rain.

One should study next the ecology and the economics of the plant: how the growing area is prepared, and how the plant is exposed to the elements. In some cases large-scale deforestation and clearing have only become possible with the introduction of metal tools. In the stone age the big obstacle for humanity was the forest which could only be overcome by using fire; and even so the big roots would remain in place. Once the ground is ready it must be used: sowing, seedbeds, bedding out, final planting, maintenance. How is the ground irrigated (irrigation canals, wells, bailer, bucket water-wheel, etc.)? Manure is more or less universal. The fight against parasites. Then comes harvesting, threshing and storing. There is often a prohibition on storing two plants of different species in the same granary.

The study of *agrarian cults* should not be neglected. In countries with paddy fields the story of the rice spirit is fundamental in relation to rice growing, and not conversely.

When studying the techniques in themselves, it may be useful to distinguish: *agriculture*; *horticulture* (very often the garden corresponds to individual property, in contrast to the field which is collective property); *silviculture* (e.g. rubber, a wild plant maintained and cultivated in the forest by its owner); and *arboriculture* (e.g. coconut palms and olive trees). A good number of the inhabitants of our colonies are horticulturists even more than cultivators.

Study the sexual division of labour, marks of ownership, and taboos. The notion of productive surplus has been very well developed by Malinowski.[35]

One should also observe the relations between individual cultivation and collective cultivation, for the same patch of ground can be cultivated collectively as a field and individually as a garden, depending on the time of year; and the impact of these modes of cultivation on the social relationships both between individuals and between the individual and the clan as a whole.

Relations between agriculture and stockbreeding, between farmers and breeders, between farmers and hunting, and between farmers and hunters, if this is relevant.

Finally, some regions will need a study of quasi-industrial production: the Polynesian headman was a kind of general entrepreneur for agricultural labour.

Industries of Protection and Comfort

Protection and comfort should be analysed as conventional needs, far more than as natural needs. All the notions we have developing since Adam Smith concerning the production of goods and the circulation of such products with a view to eventual consumption – all these are abstractions. The notion of production is particularly vague in its bearing on types of industry such as those that provide protection and comfort. It is vague not in relation to the notion of market but in relation to the idea of creation. The elasticity of human needs is absolute: if we had to, we could live as Carthusian monks or nuns. With regard to protection and comfort, there is no other scale of values but the arbitrary choices of society.

Thus, beyond the limits of our civilisation, we straightaway find ourselves confronted with people having a scale of values, a mode of reasoning (*ratio*), and a way of calculating which are different from our own. What we call production in Paris is not necessarily production in Africa or among the Polynesians. It is absurd that under the equatorial sun, a black Muslim wraps himself in as many robes as he can; but the accumulation of garments is the sign of his wealth. The garment is an object of aesthetic value, as much as it is a means of protection.

The arbitrary character of everything that bears on protection and comfort is quite remarkable: the arbitrariness is not only 'economic', but in some aspects almost exclusively social. There can be *maxima* and *minima* of adaptation. Thus the Eskimos are perfectly equipped to fight the cold, as they are to fight the heat; their clothing is the sign of a very ancient Neo-Palaeolithic civilisation. The whole Arctic world is also very well provided for. But the Tierra del Fuego inhabitants are no better equipped for this struggle than were the Tasmanians, who have now vanished: both of these peoples went through very harsh winters with a miserable cloak of loose fur as their sole item of clothing.

It is therefore essential never to deduce anything *a priori*: observe, but draw no conclusions. If we want to be in a position to assess, we must first learn to beware of common sense, for there is nothing natural in this context. The human being is an animal who does reasonable things on the basis of unreasonable principles and who proceeds from sensible principles to accomplish things that are absurd. Nevertheless these absurd principles and this unreasonable behaviour are probably the starting point of great institutions. It is not in production properly speaking that society found its impetus to advance; but clothing is already a luxury, and luxury is the great promoter of civilisation. Civilisation always comes from the outside. Huge efforts have been realised in the area of techniques of production and comfort: the whole textile industry derives from clothing, and it is from the textile industry that a large part of the division of labour derives.

Clothing

Being an object of very slow consumption, clothing represents a real capital investment. It will serve as a means of protection while walking, running, attacking; it will protect against the bush, the rain, etc. Clothes worn during the day should be distinguished from clothes worn at night; working clothes from ceremonial garments, which are often found in greater numbers. The raw material will be determined by the environment, climate, etc.

In its protective function, clothing can be studied according to the part of the body it covers.

The shoe is fairly rare across the world. A great part of the world is without shoes; another part is very well shod. The origins of footwear appear to have been above all magical (for it avoids the foot being brought into direct contact with the ground and emanations from it), and military: the Australian *sandal* allows the tracks of attacking expeditions to be erased. All forms of the sandal should be studied: how do they hold the foot? Primitive forms of buttonholes. Sandals are footwear that is imperfect, inferior by far to the moccasin from which our own type of shoes derive; the moccasin is very close to Chinese footwear, and characterises the whole civilisation of Arctic Asia and Central North America. The guild of shoemakers was probably one of the first to be constituted; its important role throughout Africa is well known. The *gaiter* often comes in military forms (the greave).

In countries with palm trees, the body is protected by *rainwear*. Rainwear is more or less the same from its Asian centre as far as South America and part of North America. The study of sarongs, loincloths and grass skirts is difficult, but most useful. How is the waist covered? The way of wearing a loincloth and saluting with a loincloth by exposing the torso can by itself form a real language. On the other hand, the warlike character of a society may lead it to develop protective items for the torso: breastplates made of cotton, of basketry, and above all of leather, coats of mail ...

The *shirt* with stitched sides seems to be of fairly recent invention.

The *hat*, which is pretty commonly seen, is very unequally distributed. The Germans used to wear a small skullcap made of basketry while it does not appear that the Gauls covered their heads; only the military wore a helmet.

Study all forms of skullcaps, turbans, helmets, broad-brimmed hats, etc. The wearing of a hat is often a sign of authority.

Moreover, some parts of the body may receive particular protection, for instance the penis (penis sheath, infibulation), and the body orifices – the latter for magical reasons.[36]

From the point of view of form, *draped clothes* should be distinguished from *sewn clothes*. Our buttons have no connection with Antiquity whereas they can be found among the Eskimos and probably throughout the Arctic world; our buttonholes certainly are of Asiatic origin. Prior to their introduction, people only knew the fibula, i.e. the safety pin. But sewn clothes require the use of patterns, that is to say the vague awareness of a kind of descriptive geometry.

Decoration of Clothes

Dyeing and decorations have played a great role in the development of clothes because of the quest for raw materials that they triggered. Raw materials had to be adapted to the desired dyes. The influence of fashion as regards dress seems to be immense. Clothes are one of the most reliable criteria for classification: thus Iroquois clothing is almost identical to Chinese. In this matter the influence of age, sex, era, etc., will also play their part.

According to the raw materials, clothing can be classified as follows:

- *Clothes made of skin*, where the minimum is represented by people who wrap themselves in a single skin, floating freely, such as was current among the inhabitants of Tierra del Fuego; in contrast, arctic clothing, though it too is made of skin, is entirely sewn. The tanning industry is very developed throughout the Arctic world, and in Sudan also; and the enormous quantity of scrapers found from the Chellean era corresponds in all likelihood to leatherworking. Study all forms of leatherwork, including leather bags, containers, etc.
- *Clothes made of leaves* are found throughout Polynesia and Indonesia; the Kiwaï Papuans and the Marind Anim use a raincoat made of palm leaves.
- The *beaten bark* of the fig tree, tapa, is used in Oceania and also in Black Africa. Some Indian fakirs are still dressed exclusively in clothes made from banyan roots.
- *Clothes made of straw* can hardly be distinguished from those made of palm. Nearly all the clothes worn for masquerades in Melanesia and in Africa are made in this way.
- Clothes made of esparto, plaits, fibers: those are the primitive forms of fabric, in terms both of material and use.

From fabrics in the strict sense one can distinguish *felt*, where the interlacing fibres are simply pressed, trodden and glued. Felting is known throughout north Asia and North America. It does not yield very impressive results, except in China and Tibet. Normally, felt is not very resistant; it tears, and it absorbs a lot of water.

Fabrics

Weaving is an important invention for humanity. The first woven material marked the beginning of a new era.

The study of any fabric implies the study of its *raw material*. Animal fabrics are made of wool (which is regarded as impure among the Egyptians); of goat or camel hair; horsehair yielded the hair shirt and crinoline. Silkworm breeding in China apparently goes back to the third millennium BC, but silk was only introduced to Greece by Alexander the Great, and to Rome by Caesar. Vegetable fabrics include linen, which was much appreciated by the Celts and the Germans; however in Europe, throughout the Middle Ages, its production was hindered by the cultivation of cereals. The taste for linen cloth only developed in our part of the world from the fifteenth century onwards. Other vegetable fabrics are hemp and above all cotton, whose history is not very clear: it was an Abyssinian plant that spread to India, but why it was not exploited in its country of origin while it became the basis for a fundamental industry in India, we do not know. Let us recall that the first cotton factories in England only date from the middle of the seventeenth century.

The study of a particular fabric presupposes the study of the *thread*, itself made of strands. The first raw material to be spun appears to have been hair. Human hair is spun throughout Australia. Notice whether the thread has one strand or several, whether it is twisted or twined; thread is twisted on the thigh everywhere in Burma. Study the way the fingers move, especially at the beginning and ending of the thread, which are the delicate moments; how do people prevent the thread from undoing? Study knots.

Study the spindle, the balance, the distaff. The spinning wheel appears later. Take photographs and, if possible, film in slow motion the way the fingers move.

Spinning can be extraordinarily delicate: for instance, the threads intended for making thin veils, which are found both in the Arab world and in the Egyptian and Hindu worlds.

After spinning comes *weaving*, in the strict sense.[37] Weaving is an industry that spreads across almost the whole of humanity, except those areas that lack the raw material (Polynesia, Melanesia, Australia). Some civilisations, now vanished, once had admirable fabrics.

To study weaving, one has to study the weaving instruments, the looms. If possible, collect some looms, noting carefully how the various parts are assembled. In studying the loom, the greatest care should be devoted to the moments where it is at a standstill during the operating process, and equally to each of the actions linking such moments. Every technical action ends with a point of stasis; it is a matter of describing how one reaches such a point and how one moves on from it to the next one. Each time, the relation between each action and each position of the loom has to be noted; the relation between every part of the weaver's body, notably his toes, and the loom. Take photographs, and above all make drawings, showing all the actions, and every step in the weaving.

Study the reels and the shuttles (shape, mode of throwing); in the absence of shuttles, what is the substitute? When the loom is complicated and involves a handover between weavers, study the process of handover from one weaver to the next.

Note all the processes involved in making a warp and putting it under tension. The technique that consists in weighting the warp with pebbles disappeared in Norway only at the beginning of the nineteenth century; this is the usual method throughout the Arctic and American worlds.

Once the warp is set, the weft must go through it. How is the thread of the weft introduced and how does it leave the thread of the warp? By hand or with a sley? Procedure for stopping. Edging.

It is always difficult to achieve great widths; the very beautiful fabrics of Peru are made on very narrow looms. Techniques using ribbons.

Classification of fabrics: simple, twilled, plaited, combed, serge. In composite fabrics – e.g. those using feathers, or those made on canvas – distinguish between the fabric that forms the background and that which forms the embroidery. A piece of velvet is ultimately comparable to a tapestry.

Starting from the second century BC, all the varieties of fabric had to be obtained from the Chinese and the Mongols. Thin veils and brocades reached the West, via Iran, only in the fourth century AD.

Dyes and dressings. When the thread has been dyed in advance, the decoration of the fabric relies on the colour of the thread. The dyeing of the thread should be distinguished from the dyeing of the whole fabric, where the resist method is often used (the dye will only reach a part of the fabric being worked on). Distinguish vegetable dyes from chemical dyes using mineral substances. Who does the dyeing? In Africa the dyer is often the wife of the shoemaker and, as such, she belongs to a caste.

The weaver. Who does the weaving? Where and when? Ideology of weaving and, if applicable, ideology of the animals who spin or weave (silkworms across the East, spiders ...). The Maori, like the Berbers, have a real cult of weaving.

Building[38]

As an essentially arbitrary phenomenon, the building of dwellings characterises a civilisation rather than a given territory. Architecture appears as the archetypal art, as creation par excellence. Building can then be studied among the industries of comfort and protection – not under human geography or the general history of civilisation, irrespective of the value of such studies. In the final analysis, building can be understood as a mode of consumption.

The researcher should not start off by looking for the typical house: each house has its own sense. It is absurd to classify a society by a unique mode of dwelling; account must be taken of all the models found in the society, with all their variations, both individual and local: houses for general or special purposes, for human or for non-human use. Only when such a study has been completed can the notion of a typical house be abstracted without running the risk of confusing houses of rich men and of poor men.

Types and Materials

The house itself can be in a shelter. Numerous troglodytes or semi-troglodytes live in France: in the Cher valley, in Ferté-Milon, in Ferté-sous-Jouarre, etc., the inhabitants use old quarries. Caves were inhabited in Provence until the Bronze Age. Elsewhere, the civilisation of the troglodytes or *cliff dwellers* of central America (Arizona, part of New Mexico, north Mexico), raises a major problem in archaeology. Houses made of clay can also form the end of the troglodytes' shelters; the house can be dug underneath, which creates a cave.

Simple distinctions between round houses and square houses seem to be inadequate. The same Gauls who had round houses built square granaries. So they were not incapable of conceiving of the two types. Throughout the north of France, in Flanders and Artois, farms made of bricks and cowsheds made of rammed clay can be seen side by side.

The simplest type of dwelling after the cave would seem to be the wind break: the Ona of Tierra del Fuego, as their sole protection against a harsh cold, make do with a screen made out of guanaco skins stretched over sticks driven obliquely into the ground in a semicircle around the fire. The Tasmanians knew of no other shelter, but they used strips of bark instead of skins.

The conical tent is widespread especially in the steppe regions. It is found throughout north Asia and in the north of America as far as Texas. The covering varies according to regions: in Siberia, deer skins give way further south to strips of birch bark, and then to pine and larch. The Plains dwellers use felt instead.[39]

In the *beehive* style of hut, the walls and the roof are not yet distinct. In the wigwam of the Atlantic coast Indians, poles driven in the ground have their tips bent and tied with transverse poles, themselves covered with grass, mats or bark. The same type of building can be found with a circular or oval shape among the Pygmies of the Congo,[40] the Hottentots and the Zulus. The principle involved in building the Eskimo igloo, using ice, is entirely different.[41]

When the cylindrical frame of the walls is crowned with a separate conical roof, we have a dwelling of the same type as the Mongol tent covered with felt, or as the Siberian yurt with its roof of reindeer skins. The same type recurs in Africa with different materials: with walls of clay and a roof consisting of arches made of basketwork covered with grass, it looks like a large mushroom.

Finally, the *oblong house*, where the ridge beam is supported by several cleft stakes can be found both in simple forms (e.g. in the Chaco) and with a complex architecture. Houses in British Columbia and throughout Oceania and Indonesia are made of wood with a double-pitched roof and protruding gable. The oblong houses of equatorial Africa have their walls made of bark, while the Muong of Indochina prefer basketry. Rammed clay walls often come with a terraced roof. Such is the case among the Hopi of North America, where the sandstone blocks are cemented with clay: access to the house is through the roof with the aid of ladders that can be withdrawn as a means of protection; the terraced roof allows the building of one or several storeys set back; people go from one terrace to the other, from one house to the next via the terraces. The principle is the same as in Arabic architecture; nothing looks more like a Moroccan town with its terraced houses than a North American *pueblo*.

When studying dwellings, one should not overlook the possibility of a double morphology. One type of dwelling is not exclusive for a given area; the whole of north Asia lives in two ways: in a conical tent for part of the year, and in a round hut for the rest of the time.

It is probably normal, in some cases, that clay houses are built on stilts: this depends not only on the soil, whether it is sandy or clayey, but at least equally on technical factors. Sometimes too, a poor adaptation to the environment comes from the fact that people remain attached to a method that once had a raison d'être, but has ceased to be adequate because of a change in the mode of livelihood or because of migration. Moreover, old means can be adapted to new ends: in Oceania, the space between stilts serves as a pigsty, and constructions on stilts provide excellent granaries. A number of large tombs serve in reality as hay cottages similar to those that are still to be seen in our mountains. From Indochina to France these cottages are placed on stone supports meant to prevent rats from climbing up; a detail of this kind can belong to a large-scale grouping of geographical and historical phenomena.

A thorough study of the different types of house found over a certain stretch of territory will make it possible to identify the limits of a given civilisation; but it is necessary to avoid the slightest *a priori*. Throughout southern Africa, people camp in circles, the huts forming a circle around the hearth: this is the kraal. But there are people in southern Africa who no longer camp in circles and sometimes do not camp at all. So we should not say that all Bantus know the kraal, or that the kraal is specifically Bantu.

Functional and Morphological Study

To study the house, proceed like an architect: if possible, get local carpenters to make small-scale models of the various types of building. Each type needs at least three models, showing respectively the foundations, elevation, and roofing. The essential task is to study the relations between the different parts.

The choice of location for a dwelling is often determined by reasons relating to magic or religion. The ground slopes, or has to be levelled, terraces have to be prepared, etc. Study the foundation rituals, which are often on a considerable scale; also the materials, and any excavation. Who does the building? In some societies, the carpenter is regularly the brother-in-law (wife's brother) of the owner. In Fiji, Melanesia and Polynesia, there are real carpenters' guilds. Note each moment, each detail and each action in the building. Deal with the techniques of building and the ideology of the techniques. Is building a collective undertaking or an individual one? Note everything to do with junction: tenons, knots, pins, nails, rafters, props. The balance of the building timbers. Does the ridge beam protrude to form a canopy, or not? The shape of the roof can be more characteristic than the shape of the house itself. A house with round walls can be crowned with a square roof; but to put a round roof on top of a square house, as do the Bamoum of Cameroon, demands the solution of a difficult problem.

A house may well be built for a limited duration (e.g. the igloo of the Eskimos). The greater or lesser durability of the materials should not be the sole focus of attention: some houses made of dried mud can last for a very long time. However, one should note the concern for different kinds of shelter appropriate to the different stages of existence, depending on age, season, etc. Thus, dwellings for adolescents are common. Nearly all negro families have their house and in addition a farm in the fields; very often the whole population spends the entire cultivation season away from the village, in the fields.

The model of ownership in Roman law is represented by ownership of land, and particularly of land with buildings. However, in nearly all African legal systems the house is regarded as the model of movable property.

In countries where the typical form of grouping is the joint or extended family, the word 'house' will sometimes have to be applied to a group of dwellings. Consider a Norwegian farm: it includes one building for each purpose: the father's house, the sons' house, shelter for the forge, the stable, pigsty, cowshed, barn, kitchen, granaries, tool shed ... The whole constitutes a single house. The same is true of the Maori house and the Sudanese house.

The *plan* of the house will show its orientation, which is often very important: the Betsileo house serves as sundial.[42] Who lives in each corner? Give the location of everyone and of every object; also the space reserved for guests. The detailed study of furniture (how it is used, beliefs related to each object) should be accompanied by a plan with a scale. The kitchen, the hearth and the fire. How does the smoke exit (chimneys only appear rather late)? Beliefs and practices relating to the domestic fire. Relations between house and garden, between house and fields; systems of enclosure. Surrounding walls made of stone are rare. Fences, hedges, etc.

Maintenance of the house. Is it resurfaced at fixed intervals? By whom and when? Where are the dead located, if this is relevant? Destruction of the house, e.g. in case of death.

The study of ornamentation implies the study of every detail of the house. The owner of the house should be asked for explanation of every ornament. Such questioning will often reveal the use of blazons, and hence the presence of an aristocracy.

Purpose of Buildings

Besides houses for private use, study with special attention houses for public purposes, particularly men's houses; if they are present, the houses of secret societies, which can be indistinguishable from temples. All Papuan villages are divided into two moieties, each of which has its own men's house. Elsewhere, the building of a men's house is an act no less important than the erection of a royal palace. It can be the sign of the emancipation of those who build it, it can provoke a war, and lead to sacrifices – or to the building of other houses.

Houses of the patriarch, of his wives, his daughters, his married sons, of adolescents.

The house of menstruating women.

Granaries, workshops, etc.

When such a study has been completed, the researcher can turn to the geography of technology. Once the various types of dwelling have been established statistically, one should abstract the notion of the architectural canon. But here, as with all social phenomena, the canon, i.e. the rule or ideal, should be distinguished from the average that is observed.

Agglomeration

The house normally has no independent existence, except in countries where the settlement pattern is essentially dispersed, but this is rare. A study of the dwelling would not be complete without a study of the village or, where relevant, the town. This issue, too often studied in purely geographical terms, should in my view be dealt with at least as much in terms of statistics and techniques.

The village is very often fortified, or else it is built in a military location. The location of a Ligurian village, a Kabyle or Maori village, a Betsileo village is the same: built on a spur allowing the inhabitants to dominate the landscape, the agglomeration is generally accessible only from one side. This is the case with the ancient [European] *oppida*.

The location of a village is not necessarily fixed once and for all: the towns of the Gauls were alternatively located in the plain or on hill tops, and were sometimes fortified, sometimes not. Study temporary camps and caves where people seek shelter; wells; all the collective services. The location of the refuse heap may be determined by religious factors. Use of refuse.

One should then study the village location from a geographical perspective, in relation to fields, to means of transportation, to roads and bridges. The study of towns is a major topic in the history of civilisation.

Some towns are fortified, side by side with towns that are defenceless. The fortified town in this case may correspond to an imperial or royal town. Thus the king's town stands out clearly in Mossi country and as far as the coast of Guinea.

Industries of Transportation[43]

Transportation industries are far more developed than is usually believed. From a technological viewpoint, the world became populated thanks to means of transport: just as the Sahara and Arabia are only habitable for camel breeders, certain parts of South America are only accessible to Indians who know how to use boats. Nevertheless, there exist societies which are still very poor in this respect: small nets are all that Australians possess to carry things, while the whole of north Asia possesses chests, which are often of large size.

Communication Routes

First of all one should observe the layout of the ground: tracks, paths and roads. Show the indigenous names on a map. The use of an airplane will be very helpful for this in savannah or desert landscapes. Tracks can sometimes be seen from the air, even in forest. Relations between villages can exist over very long distances, and relations between tribes are not rare. If appropriate, note the techniques for protecting paths, typical of the whole of Indochina; the presence of barriers, fortifications, *chevaux-de-frise* (thorn fences); sometimes also, protection is ensured by religious prohibitions and taboos.

Bridges seem to be even more common than roads: rope bridges, bridges made of creepers, in Africa and America; suspension bridges throughout Asia, Oceania, and South America. Apaches in North America used to carry their horses from one edge of a canyon to the other using transporter bridges.

Porterage

On all these routes one has to carry. *Man*, or more generally woman, was the first beast of burden. The man holds the spear and the shield; if he carried the burden, he could not protect his wife.

How do people carry things? What instruments are used? The methods for distributing the weight on the body should be observed carefully. One of the reasons for positing the kinship of Asia and part of Oceania with America is the practice of porterage with a headband. Tibetan caravans descend to Nepal, climb the Himalayas and descend again into India carrying everything on the head with the aid of a headband across the forehead. Porterage on the head; with a shoulder yoke; on the hip. Study in each case the gait of the porter, especially on uneven ground.

Next come *vehicles*. The first means of transport on land was no doubt of the trolley type: two poles are dragged along with their tips joined together and taking the load at their centre of gravity. Under the name *travoy* (from the old French *travois*), it can still be seen in North America.

The sledge is probably either prehistoric, or at least as old as the present north Asian civilisation. The Eskimo sledge remains the best.

The wheelbarrow, which implies the wheel, is very ancient throughout Asia. In the Chinese wheelbarrow the wheel was inside the tub. The theory of Mason and Powell on the origin of the cart seems correct: it proposes a trolley pulled by two horses with a wheel added at the centre of gravity. It is a remarkable thing that the Amerindians are aware of disks, and in addition they know the trolley, yet they never equipped a travoy with wheels. We can therefore assume that when they came to America they knew the travoy and the wheel, but did not have the idea of putting the one on the other.

The use of animals for transportation (*saddle animals, packsaddle animals, draught animals*) greatly modified the situation. Here, the same questions arise as with human porterage: how are things carried? What is carried? Etc.

The reindeer must have been a beast of burden in the fairly distant past, but elsewhere than in America. The Eskimos followed the wild reindeer, but they did not domesticate it. Even those Eskimos who live side by side with North American Indians who possessed domesticated reindeer were not able to tame this animal; nevertheless, the Eskimos belong to a civilisation of the reindeer.[1]

Beasts of burden exist almost everywhere. Depending on the regions, we find the llama, the yak and the horse. The South American llama that yields the vicuña belongs to the same family as the Tibetan llama. The arrival of the horse in North America transformed the whole country.[45] In everything to do with draught animals, study the harnessing and yoking. In Antiquity, the most developed yokes were the Asian ones, and among them, those of the Mongols.

The history of the cart and the wheel is among the most important of all historical developments. When observing the mode of transportation, do not fail to mention how the animals are looked after.

Water Transport

Water has never been an obstacle; water is a means of transport. Rivers have never been a hindrance to trade; they made it easier. What sort of water is being crossed? Lakes, rivers, lagoons, and especially the sea, each require an appropriate means of transport.

The most primitive form of transport on water is no doubt represented by floating wood. In all the lagoons along the coast of Guinea the natives keep afloat by holding on to pieces of wood. Several trunks joined together will form a raft, in the simple form still in use among the natives of the Amazon. The Maricopa Indians use only two parallel trunks, tied together crosswise with sticks; they propel the craft using long poles. Sheaves of reed or rush tied together in the shape of a cigar are called balsas. Like the raft, the balsa floats on account of its specific gravity, but it is not watertight. It was known even to the Tasmanians, and it is still used on the Chad and on South American lakes.

Inflated skins used as floats were the starting point for the development of boats made of skin: the kayak and the umiak of the Eskimos, the round boat [coracle] in Ireland, the latter made of an ox skin stretched across a skeleton of branches shaped into a hemisphere. Canoes made of bark (Canada, Guyana) are so light that they can be carried when it is necessary to bypass cataracts.

But the most widespread of all primitive boats is no doubt the dugout made from a simple tree trunk hollowed out with the aid of an adze and fire: it goes back to the Swiss Neolithic and is common to Africa, the two Americas, and Oceania. Such a boat can only be built when suitable timber is available. In Oceania the natives possessed simultaneously single-trunk canoes having their sides raised with planks, and double canoes [catamarans], which could be separated or tied together in a durable manner. The Melanesians travel on their rivers in simple dugouts made of a hollowed trunk which they propel with a paddle, but for the sea they use a boat equipped with an outrigger, which runs parallel with the boat and provides balance. The outrigger is typical of

Polynesia and Indonesia, whence it spread as far as Madagascar. The large boats in Oceania measure more than thirty metres in length; the double canoes in Fiji used to carry a hundred passengers and several tons of cargo.

The Polynesians are admirable navigators. Their homeland is probably somewhere in southern Asia; in the course of time, they swarmed across the whole Pacific and as far as Easter Island.

The study of boats can scarcely be undertaken except by a sailor; he or she should study the planking, the stern and the bow. The keel is a recent invention, dating back barely to the seventh or eight century AD. The invention of the stem rudder is necessarily recent since it presupposes the presence of the keel. It is the Normans who brought in this development between the ninth and the twelfth century. The invention of the stem rudder changed the entire art of navigation.

The study of the boat's ornamentation will always yield interesting results: the boat is an animate being, the boat sees, the boat feels. Very often it has an eye,[46] sometimes a neck, often teeth, whence the name of the Norwegian drakkar (dragon): it bites. Melanesian, Polynesian and Papuan boats have teeth.

The boat is a machine driven by an engine, with the aid of a particular mode of transmission. The simplest mode of transmission will be that provided by pole, paddles, scull or oars. Study the synchronisation of the paddlers or rowers, and the songs of the paddlers; note all the beliefs and all the rites concerning paddling. It is curious to note that the North American Indians who live in contact with the Eskimos never learned from them how to use the oars that Eskimo women use on their large umiaks.

The sail was a great invention. The triangular sail, at first without a mast, is known throughout the Pacific, while the Chinese junk is equipped with a square sail, generally plaited. Note all the systems of ties, all the knots and the sails.

How do people orient themselves? The stars as points of reference. Do the natives know how to take a bearing? Do they have maps? Etc.

Living on boats, and boat houses.[47]

Notes

1. On this topic see Mauss, M., 'Les techniques du corps', *J. de Psychologie*, 1935: 271–293.
2. [*poutre* 'beam' may be a mistake for *outre* 'animal skin inflated and sewn up'.]
3. Villeneuve, A. de, 'Etude sur une coutume somalie: les femmes cousues', *JSA* 7/1, 1937: 15–32.
4. Reuleaux, F., see esp. *Theoretische Kinematik*, Berlin, 1875; *Der Konstrukteur*, Berlin, 1895.
5. Noting the lack of knifes among the Seri Indians, MacGee [n. 15] concludes that this is a society with a 'primitive' character; the comment is inadequate.
6. This heading covers numerous crafts, which, however, are well-defined and follow procedures and forms imposed by tradition.
7. All industries imply a division of labour: firstly in time, if the tasks are performed by a single individual, and then between the workers, who each take up a specialisation.

8. On traps in general, Mérite, E., *Les pièges*, Paris, Payot, 1942. There is a good study of traps, with a native language description for each type, in Boas, F., *Ethnology of the Kwakiutl*, ARBAE 35 (1913–14), 1921; and *The Kwakiutl of Vancouver Island*, Mem. AMNH (Jesup) 5/2, 1909: 301–522.
9. Cline, W., *Mining and Metallurgy in Negro Africa*, Am. Anth., General Series in Anthropology 5, 1937. Hough, W., *Fire as an Agent in Human Culture*, Smiths. Inst., USNM Bulletin 39, Washington, 1926. Leroi-Gourhan, A., *L'homme et la matière*, Paris, 1943: 202–213.
10. Frazer, Sir J.G., *Mythes sur l'origine du feu*, trans., Paris, Payot, 1931.
11. The lack of pottery in a large part of the Pacific has led some to posit the primitive character of the civilisation in question, without taking into account the lack of clay in the region concerned.
12. Bobart, H., *Basket Work through the Ages*, London, 1936. Graebner, F., 'Gewirkte Taschen und Spiralwulstkörbe in der Südsee', *Ethnologica*, 2/1: 25–42. Haeberlin, H.K., Teit, J. and Roberts, H.H. (dir. F. Boas), *Coiled Basketry in British Columbia and Surrounding Region*, ARBAE 41 (1919–24), 1928: 119–484. Kroeber, A., *Basket Designs of the Indians of North West California*, Berkeley, 1905. James, G.W., *Indian Basketry*, 2nd ed., Pasadena, 1902. Leroi-Gourhan, A., *L'homme* ...[n. 9]: 284–289. Mason, O.T., *Aboriginal American Basketry*, USNM Report, 1901–02 (1904): 171–548.
13. Hodge, F.W. (ed.), *Handbook of American Indians*, Smiths. Inst., BAE Bulletin 30.
14. Dechelette, J., *Manuel d'archéologie préhistorique, celtique et gallo-romaine*, Paris, 1924–29. Franchet, L., *Céramique primitive*, Paris, 1911. Hodge, F.W., *Handbook* ...[n. 13]. Holmes, W.H., *Aboriginal Pottery of the Eastern United States*, ARBAE 20 (1898–99), Washington, 1903. Leroi-Gourhan, A., *L'homme* ... [n. 9]: 218–235. Lowie, R.H., *Manuel d'anthropologie culturelle*, trans., Paris, Payot, 1936: 147–156.
15. MacGee, W.J., *The Seri Indians*, ARBAE 17 (1895–96), 1898. [Mauss means Southern U.S.]
16. Malinowski, B., *Argonauts of the Western Pacific*, London, 1922.
17. Harrison, H.S., *Handbook of the Horniman Museum: War and the Chase*, London, 1924. Leroi-Gourhan, A., *Milieu et techniques*, Paris, 1945: 13–68. Lowie, R.H., *Manuel* ...[n. 14]: 232–242. Montandon, G., *L'ologénèse culturelle: traité d'ethnologie culturelle*, Paris, 1934: 368–495 (to be used only with caution).
18. Balfour, H., 'On the Structure and Affinities of the Composite Bow', *JAI* 19, 1890: 220–246.
19. On this point, see Lilienfeld, P. von, *Gedanken über die Socialwissenschaft der Zukunft*, Mitau, 1873–81.
20. See the works carried out under the direction of Malinowski, notably: Fortes, M. and Fortes, S., 'Food in the Domestic Economy of the Tallensi (Gold Coast)', *Africa* 9, 1936: 237–276. Hunter, M., *Reaction to Conquest*, Oxford, 1936. Richards, A.I., *Hunger and Work in a Savage Tribe*, London, 1932; *Land, Labour and Diet in Northern Rhodesia*, Oxford, 1940.
21. For planning the investigation, see Firth, R., 'The Sociological Study of Native Diet', *Africa* 7, 1934: 401–414.
22. Laufer, B., *Geophagy*, FMNH, Anthrop. Ser.18/2, Chicago, 1930.
23. Steinmetz, S.R., 'Endokannibalismus', in *Gesammelte kleinere Schriften zur Ethnologie und Soziologie*, 1: 132–260, Groningen, 1928. Kern, H., 'Menschenfleisch als Arzenei', *IAE* 9 (Supplement: Ethnographische Beiträge, celebrating 70th birthday of A. Bastian) 1896: 37–40. Koch, Th., 'Die Anthropophagie der Süd-Amerikanischen Indianer', *IAE* 12/2–3, 1899: 78–111. Volhard, E., *Kannibalismus*, Stuttgart, 1939.
24. Felice, Ph. de, *Poisons sacrés, ivresses divines*, Paris, 1936. Lumholtz, C., *Symbolism of the Huichol Indians*, Mem. AMNH 3, Anthrop. 2, 1900; *Unknown Mexico*, London, 1903. Rouhier, A., *Le peyotl*, Paris, 1927. Waterman, T.T., *The Religious Practices of the Diegueño Indians*, U. California, Published in Am. Archaeol. and Ethnol. 8/6, 1910: 271–358. For the Indo-European world: Dumézil, G., *Le festin d'immortalité*, Annales du Musée Guimet 34, Paris, 1924.
25. See Candolle, A. de, *L'origine des plantes cultivées*, Paris, 1883. Haudricourt, A.G. and Hedin, L., *L'homme et les plantes cultivées*, Paris, 1943. George, P., *Géographie agricole du monde*, Paris, 1946.
26. Bruel, G., 'Les Babinga', *Revue d'ethnographie et de sociologie*, 1910: 111–125.
27. Jenks, A.E., *The Wild Rice Gatherers of the Upper Lakes*, ARBAE 19/2 (1897–98), 1900: 1019–1137.
28. Leroi-Gourhan, A. *Milieu* ... [n. 17]: 69–95 (hunting and fishing). Lindner, K., *La chasse préhistorique*, trans. from German, Paris, Payot, 1941. Lowie, R.H., *Manuel* ... [n. 14]: 232–254. Mason, O.T., *Traps of the American Indians*, Smiths. Inst. Report (1901), Washington, 1902. Mérite. E., *Pièges* [n. 8].

29. On fishing, see Best, E., *The Maori*, 2 vols, Wellington, 1924. Roth, H.L., *The Natives of Sarawak and British North Borneo*, 2 vols, 1896. Monod, Th., *L'industrie des pêches au Cameroun*, Paris, 1929. Mason, O.T., *Aboriginal American Harpoons*, Smiths. Inst. Report (1900), Washington, 1902.
30. On the rules of fishing: Rattray, R.S., *Ashanti*, Oxford, 1923.
31. See Leenhardt, M., *Gens de la grande terre*, Paris, Gallimard, 1935.
32. Antonius, O., *Grundzüge einer Stammesgeschichte der Haustiere*, Jena, 1922. Geoffroy Saint-Hilaire, I., *Domestication et naturalisation des animaux utiles*, rapport général à M. le Ministre de l'Agriculture, Paris, 1834. Hahn, E., *Die Haustiere* ..., Leipzig, 1896. Laufer, B., *Sino-iranica* ..., Chicago, 1919. Leroi-Gourhan, A., *Milieu* ... [n. 17]: 83–119. Ridgeway, W., *The Origin and Influence of the Thoroughbred Horse*, Cambridge, 1905.
33. On cattle property marks as a possible origin of writing, see Van Gennep, A., *De l'héraldisation de la marque de propriété et des origines du blazon*, Paris, 1906.
34. On agriculture and the various agricultural techniques, see Best, E., *The Maori*, 2 vols, Wellington, 1924. Crozet, J., *Nouveau voyage à la mer du Sud* ..., Paris, 1783. Hahn, E., *Die Entstehung der Pflugkultur*, Heidelberg, 1909. Leenhardt, M., *Gens* ... [n. 31]. Leroi-Gourhan, A., *Milieu* ... [n. 17]: 120–137. Mason, O.T., *Woman's Share in Primitive Culture*, London, 1895. Robequin, Ch., *Le Than Hoa*, Paris, Brussels, 1929. Vavilov, N.J., 'Sur l'origine de l'agriculture mondiale d'après les recherches récentes', *Revue de botanique appliquée et agriculture coloniale*, Paris, 1932. The same journal published a more elaborate account of Vavilov's ideas: 'Les bases botaniques et géographiques de la sélection', trans. A. Haudricourt, 1936.
35. Malinowski, B., *Argonauts* ... [n. 16]; *Coral Gardens*. On production surplus, see also Herskovits, M.J., *The Economic Life of Primitive Peoples*, New York, 1940.
36. See Muraz, G., 'Les cache-sexes du Centre Africain', *JSA*, 1932: 103–112.
37. Harcourt, R. d', *Les tissus indiens du vieux Pérou*, Paris, 1924. Hooper, L., *Hand-loom Weaving, Plain and Ornamental*, London, 1910. Iklé, F., *Primäre Textile Techniken*, Zürich, 1935. Leroi-Gourhan, A., *L'homme* ... [n. 9]: 290–309. Ling Roth, H., 'Studies in Primitive Looms', *JRAI*, 1916–18.
38. See Leroi-Gourhan, A., *Milieu* ... [n. 17]: 254–320; see also the bibliography on architecture in the present work [Chapter 5, n. 26].
39. On the Bedouin tent, see Boucheman, A. de, *Matériaux de la vie bédouine*, Damascus, 1935.
40. See Schebesta, P., *Les Pygmées*, trans. from German, Paris, 1940.
41. On the igloo, see Boas, F., *The Central Eskimo*, ARBAE 6 (1884–85),1888.
42. On the Betsileo house, a 'perpetual and universal calendar', see Dubois, H.M., *Monographie des Betsileo*, Paris, 1938.
43. Haddon, A.C. and Hornell, J., *Canoes of Oceania*, 3 vols, Honolulu, 1936–38. Harrison, H.S., *A Handbook to the Cases Illustrating Simple Means of Travel and Transport by Land and Water*, London, 1925. La Roerie, G. and Vivielle, J., *Navires et marins: de la rame à l'hélice*, Paris, 1930. Leroi-Gourhan, A., *L'Homme* ... [n. 9]: 119–165. Mason, O.T., *Primitive Travel and Transportation*, Washington, 1896. Thomas, N.W., 'Australian Canoes and Rafts', *JAI* 35, 1905: 56–79.
44. Leroi-Gourhan, A., *La Civilisation du renne*, Paris, 1936.
45. Wissler, C., 'The Influence of the Horse in the Development of Plains Culture', *Am. Anth.* 16, 1914: 1–25.
46. On the boat's eye, see Hornell, J., 'Survivals of the Oculi in Modern Boats', *JRAI* 53, 1923: 289–321.
47. **Chapter Bibliography**. Ankermann, B., 'Kulturkreise und Kulturschichten in Afrika', *Z. f. Ethnologie*, Berlin, 1905; 'L'état actuel de l'ethnographie de l'Afrique méridionale', *Anthropos*, 1906. Boas, F., *The Kwakiutl* ... [n. 8]; *The Central Eskimo* ... [n. 41]: 399–669. Bogoras, W., *The Chukchee: Material Culture*, Mem. AMNH (Jesup), Leiden, 1905. *British Museum Handbook to the Ethnographical Collections*, 2nd ed., 1925. Dixon, R.B., *The Building of Cultures*, London, 1928. Espinas, A., *Les origines de la technologie*, Paris, 1897. Graebner, F., *Methode der Ethnologie*, Heidelberg, 1911; *Gewirkte Taschen* ... [n. 12], Berlin, 1907; 'Kulturkreise und Kulturschichten in Ozeanien', *Z. f. Ethnologie*, 1905. Haddon, A.C., *The Decorative Art of New Guinea*, Dublin, 1894; *Evolution in Art*, London, 1899; *Reports of the Cambridge Anthropological Expedition to the Torres Straits*, Cambridge, 1901–02. Harrison, H.S., *Handbooks of the Horniman Museum: From Stone to Steel; War and the Chase; Evolution of the Domestic Arts*, pts 1 and 2; *Travel and Transport*), London, 1923–29. Leroi-Gourhan, A.,

L'homme ... [n. 9]; *Milieu* ... [n. 17]. Lowie, R.H., *Manuel* ... [n. 14]. Mason, O.T., *Influence of Environment upon Human Industries or Arts*, Smiths. Inst. Report, 1895: 639–665; *Technogeography or the Relation of the Earth to the Industries of Mankind*, Washington, 1894; *The Origins of Invention*, Washington, 1895. Noiré, L., *Das Werkzeug und seine Bedeutung für die Entwickelungsgeschichte der Menschheit*, Mainz, 1880. Nordenskiöld, E., *Comparative Ethnographical Studies*, Göteborg, 1919; *An Ethnographical Analysis of the Material Culture of two Indian Tribes in the Gran Chaco*, Göteborg, 1919. Powell, J.W., *Relation of Primitive Peoples to Environment*, Smiths. Inst. Report, 1895: 625–647. See also all the reports of that Institution. Ridgeway, W., *Origin* ... [n. 32]. Roth, W.E., *Arts and Crafts of the Guiana Indians*, ARBAE 38 (1916–17), 1924. Schurtz, H., *Das afrikanische Gewerbe*, Leipzig, 1900; *Urgeschichte der Kultur*, Leipzig and Vienna, 1900. Weule, K., *Kulturelemente der Menschheit*, 15th ed., revised, Stuttgart, 1924; *Die Urgesellschaft und ihre Lebensfürsorge*, Stuttgart, 1924. Wissler, C., *The American Indian*, 3rd ed., New York, 1938; *Material Culture of the Blackfoot Indians*, New York, 1910.

5

Aesthetics

Aesthetic phenomena form one of the largest components in the social activity of human beings, and not merely in their individual activity. An object, an action, a line of poetry is beautiful when it is recognised as beautiful by the majority of people of taste. This is what people call the grammar of art. All aesthetic phenomena are in some degree social phenomena.

It is very difficult to distinguish aesthetic phenomena from technical ones, for a particular reason: a technique is always a series of traditional actions; a series, that is to say an organic concatenation, designed to produce an effect that is not only *sui generis* – as in religion – but also physical. Now, very often the aesthetic work too consists in an object. Thus the distinction between techniques and arts, especially when we are dealing with creative arts, is only a distinction made by collective psychology: in the one case the object has been produced and is thought of in relation to its physical purpose; in the other, it has been produced and is thought of in relation to the pursuit of aesthetic sensation. The outsider will make the distinction by questioning in the first instance the maker or creator. There is technique in art and there is a technical architecture; but the aesthetic object can be recognised by the presence of a notion more complex than simply that of utility.

As soon as modelling (*la plastique*) appears, one sees the rise of notions of equilibrium and, therefore, of notions of rhythm; as soon as the rhythmical (*la rythmique*) appears, art appears. Socially and individually, man is a rhythmic animal.

The notion of utility characterises the notion of technique; the notion of (relative) lack of utility characterises the notion of aesthetics: the aesthetic phenomenon is always conceived of in the minds of those concerned as a form of play, as something superadded, as a luxury.

Where is the aesthetic to be found? Firstly, in the whole range of techniques, and especially in the higher techniques: a garment is an adornment even more than a protection [against the elements], a house is an aesthetic creation; a boat is often highly decorated. Among the peoples that concern us here, ornamentation forms part of technology; and to it there are added in addition elements of religion such as religious representations and equilibria. The aesthetic dimension contributes to efficacy, no less than do the rituals (the number of purely secular objects seems rather limited). Conversely, there is always an element of art and an element of technique in every religious object.

One of the best criteria for distinguishing the aesthetic component in an object or an action is the Aristotelian distinction, the *theoria*:[1] an aesthetic object is an object one can contemplate; an aesthetic phenomenon contains an element of contemplation, of satisfaction extrinsic to immediate need, a pleasure that is sensory but disinterested. In all these societies one finds a capacity for disinterested enjoyment, for pure sensitivity and even a sense of nature.

The aesthetic domain can be highly developed: the aesthetic of games, of dancing, of behaviour itself. One component of rhythm consists in the representation of the behaviour itself. To study aesthetic phenomena is to study first and foremost an aspect of the object and of the behaviour. So one can gauge in each object the aesthetic behaviour it embodies, its aesthetic component.[2]

I defined technical phenomena as consisting in actions that combine to produce a result that is physically or chemically determined. I shall define aesthetic phenomena by the presence of the notion of beauty. It is impossible to find a definition of beauty that is not subjective. Thus one needs to list all the games and all the activities that create a pleasure corresponding to the beautiful, from a dye (*teinture*) to a painting (*peinture*).

Another formulation allows us to define the beautiful via the notion of pleasure and enjoyment, enjoyment for its own sake, which is sometimes pursued with mad intensity. Enthusiasm and catharsis: among the Zuñi of Central America there exist festivals which end with general purging and vomiting.

A further definition again is that based on rhythm, as studied by Wundt and, with him, by the whole school of Völkerpsychologie.[3] In his *Primitive Art*[4] Boas connects all art to rhythm, for where there is rhythm, generally there is something aesthetic; where there are tones, variations in touch and intensity, generally there is something aesthetic. Prose is only beautiful when it is to some extent rhythmic and to some extent chanted. Differences in tone, touch and feeling – all this is rhythm and all this is art.

Lastly, in most of the societies that belong to ethnography, there exists an important phenomenon, namely the mixture of arts. Most of the arts are conceptualised simultaneously, by people who are wholes (*des hommes totaux*): a decoration is always made in relation to the object being decorated.

The significance of aesthetic phenomena in all the societies that have preceded us is great. In this respect contemporary societies show a marked regression compared with preceding civilisations. Robertson Smith has a fine comment on the gloomy character of the post-Japhetic religions and on the joyousness of paganism.[5]

A second way of studying the aesthetic domain consists in studying precisely the distribution of this notion of beauty in the society under study. The notion is not found in all classes of the society in the same form, and it applies to different objects.

The aesthetic always carries with it a notion of sensory pleasure. There can be no beauty without sensory pleasure. A big Australian *corroboree* is called 'one which unravels the belly'. One should therefore note in every aesthetic phenomenon the problem of the mixing of the arts; in a *corroboree* there is everything, including painting, both the painting of bodies and the painting of objects.

On this basis, it is desirable to study each art, each artistic system, each mixing of the arts, from all possible vantage points and firstly from that of psycho-physiology and the perception of colour.[6] One should then observe the contrasts, the harmonies and disharmonies, the rhythms and the relations between different rhythms, the representations and relations between rhythms and representations. This is a difficult study, but an interesting one for the graphic arts – it is far more complicated in its application to the acoustic arts.

One should analyse the differences in sensitivity within the society: some individuals are highly perceptive, while others remain very insensitive. Study next all the emotions involved: those of author, actor, hearer and spectator; also the interfusing of the whole with the general principles of psycho-physiology. Study the creative faculties, the mysteries of intuition and of creation *ex nihilo*. How did this song originate? People generally know to whom it was revealed, where, under what conditions, and whether an old verse or an old song has been modified. Record also the whole sociological side of aesthetic phenomena, the role of festivals in public life. This involves the notion of the fair, of enjoyment and play. All of this coexists in the aesthetic phenomenon, in a mixture that is often inextricable. Note the religious significance of aesthetic phenomena, which are closely linked to religious phenomena. This leads on to the theory of collective representations of art. Here one encounters a great theory to which I expressly subscribe, namely Preuss's teaching on the common origins of religion and art: the religious origin of art and the artistic origin of religion.[7]

Once aesthetic phenomena have been defined and circumscribed in this way, one should at last study their ethnographic aspect, that is to say the artistic history of civilisation. A large part of our history of civilisation consists of history of art, simply because the latter particularly interests us.

The cartography of the plastic arts emerges as absolutely necessary; it forms part of the description of types (*typographie*) and has not been sufficiently studied. Thus, the shape of certain objects characterises a society – for example, the beaked pot or beaker invented by the Celts. It is the whole range of typological contacts that makes it possible to trace civilisational wholes, or successive layers and linked sequences of civilisations. But at the same time research is needed on what makes an era or society distinctive: the study of shared elements and the study of divergent or unique elements should proceed side by side. The character of a society's art needs to be portrayed in its entirety: one should make an individual portrait.

On this basis, study each individual aesthetic phenomenon, starting with the objects. In large part, the study of aesthetics consists simply in collecting objects. Collect everything, *including* what is easily collected, jewels in particular. Jewels, even very primitive ones, are art; a bodily ornament is art. In a similar vein, study all the objects used in ceremonial – embroidery, feather decorations and the like. A great many arts are ceremonial arts, where the impression of wealth and expense is particularly sought after. There is enjoyment in materials, and enjoyment in the use of these materials: jade is one of the most beautiful materials that exists. An item of clothing is nearly always a ceremonial garment. The impression of luxury plays a major part in the notion of art.

Next come sculpture and painting. Sculpture covers something quite different from what we understand by the word. We have a definition of sculpture in the round that assimilates it to a statue; but a decorated stake or a decorated pipe is equally sculpture. From another point of view, it is not the material by itself that makes something an art object; it is not because an object is made of marble that it is a work of art.

As far as possible, study everything *in situ*. When the object itself cannot be removed, communicate a photograph, or a print (*estampage*) redrawn after the photograph, e.g. for body paintings. Take all the everyday objects, one by one, and ask the informant whether they are beautiful. The whistle is an art object throughout America. Almost always, an art object hides a meaning, a particular shape presents a symbol. It is up to the fieldworker to find the exact meaning of this symbol. We [Westerners] study symbolism starting from the notion of a pure symbol as in mathematics. But what characterises a symbol is the way in which one form of thing is thought into another thing. One tries to think the thing that the art object signifies; here is a whole language that has to be deciphered. Finally, many art objects have a religious value – why? And they have an economic value – again, why?

Study carefully all the circumstances surrounding each artistic object and event: where, who, when, in what capacity, for whom, for what purpose. An art object is by definition an object recognised as such by the group. It is therefore necessary to analyse the feelings of the individual making use of this object. In this kind of enquiry, even more than in any other, the European observer should be wary of his or her personal impressions. The form in its totality should be analysed by the native with the native's visual sense. After the analysis of the whole, move on to the analysis – still the native's – of each motif and each system of motifs.

After the detailed study of the various subjects making up the object, move on to study its type, that is to say the object as a whole. An aesthetic object is always a whole (*ensemble*), so it has a general form – a type. And when several objects present the same type, we can then say that this type is one that is generalised in a particular industry in a particular society. Here we enter the realm of typology, which offers a starting point for studying the relations between arts and societies.

All aesthetic phenomena can be divided into two groups: pure artistic phenomena and play [or games – *jeux*]. All aesthetic phenomena are ludic phenomena, but not all games are necessarily aesthetic phenomena. In the artistic phenomenon the notion of entertainment, of relatively disinterested pleasure, is accompanied by the sensation of the beautiful. We can also distinguish arts from play fairly clearly by the serious character of the former – the enjoyable activity of play versus the serious activity of art. Games form part of aesthetics; they are a method of creating disinterested enjoyment; they are traditional acts, generally carried out collectively.

The classification of arts proposed by Wundt distinguishes between plastic arts, comprising music and dance, and ideal arts, which are governed by an idea, held by author and spectators alike. But in this I only see an expression of our contemporary pedantry in matters of art. The Japanese see no difference between a painting and make-up.

Play[8]

Games are traditional activities whose aim is sensory pleasure – itself aesthetic to some degree. Games are often the origin of crafts and of numerous higher activities, ritual or natural, which were first tried out in the 'unnecessary' activity that takes the form of games.

Games are distinguished according to age, sex, generation, time and space. An investigation of games should start with a psycho-physiological study of the activity of playing: the action involved, becoming tired, the relaxation and pleasure provided by the game. The relations between body and mind while playing: study everything that in this context belongs to the realm of psycho-physiology and also psycho-sociology. The people I play with – are they or are they not from my family? Furthermore, games of physical skill involve all the techniques of the body.

Culin distinguishes games into ritual and non-ritual, games of chance and games that have nothing to do with chance, games of bodily skill and games of manual dexterity. This classification ignores the notion of the agonistic or competitive, that of questions that one asks the game to answer, which seems to me to be of prime importance: games are agonistic, or they are not, they pit two sides or two individuals against one another, or they do not. These distinctions will intersect ritual versus non-ritual games, physical versus oral: a physical game, like an oral one, can be ritual or non-ritual. Games can further be distinguished into public versus private, even if the latter always imply at least a minimum of publicity.

Physical games can easily be divided into games of skill, games involving or not involving chance, games with or without an element of divination; and games of luck properly speaking, which are nearly always games of skill. Another classification distinguishes games according to the players: their sex, age, profession and social class. Moreover, such and such a game is played at a particular season, in a particular place; many games are nocturnal. Games often take place in the public square, which is sacred ground. Some involve the entire population.

For each game study the mix of art and play, of religion and play, of drama and play, of physical and verbal.

A further division cuts across the preceding ones. Many games are imitations of useful activities, but in this notion of mimicry we should also distinguish what is true mimicry, whether verbal or physical.

Some very simple games have as their sole aim the relaxation produced by laughter, an effect of surprise; others can be far more complicated, for example acting games. Drama is always mimicry, which can go very far. I would include here living animals treated as toys as a result of the child's cruelty. Still other games tend towards the acme of intelligence: mathematical games, sticks, knucklebones. Primitive forms of chess board were established for North West America by Tylor; spillikins are a major game in America. Questions of divination and even cosmology come into all this, side by side with games of skill pure and simple, such as the mora,[9] or riddles.

Games can also be classified according to their consequences, by the element of divination and success that they entail. Very often the game allows the determination of luck; even skill is a matter of luck. The spinning top is a religious game in America.

Finally, for the individual, a game can be very serious, as may be seen among the Kanaks [of New Caledonia] or the Papuans, where the future entrant to a drum competition rehearses his piece privately for a whole season.

Physical Games

Physical games entail a maximum of bodily effort, and a maximum number of objects to be manipulated. They are very generally accompanied by verbal games. Material games are not to be separated from physical games. The maximum of toys is represented by North Asia and Far East Asia.

The most widespread game, reported worldwide, is the string game or cat's cradle. It is one of the most difficult games to describe. The fieldworker should learn how to make every figure so as to be able to reproduce the movements afterwards. Use words and sketches since film blurs the figures. To make the sketch indicate the position of the string at each moment and also the direction in which it will be moved so as to pass from one position to the next. The written description will call on a precise vocabulary: everything that happens on the back of the hand will be referred to as dorsal, everything that happens on the palm as palmar. Thus each finger has a palmar and a dorsal surface. Movement proceeding towards the little finger is called radial, while movement towards the thumb is ulnar. Lastly, the positions of the string in relation to the fingers can be proximal (near the palm) or distal (near the fingertip).[10] This terminology can be applied equally well in studies of wickerwork or basketry, ropemaking and esparto goods.

Material games can be divided into permanent games and non-permanent games, children's games and adults' games.

Among permanent games the first to be mentioned are dolls; then all the equipment for musical games: rattles, clappers, etc.; games with weapons and with bats; all the Jack-in-the-box games, the diabolos; ball games, general throughout America; then pebble games, hopscotch (Parisian children who play hopscotch 'go to Heaven').

Ball games when played by adults generally have a ritual character. They are games of skill and games of strength, often played collectively; they correspond to a social expression of prestige by determining the side which will be victorious; it is a matter of winning, of being the strongest, the champion. A divinatory element is mixed in with all this: the winners have the gods on their side; the gods have played alongside them, just as in war they have fought alongside the winners. In a ball game, record the location and the terms of engagement.[11] Most of the great temples of Central America are sanctuaries for ball games, and most of the great rituals correspond to matches in these games.

Games of skill typologically akin to the greasy pole or to kite-flying also have a ritual character.[12] The history of the royal family of Siam [Thailand] is linked with the history of the kite. Tournaments and races for kites are typical of the entire Pacific and of the Indian Ocean. The cup-and-ball game existed in the Magdalenian, and is found today among the Eskimos. In the disk game the object has to be pierced while it rolls, and symbolises the solar disk.

Among physical games are included also athletic games, individual or collective, like tug of war or the game of hoop and whoop.[13] Polo comes to us from Persia and derives from the game of chess, while water polo is said to be a Malayan invention.

Verbal Games

I will be very brief on verbal games, which we shall meet again when talking of literature.

Under verbal games come all riddles, enigmas, rhymes, puns, including scatological jokes and competitions in uttering obscenities. All this is at the root of literature. Songs, that is to say [oral] literature, accompany almost all games of dancing.

The existence of a category of 'games of chance' is scarcely valid except for our modern civilisations: we have invented new mental categories. Everywhere else, a game of chance is a game of chance *and* a game of skill: knucklebones, dice, the game of mancala throughout Africa.[14]

The Arts[15]

The arts are distinguished from games in that they entail an exclusive quest for beauty. However, the distinction between games and arts proper should not be regarded as absolutely rigid.

To study the arts, we shall proceed as we did for techniques, by starting with the body. All the arts can be classified into plastic and musical. The former can be defined by the use of the body or of a temporary or permanent object; consequently they include all the bodily arts: the art of adornment (*ornementique*) and finery, including painting and sculpture, since people sculpt their bodies when they deform and tattoo them. A jewel is intended for wearing; the art of adornment is far more developed in these societies than in our own. After the decoration of everyday objects comes decoration for the sake of decoration – art as ideal – which makes up only a tiny part of art. Under the musical arts fall poetry and drama, as they were conceived by Plato.

A division that appears to me more logical would proceed otherwise. I would start with one of the musical arts, namely dance. Dance is very close to play – the progression from one to other is almost imperceptible; and dance is at the origin of all the arts. Certain peoples – the inhabitants of Tierra del Fuego, the Australians – know of only very few arts, and put all their artistic effort into dance. The Australians have an important artistic life; they have operas – the *corroborees*, which include actors, sets, poetry, drama ... We are far too inclined to think that our divisions are imposed on us, once for all, by the human mind; the categories of the human mind will continue to change, and what seems well established in our minds will one day be completely abandoned.

Plastic Arts

I shall begin with the plastic arts, which have the advantage here of coming immediately after techniques. Not all techniques are arts, but plastic arts are techniques. The distinction in the work of the craftsman is faint, and difficult to find; it is a distinction of viewpoints, which the native will explain. We shall therefore regard all the plastic arts as techniques but as ones that are more aesthetic than techniques pure and simple. All art is rhythmic, but there is more to art than rhythms.

The plastic quality of an art is defined by the creation of an object, whether temporary or permanent. A big mound or a big tumulus is a work of art, and so are the tattoos of the Marquesas Islanders. Elsewhere, people paint their faces or their bodies for a particular ritual; feather adornments in the Mato Grosso are made to last only for two or three days.

So a study of the plastic arts should begin with the collection of all the art objects, including the most humble ones: paper dolls, lanterns in bladders, etc. A tree may be sculpted on all sides, in which case the craftsman has a feeling for volume and relations; the handle of a fork used by cannibals is sculpture, and so is a handsome specimen of American whistle.

In studying the plastic arts, one should use a classification drawn from the body, as we did for techniques. The first plastic art is that of the individual who works on his or her body: dance, gait, rhythm of the gestures, etc.

Like techniques, plastic arts can be divided into general ones and special ones. The general techniques of plastic arts comprise first of all dyeing, together with its derivative, painting. Dyeing and painting lead on to drawing, which makes possible the distribution of tones over the various parts of the area to be decorated. A purely graphic drawing is seldom directed to producing an aesthetic effect; nevertheless, it can achieve this effect, for instance thanks to the division of the paper. We must not forget also the rhythmic quality of drawing, which is a rhythm of markings. Study all the materials used for dyeing, painting and drawing: chalk, charcoal, ochre ... Take a sample of the raw material at various stages in its use. What colour mixes are produced, with what components? Carry out the same work on varnishes and resins, recording the indigenous terms. How are paintings fixed? Consider the origins of the pen, the pencil and the brush.

The special plastic arts can be classified according to the objects being created or decorated, as was the case for industries. They form a whole body of techniques which are combined in the creation of a particular object, for particular purposes. Here at last the notion of need comes into play – aesthetic need in particular.

The starting point is decoration of the body. The first decorated object is the human body, and more specifically the male body. The direct ornamentation of the body can be called *cosmetics*. Humans have always sought to add on to their person something socially recognised as beautiful, and incorporate this element in their selves. We shall keep the term indirect ornamentation or *finery* to refer to objects that are movable. Then comes the ornamentation of objects from everyday life, whether movable or immovable; and finally we have pure ornamentation, or ideal arts: sculpture, architecture, painting and engraving.

Cosmetics[16]

Cosmetics covers beautification that has been added on to the body and can consist in what to outsiders may appear as disfigurement. For all works of art realised on the body take a photograph and make a drawing (preferably giving exact measurements). In societies that practise cranial deformation, like the Mangbetu of the Belgian Congo, bring back deformed skulls. The observer should distinguish between public and private cosmetics, permanent and temporary ones, between total and partial ornamentation of the body. These divisions do not necessarily match up with each other.

One method of proceeding is with an inventory, following all the rules that apply to producing a good inventory: where, who, when, in what capacity, on whom, for whom, why, how. Note the aesthetics of each object: the natives find it beautiful; but why? In another direction, attempts should be made to elicit the symbolism of each decoration.

All decorations for dancing should be studied individually – both direct decoration of the body and ornaments added on to it, such as masks.

For the temporary decorations, collect all the materials: oils, urine, soap, spittle, blood used as glue or for ornamentation, studying each individual effect as well as the overall result. Tattoos and bodily painting may indicate the clan, family or individual. Sometimes too they indicate a solemn event: a dramatic ceremony, death ritual, initiation, war. Who has the right to bear a particular adornment or coat of arms?

As for permanent ornamentation, we come first to scarring and deformation. The tattoo is a sign or symbol, in particular of social rank or birth, and even of nationality. Populations that practise deformation of the ears do so in order to mark each member of the group with a single sign.

The same questions are to asked here as with temporary ornamentation. In addition, always study the symbolism and the religious, initiatory or jural value of the mark. There are rights and duties in tattooing and scarring: no one can shirk them with impunity. Study each deformation individually, distinguishing by sex, age and clan. Indicate the depth of the deformation, whether it affects the epidermis or the whole skin (stamping, moulding). Study deformations affecting bone: deformations of the fingers, amputation of the little finger, or of toes. Deformation of the skull, which is frequent; deformation of the ears ... Flattening or sharpening of the nose. Take photographs of skulls, or mouldings, look for ancient skulls. Very often, the peoples who practise cranial deformation are peoples with cradles.

Fat deliberately cultivated by women (steatopygia) is typical of the whole Turkish world and part of the Black world. Amputation of the breast, for instance among the Amazons.

Deformation relating to hair: the growth of head or pubic hair may be associated with vegetation. The hair style is determined by fashion, and also by the rank, clan, family, age and social status of the individual. How do people shave their heads? What fixatives are used for the hair? Mixing of the hat and the hair style, braiding with pearls.[17] Finally, the study of depilation.

The orifices of the body are points of danger that need to be protected: deformations of the eyes, eyelashes and eyebrows; colouring of the eyes, whether temporary or permanent: the evil eye. Deformations of the mouth: the labret, culminating in the lip plate. Holes pierced in the tongue, for instance among the Maya high priests of ancient Mexico. The removal of incisors in Australia is sometimes related to a cult of water – water must not be bitten. Sometimes too it is related to a cult of speech – the extracted tooth is crushed and then sent to the future mother-in-law who must swallow it; from this moment on, son-in-law and mother-in-law may no longer speak to each other.

Deformations of the ears: ears made to stick out, or to lie close to the skull; stretching or piercing of the earlobes. Deformations of the nose: perforation of the nasal septum, permanent or not. Deformation of the sexual organs: the scar is supposed to make the organ beautiful and clean, and is also a tribal marker: infibulation, sewing, subincision and incapsulation for male organs. Circumcision is a form of tattoo; it is first and foremost an aesthetic operation. For women, sewing of the labia, excision of the clitoris, elongation of the clitoris, elongation of the vulva ... Deformation of the scrotum or anus.

Scars and deformations as a whole merit the term *tattoos*.[18] Tattoos are permanent deformations, since they require pinpricks that are generally indelible. Tattooing in the Marquesas is done with an indelible pigment introduced under the skin with the aid of a needle. Polynesian tattoos use fairly thick lines to link up different areas of tatooing. In Africa tattooing simply aims to produce strips of flesh arranged according to a pre-established design. Tattooing lives on in our societies: it was formerly current among the rank and file of the army and continues today among isolated younger men such as sailors and colonials, and also among the criminal strata of the population. General tattooing should be distinguished from special tattoos, which are always precisely located; each important part of the body is supposed to have eyes, to look out on the external world. A great many tattoos are made on parts of the body where blood can be seen to pulse, namely the ankles, neck and wrists. A handsome Maori is a living picture, the product of accomplished and traditional artistry. Record the design in detail, as well as the symbolism of each design and the effect that is aimed for. All these primitive forms of writing must be studied individually. If the symbolism is known and understood, we are already in the realm of writing.

Finery

We move on from cosmetics to the ornamentation of the body, to ornaments that are added on to it. The notion of finery corresponds to the pursuit of artificial beauty, so to speak, a beauty which is enduring and full of symbols. The language of flowers in Polynesia and Melanesia is highly developed. A certain amount of time is spent on the pursuit of finery, as in the ritual of plaiting the hair among the Marind Anim, Papuans from the mouth of the Fly River in Dutch New Guinea [Irian Jaya]. The position of women as regards finery has evolved a great deal; Australian women are poorly adorned while the men are highly adorned. The history of finery among Chinese women, in towns, at court, in the countryside.

Clothing is more finery than protection. The lack of clothes should be noted as much as their presence. Clothing varies greatly according to age, sex and ceremonies. Always proceed by means of an inventory, not omitting a single detail. What impression is the wearing of a garment meant to produce? Clothing is generally a sign of wealth and it possesses value, often monetary. The American North West maintains accounts in blankets, of which the whole supply is kept shut up in chests. It belongs to the clan and to the individual, and constitutes for them the series of insignia. Very often, people wear on themselves everything they can: why are the Hausa of Nigeria so well wrapped up?

A further distinction should be made between possession and exhibition. The clothes and jewels that are worn do not all of them necessarily belong to the person wearing them; the notion of the paraphernalia or of the supplementary dowry, which are always individual property.

Finery should be studied as a whole and with each item taken separately. Clothing is normally accompanied by dyes, embroidery and designs. Let us not forget that fabrics made of gauze, known in Asia from time immemorial, were introduced to Europe only after the Crusades: 'gauze' comes from Gaza.

Finery is generally located at the critical parts of the body, at the body orifices: the insertion of the labret in the lips, of rings in the earlobe or nasal septum; all the knots worn at the joints, all the bracelets, and necklaces (some of which are intended to cause deformation of the neck). The history of decoration of the head. The hat is either a protection or an adornment. Acoustic jewels: neck bells, tinkling bells.

Jewels can also be classified according to material: *ars plumaria* [art of feathers] in South America, jewels made of bone or ivory, rings made of wild boar's teeth in Indo-China and Polynesia. Jewels made of shells, or teeth. Finally, work in gold and silver is often no more than a copy in metal of jewels made of bone, shell, ivory, etc.

Lastly, the *mask*[19] is only a huge ornament, the wearing of which results in a complete disguise: the masked individual is other than himself. We are in a position to observe the entire evolution of the mask starting with the very elementary forms found in Australia where a widow piles up an impressive quantity of plaster on her head; her absolute mourning will only end when her hair falls out, together with this fixed mask. Masks seem to date from the Solutrean. They have developed a great deal, especially in Tibet, whence they spread as far as Malaysia. Masks can be of all kinds: a very heavy painting, in the last resort removable, is the beginning of a mask. Masks made of clay or kaolin. The masks of the Bismarck Archipelago, in northern Melanesia, represent the entire history of the clan and of the individual wearer. Some masks are intended to hide the whole of the individual; throughout Melanesia, the masked individual disappears completely behind the mask.

In some societies the mask is fundamental in ritual; each individual wears his own mask indicating his situation within the clan. The arrival of the masks in a ceremony corresponds to the arrival of the entire clan, including the personified ancestors. The ritual of the *katcina* among the Hopi and Zuñi of Central America.

Humanity as a whole is familiar with masks; even the inhabitants of Tierra del Fuego have very fine ones. Very often the mask does not represent a man, but a spirit, and sometimes it is one particular mask. Among the Marind Anim, a major ceremony represents the sea: the men arrive with their head-dresses of feathers, which they wave around to simulate the motion of waves.

Each mask should be studied individually. When they form a masquerade, study the relations between the masks, both in drama and in religion; the symbolism, myth and history of each of them, the relations with the name and forename. The mask lies at the origin of the notion of the person.[20] A mask can reincarnate an ancestor, or incarnate an auxiliary spirit. Many masks are burnt after being worn only once.

The mask is a sculpture in the round; the dimensions can be impressive and the design very elaborate. For each mask, study all the ritual and all the technology in its manufacture, its painting and its sculpture, also its design, and the art of wearing it. There exist double masks and treble ones, as well as masks with flaps. Generally, the mask forms part of a coat of arms; the great Chinese dragon is a mask and also a coat of arms. Some of our own masks are coats of arms. The Gorgon corresponds to a coat of arms. In the art of the mask, an effort is made to attain an expression that is permanent and average: during the performance the individual moves, but the mask remains motionless. It is an item of finery, but one already independent of the person.

Ornamentation of Everyday Objects, Movable and Immovable

The range of decorated movable objects varies enormously. Some peoples – the American North West, parts of Polynesia and Melanesia – decorate everything; others decorate next to nothing, or they do it poorly. But an aesthetic value can be placed on the very lack of decoration. All the same, overall, it seems that it is in our Western societies that the non-decoration of movable objects is on the increase. There is evidence of decoration starting in the Aurignacian.

To undertake a thorough study of this type of decoration, start with an inventory of the decorated movable objects, following the rules common to all inventories: for whom, for what; location of each item in the house; aesthetic value additional to practical value; collective value; economic value and individual value of the decorated object; the object evokes a memory, possesses a magical value and greater or lesser efficacy; it may or may not be animated, may or may not have an eye, etc.

In the course of this study, always distinguish between an object and the object's aesthetic value; and as regards the aesthetic value, distinguish its elements – form, decoration, material – from the whole that they compose, or the type of object. Whole and parts, and their relationship: that is the type. The ensemble of the types of instruments and of aesthetic objects used in a particular society at a particular time, constitutes its style. Elements, themes, motifs, forms, types and style. Style corresponds to the overarching aesthetic within which a society wishes to live, at a given point in time.[21] The determination of this point in time is difficult to establish because this is where the notion of generations becomes relevant. We know that fashion changes with the generations, but we do not know where generations begin or end. Thus things acquire a style, or borrow a style, then abandon it, and this applies even in primitive societies. One should beware that there are not necessarily any direct links between style and civilisation; the spatial extent of a style does not necessarily correspond to the extent of a civilisation: it is an indication, but not necessarily proof. Nothing is more dangerous than such inferences.

After collection comes the individual study of each object. Efforts should be made never to proceed from general notions such as imitation of nature, copying or stylisation, geometry – *all these things should be examined from the point of view of the native*, without ever calling on universal principles. Explanations and hypotheses can come at the end of the work, but the starting point should always be the individual study of each object.

Different ways of classifying objects can be envisaged. One is according to technique – drawing, painting, sculpture. Another is based on the material that is being decorated – wood, stone, basketry, fabrics, metals, feathers. The most elementary of the plastic arts is obviously graphic design, which can always be reduced to plane drawing even when it is applied to a volume. After graphic design comes engraving, followed by painting and free-standing sculpture, i.e. sculpture in the round. But each object may well present all these different arts simultaneously; everything is done at the same time. Arts and techniques are interrelated, hence nothing should be seen in isolation – embroidery can appear on pottery (corded ware); the use of a roulette, knife, or stamp in ornamentation should be recorded. The arts can also be distinguished according to the techniques they embellish: the arts of pottery, basketry, esparto goods, weaving, decoration of woodwork ...

I shall limit myself here to just a few words on drawing,[22] the most elementary of arts. Any art, type, or element of a type, is necessarily reducible to a projection and a design, or simply to a design. In the shape of a pot there is a design open to representation as a drawing: it is always possible to extract a design from any form. Now a drawing or design is always made up of several elements, even when it consists only of a single line. Every drawing involves both expression and impression – expression on the part of the artist who is expressing himself, and impression on the part of the spectator who receives the impact. Both aspects should be studied: the [artist's] knife stroke has determined the incision; and the sequence of incisions has produced an impression.

From another point of view, drawing is an abstraction from painting: every painting can be reduced to a drawing; two colours side by side are separated by a line. Here a distinction is needed between the elements of a drawing: a drawing includes a certain number of lines which combine to create a *motif*. The motif is in reality the unit of the design. Decoration may be called anthropomorphic, theriomorphic or floral. However, the difficulty in interpretation lies in the fact that the design signifies what the people want it to signify, be it geometrical or an imitation of the natural order.

An important geometrical decoration is the swastika,[23] which is attested from the lowest Neolithic and symbolises sometimes the sun, sometimes the sky, sometimes a starfish, etc. The spiral requires a technique – it calls for the string compass; but we know of Australian spirals drawn without any spiral technique. Study therefore the history and nature of each design, and of each element in the design. When it is relevant, describe how it has travelled: the motif of the dragon with its tongue hanging out is found on both sides of the Pacific, in China and North West America.

The human figure pure and simple is rarely represented; generally it appears highly stylised. In fact, things are at once stylised and naturalised – thus one should distrust any interpretation which is not given by the natives. Generally, a design does not stand on its own; similarly, a graphic motif includes both graphic and decorative phrases. The notion of art as phrase: not only does the artist say things, but he puts them in order; the decorative phrases can be multiplied on one object and distributed differently over the parts of that object.

In any decorated object distinguish between the basic decoration or decorations, which generally cover the largest fields of the object, and the frame; and between the field and its edges: friezes, framing, borders. One field may be inside another. Never study an aesthetic element without mentioning the relations between that element and the whole and without seeing how the various elements are arranged so as to form a picture. The décor of the main field and all the motifs present in the various divisions of the field are all methods of highlighting – they are there to accentuate something (compare the English word 'enhance'[24]). Besides the design, the décor includes highlighting and colours, whether opposed or complementary. Consider the relations between the design and the raw material on which the design is superimposed; the design may be incised with a line or in depth, with the help of a roulette or a burin.

But design and painting do not by themselves determine the aesthetic character of the object; there is also its *form*, which is always related to its material. The form entails a pursuit of balance – the object must be able to stand (a pot will need a base) – and a pursuit of aesthetic quality. It must also be adapted to practical use; certain technical elements alter its form, e.g. the handle of a pot, its tripod, spout, etc.

Granted the general form of an object, its décor will vary according to its dimensions; a small jar may be repeated in a big one. One must therefore study all the relations between the elements of the form of an object and the volume of the object. The whole undertaking will yield the series, that is to say anything within a typical form that presents variations, from the small pot up to the very large one.

An object has a graphic form and a three-dimensional form. The relation between these two kinds of form constitutes the type of the object. Within each type, collect all the series in which the object appears.

The collection of types from a particular society gives a notion of its *style* and of its aesthetic specificity. When an element is not so much dominant as specific and arbitrarily chosen, it becomes typical of the society or even of a group of societies (an example is the three-fingered hand among the Maori). The ensemble of the aesthetic elements typical of a society constitutes the style of that society.

The study of these rhythms and equilibria that make up a style, and the study of small objects carrying numerous designs, and of large objects carrying few designs – all this constitutes the study of an art or an artistic realm. Once this art is analysed, one can study its distribution: for example, the study of interlacing designs.

In sharp contrast with our own arts, in the societies we are concerned with painting and drawing are most of the time not isolated from the object they decorate. Generally, a mix of arts is heaped onto a single object, the time factor being irrelevant. The design is fixed onto the object; it is we who have invented art for the sake of art and who have detached the design from what it ornaments. And yet, very early on, drawings were made on sand, on rocks, on all kinds of thing that can at a pinch be considered akin to paper. Decoration of wooden vessels in North West America, decoration on hide, decoration of the tent or house, both outside and in.

Each object should be measured and accompanied by accurate photos, as well as by photos of the whole, such that one can ultimately attempt to envisage the characteristics of the plastic arts whose ensemble constitutes what we call art. The researcher will not set off as an aesthetician, but may return as one. Within your general assessment include an assessment of the plastic arts, taken as a whole, in relation to other social activities: what place do they occupy, what are their relations with the other activities? Rather than speaking in terms of the magical-religious character of Black art, mention the links that connect such and such art with magic and with religion in some particular Black society. A shield is marked with a coat of arms: which coat of arms?

Ideal Arts (*Arts idéaux*)[25]

According to our usual classifications, plastic arts include the non-ideal arts we have just been studying, as well as the ideal arts. But in fact all arts are ideal arts. When they invented paper, our ancestors detached painting from the walls supporting it; but this separation did not make painting more ideal. The fact that a motif is found on some practical object does not make the motif a practical one; it is just as ideal as the paper on which a drawing has been made.

The four ideal arts are drawing, painting, sculpture and architecture. The notion of ideal art, of art that is only the representation of the ideas and feelings of the authors and spectators, is a modern one. One of its extreme forms, the doctrine of art for art's sake, is a nineteenth-century phenomenon; in literature, it was launched by Théophile Gauthier, Baudelaire, and their successors in France, and prior to Baudelaire, by the great English Romantics. There is no such thing as ideal art, but on the other hand art has lost its symbolic/religious decorative value. Ideal art is a certain conception of art.

We can embark upon this study at one end or the other – it does not matter which. We can start with architecture, which is the total art, and end with sculpture, painting, and drawing, or we can start with drawing and end with architecture. It is easier to start with drawing and painting.

We do not know precisely how far all societies have truly practised sculpture or architecture or, most of all, drawing; however, architecture is already clearly present in the laying out of a clearing for initiation in Australia.

We have already seen that, technically, *painting* derives from dyeing and dressing skins. In any case, painting should be studied simultaneously with drawing. It is only rarely that one finds designs that are merely drawn without at the same time being painted. In the case of drawing, study first of all the relation of all decoration with pictography: this raises the fundamental question of symbolism. A big churinga, or a big sacred bull-roarer among the Arunta of Australia, narrates through its decoration all the heroic deeds of the ancestor whose incarnation it is. Questions of pictography, but also technical questions: the sense of perspective on inscribed bamboos in New Caledonia, the sense of balance. In paintings, study the mode of representation of spiritual or natural objects: a rose ornamenting a pot is *the rose*. Study too the question of ownership of colours: in Tonga, colours are the property of the king, hence many colours are taboo.

When made by means of a knife, painting and drawing are called engraving (*gravure*). There exist very ancient engravings on wood, and paintings on stone, which are wholly modern. There also exist engravings on trees – which brings us close to sculpture. We can see how *sculpture* is closely connected with painting and engraving: a carved post is sculpture in the round by definition. Spearheads, arrowheads, door lintels, kris handles are sculpted – the thickness and curves of the blade are sculpture. The study of pipes, which is now being extended to the whole of South America, is yielding remarkable results. Certain objects are naturally sculpted: gourds, calabashes, large pieces of pottery. Among some peoples there exist items that are always sculpted, such as seats or headrests. Figures do not necessarily have to be isolated and treated as figures in order to qualify as sculpture in the round. Throughout North East Asia, huts are decorated all over with dolls, which form a sculptural whole. Sculpture is attested since the Upper Palaeolithic – the bisons of Val du Roc.

Lastly comes *architecture*, which dominates all the arts. Every art is basically an architectural art: every artist is an architect. A house in North West America is decorated to the utmost. There are guilds of architects and carpenters throughout South America, Polynesia and Melanesia.[26] Study especially how the architect puts forward his suggestions. What is the difference between public houses and private ones? The men's house is an important element pervading social life; it is richly decorated and full of meaning, since the whole social organisation is to be seen inscribed on it. Cover terraced architecture and the pursuit of aesthetic effects in the sculpture. The cliff-dwellers of Central America have a remarkable architecture.

Musical Arts

Throughout the following pages, we shall be considering phenomena that are increasingly distanced from the material. We shall no longer be studying things that can be held in the hand or that are visible, but above all states of mind. However, musical art includes objects – for example, the whole paraphernalia of drama – just as there are economic objects (money), jural objects (insignia of rank), and religious objects (many of which belong to the plastic arts).

The musical arts all remain closely connected with the plastic arts: for the dancer, dance is a technique of the body which includes aesthetic movement. In all the arts there is a notion of sensory harmony. The notion of musical arts, which is nowadays being generally abandoned, is nonetheless the basic notion of art for the Greeks – witness [Plato's] *Phaedra* and *Republic*.

In the musical arts we find two elements: a sensory element corresponding to the notions of rhythm, balance, contrasts and harmony, and an ideal element, an element of *theoria* – the dancer sees herself dancing and experiences the joy of it; the simplest of the musical arts includes an element of imagination and creation. Some children have an instinct for dance, they feel themselves dancing.

Music offers one point of superiority over the other arts: it carries with it a freshness, a rapture, an upsurge of enthusiasm, a real ecstasy, which was spoken of by Plato and after him by Nietzsche and Rohde. The musical arts include dance, music and singing; poetry, drama and literature. These arts are interrelated and linked with various institutions.

Drama is nearly always musical, danced and pervaded by poetry; finally, very generally, it implies efforts at individual adornment, at architecture and painting. This brings up the plastic arts notion of the actor and his or her ornamentation. Nothing is more important in art than artistic education; nothing is more the product of education and habit than an art. Consider the relations of the musical arts to the other arts and to all the other social activities.

The forms of social life are in part common to musical art and the musical arts: rhetoric, mythology and theatre penetrate the whole life of a society. Lastly, note the importance of rhythm: work derives from rhythm even more than rhythm derives from work.[27] Man is a rhythmic animal. Among rhythmic animals, which are rare, we can cite the dancing bird, a bird from Australia which gives its dance a rhythm and a form.

Consider the relations between all the arts and vocal technique and, more generally, all the techniques of the body. Study the distribution of art objects, and of the artistic calendar. Major weeks of religion and art, seasons of art and games, for instance in Hawaii; festivals for the year's end and the new year throughout the Asiatic world, notably in the Thai-Muong ensemble. The peasants spend a fortune and run into debt in order to play a fittingly exalted role in these festivals.

The work of art and the musical event occupy a far more important position in exotic societies than in our own. These arts present an importance that is at once social, artistic, psychological and even physiological: an Arunta who loses his *corroboree* loses his soul and his purpose in life; he lets himself die.

Dance[28]

Dance is always sung, and often mimed with music. Danced mime has been a great vehicle of civilisation; travelling entertainers have been able to import elements of civilisation in the same way as a religion or an art.

Diderot defines dance as 'music of bodily movements for movements of the eye'. Nearly always sung, and always mimed, dance is also rhythm of the body or part of the body. Ballet is the only survival of it in our societies, but ballet is mute – a mere pantomime. In the societies that concern us, ballet corresponds rather to an opera that is danced and sung; mimicry, which is very expressive, is always understood (symbolically or not) by the spectators, who take part in the drama.

A study of dance will necessarily start with a study of the body technique it entails – a psycho-physical study of rhythm. Certain Australian dances regularly end with the exhaustion of the dancer. Dance is often closely connected with acrobatics; it is everywhere an attempt to be something other than one is.

In all research on dancing distinctions should be made between the protagonist; the chorus, which dances; and the spectators, animated by the rhythm. The whole event culminates among the protagonists, and sometimes also among the chorus, in states of ecstasy where the individual exits from himself. These multiple ecstasies can extend to the spectators *en masse*, male and female; phenomena of this type are widespread throughout the Black world, among the Malagasies and among the Malays.

The methods of study include the analysis of each dance, using the ordinary procedure of the inventory: who dances, where, when, why, with whom, etc. Dancing in two lines with the sexes facing each other exists in the Black world; ring dancing is widespread in America, Africa and Europe. The dance should be described with reference to all the dancers, at every moment.

Each dance has to be broken down into all its components: the dance itself, the chorus and the spectators; the music, the miming that dominates everything; and the effect it has on the spectators. Note the details, including the silences and standstills. The dance is often a masquerade, with the important dancers wearing masks.

The distinction between dances of mimicry and dances of feeling seems inadequate. Dances should rather be distinguished according to their object: a dance represents a legend or a tale, be it tragic or comic (e.g., on the sculptures at Angkor, the actor who represents a god); or a dance is anthropomorphic, or theriomorphic, etc. Dances can also be distinguished according to their function: funeral dances, totemic dances, or dances pertaining to jural status (e.g., the bride's dance); they may accompany wrestling, or a hunting expedition; war dances, dances for play or work ...

Distinctions should also be made according to the indications of the dancers, who are generally quasi-professionals of high standing, often forming troupes. They should be asked about the history of their dance ([perhaps] it was revealed to them in a dream by an ancestor or totemic spirit); also about how it is taught.

There is hardly a single rhythm to be found in North West America that is not danced. The dancer is usually animated by a spirit; he only dances when moved by a superior power. Very often, the dance is an item of property; once transferred to another owner, it is no longer danced.

Music and Singing[29]

Music can be defined as a phenomenon of transport, a 'marvellous stroll in the world of sounds and harmonies'.

The sense of music seems most unevenly distributed across societies. Rhythms, melodies and polyphonies vary to a large degree from one society to another, and also within the same society between sexes, generations and classes: noble music, vulgar music, military music, church music, cinema music. Music is a system. So, an uneven distribution of musicality within a society, combined however with an extreme homogeneity of the whole phenomenon.

Methods of observation. The instruments should be studied first. Where it exists, the instrument is a limiting factor for music and a supporting factor. Thus, everything one learns from the study of instruments will present a certain objectivity, provided the instrument is observed when being handled by the artist: study the tuning and the rhythm while in the field. In addition, interview the musicians and if possible live with them. In some societies one comes across choruses that include the whole assembly. A theory of music exists wherever the panpipe exists. People distinguish the lengths of the pipes and thus appreciate the absolute pitch of the notes and their intervals. In Bougainville Island Thurnwald watched economic competitions or potlatches that began with competitions on the panpipes; the two orchestras tune their pipes together before starting to play.

Our European music is one instance of music; it is not music as such. Thus, the notion that the major scale is the typical scale has to be abandoned, and so has the notion that there are scales radically different from our own. Our scale is just one choice among possible scales, which have some common features and some contrasting ones. Our major scale is one instance among other scales and among other modes, whether ancient or exotic. Such scales are all defective; there are always notes that are missing. The notion of an ideal scale should therefore be expunged.

From another point of view, any music is made up of melody and rhythm. But there is no melody without rhythm and, possibly, no rhythm without melody. The relations between rhythm and melody, between long and short notes, stressed and unstressed notes, low and high notes; this is clear-cut neither in language nor in music. European rhythms rank among the poorest. Our ideal is a certain rhythmic monotony, while music outside the European tradition usually has rhythms that change at very brief intervals.

If these rhythms are varied, it may be because they correspond to dances; they punctuate a mimed dance which includes a variety of figures, and the rhythm changes with every gesture in the mime. In other contexts, the endless repetition of the same phrase accompanies a physical effort; an example is the song of those paddling a canoe. One also finds abbreviations even in relation to that rhythm – abrupt breaks, instantaneous halts.

But the work song is the origin neither of singing nor of work, contrary to the claims of Bücher; work songs are merely a particular form of song. Marching or walking songs are fairly rare, while work songs are common, especially among women. In other songs one finds considerable variations in rhythm, which alter both the emotion of the song and the song itself; abrupt abbreviations, and also lengthening – it is what we call the poetic licence granted to the librettist.

The whole world is familiar with unison and indeed it does not distinguish very clearly between a higher octave and a lower one, or the fifth. In a chorus chords and polyphony are very variable, but the melody usually remains fairly well defined.

Moreover, it should be noted that music extends to quite other things than among ourselves. In tone languages a certain degree of singing is always necessary; it is part of the phonetics of the language, and the tone is equivalent to whole syllables. Our languages are languages that have abandoned their music. In most cases it is a matter of using melody and rhythm in the language; there is much more on-going musicality than with us. So, many things we do not believe to be sung are in reality sung.

Having studied each musical type, move on to study the variations: extempore individual variations, and systematic or collective variations. In Australia, whole populations are capable of learning a musical drama: the undertaking involves bringing together in time the song, drama and actions of a considerable crowd.

After these precise studies, one can just touch on an issue that is fundamental but that can only be studied following preliminary observations: the question of the origin of the various types of music. There is hardly anything more impenetrable than the music of one society is to the music of another, or the music of one age to another; on the other hand, nothing is easier to borrow than a type of music or art. Instances of non-borrowing should be studied as well as instances of borrowing; here there is neither natural evolution nor supernatural evolution. In each society, invention takes place according to definite modes that vary depending on locations, generations, etc. Questions about invention are generally badly phrased. We always have the impression of individual invention; this is the only way in which we conceive of it, because among us the inventor is supposed to be a potent individual responsible for all creativity. But outside our societies invention is not generally believed or understood as the work of a single individual – it is revealed.

From another point of view, borrowings from and contributions to a given musical style should be conceived in the following way: people start with the local music and contribute to it what they can and what it accepts.

There is no doubt that originally humanity sang as much as it spoke. One of the great mistakes of psychology is the separation it has made between singing and speaking. There is an enormous mass of what were originally songs, but it is only perceptible in dance as concerns rhythm or via an instrument as regards melody. It is the instrument that has enabled us in singing to get rid of false harmonics, and it is the instrument that has detached the notes, one from another – pauses became necessary as soon as there was an instrument. Even as regards rhythm, the pause of the drumstick on the drum isolates the rhythm and isolates the volume (*force*), however short and weak the tempo and volume may be. The instrument is the means used by music to detach itself from itself.

Not only have the rhythm and melody been detached in this way, but so has the scale of notes. Ever since it became necessary to tune instruments one against another, and no longer simply to adjust voices, people were forced to arrive at what we call the normal range. The whole extent of tonality became fixed because of the necessity to arrive at it technically, and above all in the relation to the song and the melody. In addition it was necessary to adjust instrument and voice – hence the importance of the range.

The geographical distribution of musical instruments raises one of the most important questions for ethnography as a whole: the great *vina* and the instruments akin to it spread exactly across the whole region of the world that was familiar with Indian civilisation. The mouth organ can be found everywhere that was penetrated by Chinese and Indo-Chinese civilisation. The bell comes from Tibet or from North India.

Whenever there is an orchestra, each instrument should be studied as well as its relations to all the other instruments; consider the relation with song, dance and mime. Never forget the chorus: singing is fundamental. Even the shape of the instrument is interesting, the object itself remaining the same. Study the horns and their length; study the slits in the wooden drum, and the methods of attaching the drum skins.

Once the elements of the musical instruments and all the activity of the music-makers have been studied, observe how the whole system functions. While making a recording, note carefully to which dance steps and mime gestures each moment of the score corresponds. It is not a matter of simple melodies, but of real problems in harmony. Always use a chronometer.

When making a collection of songs and music the following principles should be observed: study the occasion for the music; religious songs, magical songs, shamanistic ceremonies, divination ceremonies, work songs, nursery songs, marching songs, war songs, peace songs; dances, calls, salutations; pornographic songs, songs of rivalry, songs for games ... The study of threnodies, psalmodies, etc.

For us a song is a single isolated song. But this is a rare phenomenon outside our own societies. There exist isolated dances accompanied by songs, but the song that one hums to oneself is rare; a song composed without any reference to elements of dance or mime is unknown in Australia.

Distinguish the music of the learned from popular music, the music of children from that of adults, and the music accompanying rituals – and which rituals.

We usually classify poetry and literature very far away from music, in a realm where I personally do not at all envisage them. The ideal for poetry is sung poetry; poetry is ideal in so far as it is musical.

The classical distinction is between prose, poetry and drama. But in fact all began with musical drama, including comedy. It is we who have divided up and decomposed the whole complex.

Drama[30]

Drama exists everywhere. One of the few things we know with certainty concerning the Tasmanians, who are now extinct, is the importance among them of ceremonies corresponding to the Australian *corroboree*. Drama is found among the people of Tierra del Fuego and among the Pygmies. All ritual is essentially dramatic; this can clearly be seen among the Australians. We have evidence of the masquerade, accompanied with dances, from as early as the Aurignacian, i.e. Middle Palaeolithic; it corresponds to representation of myth. The high point of dramatic art is to be found in religion; drama presents a large component of religion, and also of poetry. It corresponds to the search for another world, in which people have a degree of belief. Let us add that everyone participates in the drama; in an Australian *corroboree*, men, women and children dance and sing: everyone is simultaneously actor and spectator.

The labour involved in a musical drama is infinite. Study the relations between drama and mime; the overall plan of the composition. Usually, the subject is revealed to the author who has attended a dance of the spirits; the invention is the repetition of a vision. Record the methods of apprenticeship and the mode of transmission, be it in direct line or from one tribe to another.

Study the guilds of actors and tumblers; let us not forget that one whole population, setting off from Afghanistan, has been able to subsist as tumblers. Puppets are found throughout Africa and Asia. Almost everywhere, people have come to objectify to themselves their own dramas.

Study everything that relates to each character and everything that relates to the whole set of characters. Establish the full *libretto* of the drama. Nowadays we distinguish between drama, tragedy and comedy; the full energy of German romanticism was required in order to put things back in order. This distinction of drama, tragedy, comedy is a purely literary one; the ancient Greek tetralogy consisted of three heroic tragedies, leading to sacrifices, and one comedy; the whole, made up of tragedies and comedy, formed the drama. It is we who have atomised the whole complex.

The reactions to which humanity is susceptible are of two types: reactions of exaltation, and reactions of laughter and relaxation. Relaxation is common to all the effects of art, especially relaxation due to a series of expectations that have transported you elsewhere, into a setting which is not your own, one where even if you participate in the action, you know that it is in a different mode from the one in which you would participate in the same action in ordinary life.

Distinguish then, within the drama, between everything that leads to exaltation and everything that turns things to ridicule. The spectator/actor will achieve a good catharsis provided he has escaped from the world of humanity and lived for a moment in the company of heroes and gods. Drama thus entails a process of sacralising what is lay and making heroic what is banal; it also entails a process of casting ridicule on things that are great. Observe the importance of obscenity.

Poetry[31]

Poetry exists from the moment when singing is added to words, since the text, being necessarily rhythmic, corresponds to verses. Oral literature follows rules that differ from those observed by written literature; it enjoys different privileges, because in it people normally aim for rhythm and composition. Poetry meant for reading is less perfect than poetry composed for recitation.

Poetry is generally of formulary character. It is not merely a matter of phrases intended to produce an effect on the audience by means of their rhythm, but of formulae conceived for repetition. The aim is to concentrate attention. The formula is sometimes poor, but it is impregnated with a considerable number of other elements and it sometimes contains the myth of a dramatic representation. A poem very often corresponds to a rubric; it is the theme to which people dance. The Malayan *pantoun*, the Japanese haiku are far more complicated than our sonnet.

While listening to a tale, pay attention to the moment when the narrator utters such formulae, which are generally sung, though sometimes very faintly. Poetry should be looked for in places where we do not put it – it should be looked for everywhere. There are rhythmic law codes (the code of the Rade [or Rhade] in Indo-China, the [Roman] Law of the Twelve Tables). Transmission through rhythm and formulae is the sole guarantee of the survival of oral literature; collective poetry imposes itself on everyone.

In Africa one finds a highly developed epic poetry; the griots of Niger can recite ten or fifteen thousand verses. The poetry of the herald, the poetry of feasts: the king drinks. All ceremonies are marked by poetry; the herald often speaks in verse, or gives rhythm to his prose. Proverbs and legal maxims are told in rhythmic form.

In Indo-China girls and boys sing alternately.[32] Throughout Polynesia, poetry is divided into learned poetry and popular – poetry of the court and the higher castes and poetry of the people, which sometimes overlap. The technical highpoints of poetry are presented by the Malayan-Malagasy grouping.[33]

To indicate rhythm use the Latin notation of longs and shorts, indicating intensity with the help of an acute accent. Distinguish feet and mark the caesura. Make a recording of the melody whenever possible.

The presence of rhythm generates repetition; the primitive form of verse is the repetition of the same verse. But repetition can present variations, by means of alliteration and assonance. Regular assonance at the end of a verse is rhyme. The notion of groups of verses, strophes and antistrophes.

Always record the instrument used to sing a particular poem.

Besides alliteration, assonance and phonic balancing, note also semantic balancing; the balancing of sounds is fundamental – for example, in Semitic poetry. In Semitic poetry there very clearly exist rules of proportion. The effect of poetry is not only physical, but also moral and religious. The different parts of the Greek chorus are sung in specific languages. The modes are typical musical phrases which are connected in a fixed order; Hebrew psalmody in the bible is made up of thirty-two modes. The poetry varies with the musical mode; this notion of modes applies to poetry as much as to music.

All this the bards, heralds and professional poets will be able to explain clearly. Study the poets and artistic inventors. A poem is generally revealed by spirits. Very often, poetic language differs from everyday language. The Australian Arunta sing verses in an archaic language, or in one that is different from their own.

Note the types of poetic licence: one can change the length of words or the intensity of syllables; one can cut syllables or add them. Study the metric formulae. For the convenience of the enquiry, one could distinguish between epic, lyric and dramatic poetry. But most of the time, one finds a constant mixing of all the genres.

Prose [34]

Literature, as we conceive it, is written literature, but in the societies that belong to ethnography, literature is made to be repeated orally; and the more you repeat a story to a child, the more he or she enjoys it. However, this literature generally contains an extra-literary meaning; it is not meaningless like our own. The tale is not intended solely for the profit of the story-teller or for the amusement of the public; in large measure it is intended to say something. In a legal hearing, the adventure of the spider or of the hyena can serve as a legal precedent. Let us recall that in France the novel dates from Mme de Lafayette [1643–93] and only really developed in the eighteenth century.

The greater part of the literature is in verse, and even magical formulas (*formulettes*) are generally versified. Very often, the epic is linked with the cult of the ancestors. Taken as a whole the deeds of a family will provide an epic; the ideal of a princely Kwakiutl family is to appropriate the coat of arms of another princely family. Compare the cycle of Arthur and the Knights of the Round Table.

The interest in literature is therefore different in nature from ours. The recitation is always half religious, and half epic. Among the Cherokee Indians stories are told in wintertime: 'I have enchanted you, the night has seemed less long'. Among the Pueblo Indians people tell their myths at night, and this, they say, makes the stars move onwards. The notion of literature as pious work, for the edification of the audience.

As soon as an effort is made to speak well and not simply to speak, there exists a literary effort. When the literary effort is sustained and is widely adopted in literary circles, there exists a style. Exactly as one can define a pictorial or musical style, so one can define a literary style by the whole range of effort that characterises speaking well.

The importance of oral literature and its ability to endure are not generally recognised. Prose is very widespread. In Australia it includes all the tales and myths attached directly to rituals or to geographical features. The language of etiquette in North America is highly developed. In Australia, people change their voices to talk in front of the Council. Study the capacities of memory and its resources, and the literary factors facilitating memory. There are professional storytellers throughout the Sudan, throughout Berber territory, and throughout Southern Africa.

A group of tales forms a kind of novel or cycle. Certain tales are grouped in relation to certain cycles; and present a certain spread that can be represented on a map. Such a distribution of tales can serve as a starting point for historical research. Tales can be distinguished from myths by the lesser degree of belief that adheres to them. Telling a myth is a religious act that takes place only in certain circumstances. Telling a tale is far less serious and may have as its aim simply the entertainment of the audience.

The passage from tales to myths, and from myths to tales is constant; people sacralise the most ridiculous events, and treat with irony the most serious ones. The simplest procedure is to classify by cycles.

For an inventory of the literature one should rely on professional storytellers, who are known as such and are easy to find. The classification can be carried out according to any scheme: court adventures, war tales, love tales; tales told to men only; or to women, or children. Tales about love are less numerous than is generally thought, and tales about crafts or tradesmen more numerous. Tales of adults for children. Do not seek the original text, *for there is none*; the narrator improvises, and his contribution may be far reaching, for instance, in *The Thousand and One Nights*. But make an effort to collect all the variants of a single theme, adding all possible commentaries.

A tale is a story made up of several themes. Each of these themes must be studied in itself. The most literary aspect will be the adjusting of the themes, one in relation to another. Thus a tale should be divided into a series of scenes forming a little drama: introduction, the various themes, their adjustment, the ending.

The analysis of specific features makes it possible to construct the history of a theme, or even of a tale: the tale of the magic carpet comes from the country of carpets, i.e. northern Iran, whence it spreads into Europe on the one side, into Polynesia and as far as North America on the other. One finds the tale of the magic carpet in all the countries that possess mats and carpets. Tales offer moral and jural authority, and they serve as precedents.

The anecdote differs from the tale in that it is more prosaic and less historical.

A type of literature that is very difficult to record is mottoes. It is very important throughout the Black world, where mottoes play a role of prime importance: every individual or every family has its motto, which may be represented on its weapons. Study the figurative representations of every tale and every theme.

Etiquette too involves an enormous literature: the literature of the heralds in Melanesia, the drum competitions of the Eskimos. American Indians attach great importance to etiquette, both vis-à-vis the gods and vis-à-vis men. The high point of etiquette is to be found in countries with a caste system (Japan, Samoa).

Study syllogisms or modes of proof. Study metaphor.[35] Rhetoric is universal, and is made of repetitions of or allusion to a myth, a tale, a traditional custom: the *Mahâbhârata* and the Nordic sagas each correspond to the sum of human wisdom; each page of the Gospels presents allusions and clichés.

Notes

1. [Greek *theóreó* means 'view, contemplate'.]
2. See Fechner, G.T., *Elemente der Psychophysik*, Leipzig, 1889.
3. Wundt. W., *Elemente der Völkerpsychologie*, Leipzig, 1912.
4. Boas, F., *Primitive Art*, Oslo, 1927.
5. Robertson Smith, W., *Lectures on the Religion of the Semites*, London, 2nd ed., 1894.
6. See the issue of *J. de Psychologie* devoted to the psychology of art (Jan–March 1926).
7. Preuss, K.Th., *Religionen der Naturvölker*, Leipzig, 1904; 'Der Ursprung der Religion und Kunst', *Globus* 22, 23, 24; *Der Unterbau des Dramas*, Leipzig, 1930.
8. See notably: Gross, K., *Die Spiele der Menschen*, Jena, 1899; *Les jeux des animaux*, Paris, 1902. Hirn, Y., *Les jeux d'enfants*, trans. from Swedish. Paris, 1926. Bett, H., *The Games of Children*, London, 1929. Roth, W.E., 'Games, Sports and Amusements', *North Queensland Ethnography Bulletin* 4, 1902. Kaudern, W., *Ethnographical Studies in Celebes*, vol. 4, *Games and Dances in Celebes*, Göteborg, 1939. Hervey, F.A., 'Malay Games', *JAI* 1903: 285–304. Best, E., 'Games and Pastimes of the Maori', *Dominion Museum Bulletin* 8, Wellington, 1925. Weule, K., 'Afrikanisches Kinderspielzeug', *Ethnologisches Notizblatt* (Berlin) 2, 1899. Griaule, M., *Jeux et divertissements abyssins*, Paris, 1932; *Jeux dogons*, Paris, 1938. Culin, S., *Games of the North American Indians*, ARBAE 24 (1902–03), 1907. Stevenson, M.C., 'Zuñi Games', *Am. Anth.* 5, 1903: 468–498. Nordenskiöld, E., 'Spiele und Spielsachen im Gran Chaco und in Nord Amerika'. *Z. f. Ethnologie* 42, 1910: 806–822. Piganiol, A., *Recherches sur les jeux romains*, Strasbourg, 1923.
9. [An Italian game, played with the fingers.]
10. Handy, W.Ch., 'String Figures from the Marquesas and Society Islands', *Bernice P. Bishop Museum Bulletin* 18, 1925. Dickey, L.A., 'String Figures from Hawaï', *Bernice P. Bishop Museum Bulletin* 54, 1928. Victor, P.E., *Jeux d'enfants et d'adultes chez les Eskimo d'Angmagssalik: les jeux de ficelle (cat's cradle)*, Copenhagen, 1940. On cat's cradles, see also Jayne, C.F., *String Figures: a Study of Cat's-Cradle in Many Lands*, New York, 1906.
11. On the ritual aspect of the ball game, see Blom, F., 'The Maya Ballgame Pokta-pok (called Tlachtli by the Aztec)', *Middle American Papers* (Tulane University, New Orleans) 4, 1932: 485–530. Karsten, R., *Ceremonial Games of the South American Indians*, Helsinki and Leipzig (n.d. [1930]).
12. See Larsen, H., 'The Mexican Indian Flying Pole Dance', *National Geographic Magazine*, 71/3, March 1937: 387–400.
13. [Tug of war, hoop and whoop: in English in the original.]
14. See Culin, S., *Mancalah, the National Game of Africa*, Reports of USNM, 1893, Philadelphia, 1894.
15. Grosse, E., *Die Anfänge der Kunst*, Friburg, Leipzig, 1894. Haddon, A., *Evolution in Art*, London, 1895. Hirn, Y., *The Origins of Art*, London, 1900. Boas, F., *Primitive Art*, Oslo, 1927. Sydow, E. von, *Die Kunst*

der Naturvölker und der Vorzeit, Berlin, 1923. Luquet, G.H., *L'art et la religion des hommes fossils*, Paris, 1926; *L'art primitif*, Paris, 1930; *Le dessin enfantin*, Paris, 1927. The publications of the international congresses of popular art (Prague, 1928) and of aesthetics (Paris, 1937): see *Institut international de coopération intellectuelle. Art populaire ...*, Paris (1931), and *2e Congrès international d'esthétique et de science de l'art*, 2 vols, Paris, 1937. See the works of Lalo, C., *L'esthétique expérimentale contemporaine* (1908), *Les sentiments esthétiques* (1910), *Introduction à l'esthétique* (1912), *Notions d'esthétique* (1925), etc. See also *J. de Psychologie* [n. 6]; Delacroix, H., *Psychologie de l'art*, Paris, 1927. Ribot, Th., *Essai sur l'imagination créatrice*, Paris, 1900. See also the works of Wolfgang Koehler, P. Guillaume, etc. on the theory of 'form' [*Gestalt*].

16. Best, E., 'The Maori as he was', *New Zealand Board of Science and Art Manual* 14/2, Wellington, 1924. Cole, F.C., *The Wild Tribes of the Davas District*, FMNH, Anthrop. Series, 12/2, Chicago, 1913. Handy, E.S.C., 'The Native Culture of the Marquesas', *Bernice P. Bishop Museum Bulletin* 9, Honolulu, 1923. Hofmayr, W., *Die Schilluk*, Anthropos Ethnologische Bibliothek, 2/5, 1925. Kroeber, A.L., *Handbook of the Indians of California*, BAE Bulletin 78, Washington, 1925. Schebesta, P., *Bambuti: die Zwerge vom Kongo*, Leipzig, 1932. Thomas, N.W., *Natives of Australia*, London, 1906.

17. See Torday, E. and Joyce, T.A., *Notes ethnographiques sur les peuples communément appelés Bakuba*, Annales du Musée du Congo belge, series 3, vol. 2/1, Brussels, 1910.

18. Hambly, W.D., *The History of Tattooing and its Significance*, London, 1925; 'Tattooing in the Marquesas', *Bernice P. Bishop Museum Bulletin* 1, 1922. Kraemer, D.H., 'Die Ornamentik der Kleidmatter und der Tatauierung auf den Marshallinseln', *Archiv f. Anthropologie*, 1904/2: 1–28. Lévi-Strauss, C., 'Le dédoublement de la représentation dans les arts de l'Asie et de l'Amérique', *Renaissance*, 2/3, 1944–45: 169–186. Ling Roth, H., 'Tatu in the Society Islands', *JAI* 35, 1905: 283–295. Meyrac, A., *Du tatouage*, Lyon, 1900. Pales, L., 'Le problème des chéloïdes et le point de vue colonial', *Médecine tropicale* 2, 1942: 183–296. Von den Steinen, K., *Die Marquesaner und ihre Kunst*, Berlin, 1905, 3 vols (vol. 1 entirely about tattoos). Teit, J.A., *Tattooing and Face and Body Painting of the Thompson Indians of British Columbia*, ARBAE 45 (1927–28), 1930.

19. See especially: Schneider-Lengyel, I., *Die Welt der Mask*, Munich [c.1934]. Lewis, A.B., *New Guinea Masks*, Chicago FMNH, 1922. Nevermann, H., *Masken und Geheimbünde in Melanesien*, Berlin, 1933. Wirz, P., *Beiträge zur Ethnographie des Papua-Golfes, Britisch Neuguinea, etc*, Leipzig, 1934; *Die Marind-anim von Holländisch-Süd-Neu-Guinea*, vol. 2, Hamburg, 1925. Reche, O., *Der Kaiserin-Augusta-Fluss*, Hamburg, 1913. Leenhardt, M., 'Le masque calédonien', *Bulletin du Musée d'Ethnographie* 6, Paris, July 1933. Filchner, W., *Kumbum Dschamba Ling*, Leipzig, 1933 (Tibetan masks). Fewkes, J.W., *Tusayan Katcinas*, ARBAE 15 (1893–94), 1897: 245–315; *Hopi Katcinas*, ARBAE 21 (1899–1900), 1903. Griaule, M., *Masques dogons*, Paris, 1938.

20. Mauss, M., 'Une catégorie de l'esprit humain: la notion de personne, celle de "moi"', *JRAI* 68, 1938: 263–281.

21. Kroeber, A.L., 'Decorative Symbolism of the Arapaho Indians', *Am. Anth.*, 1901: 301–336. Lumholtz, C., *Decorative Art of the Huichol Indians*, Mem. AMNH, 1904/3: 281–326. Speiser, F., 'Über Kunststile in Melanesien', *Z. f. Ethnologie* 68, 1936: 304–369. Wassen, H., 'The Frog-motive among the South American Indians, Ornamental Studies', *Anthropos* 29, 1934: 319–370.

22. [French *dessin* means both 'drawing' and 'design'. The choice of translation is often difficult.]

23. On the swastika, see Wilson, T., *The Swastika ...*, USNM Report, 1894.

24. On the notions of field, border, and frame, see especially the works of the theoreticians of 'form' [n. 15].

25. [Mauss is using *idéal* in the sense of 'pertaining to ideas or conceptions', not in the sense of 'satisfying one's idea of what is perfect'.]

26. Brigham, W.T., *The Ancient Hawaian House*, Honolulu, 1908. Conrau, G., 'Der Hüttenbau der Völker im nordlichen Kamerungebiet', *Globus* 74, 1898: 158 ff. Dugast, R., 'L'habitation chez les Ndiki du Cameroun', *J. de la Société des Africanistes* 5, 1940: 99–125. Maunier, R., *La construction collective de la maison en Kabylie*, Paris, 1926. Kaudern, W., *Ethnographical Studies in Celebes ...*, Göteborg, 1925–29, vol. 1: *Structure and Settlements in Central Celebes*, 1925. Kishida, H., *Japanese Architecture*, Board of Tourist Industry, 1935. Kon, W., *Construction de la maison paysanne au Japon*, Tokyo, 1930. Koch-Gruenberg, Th., 'Das Haus bei den Indianern Nordbresiliens', *Archiv f. Anthrop.* 7/1, 1908.

Mindeleff, C., *Navaho Houses*, ARBAE 17/2 (1895–96), 1898: 469–519; *The Cliff Ruins of Canyon de Chilly, Arizona*, ARBAE 16 (1894–95), 1897: 80–118. Sapper, C., 'The Old Indian Settlements and Architectural Structures in North Central America', *Smiths. Inst. Annual Report*, 1895: 537–555. Wauchope, R., *Modern Maya Houses: a Study of their Archaeological Significance*, Washington, 1938.

27. See Bücher, K., *Arbeit und Rythmus*, Leipzig, 1902.

28. See Sachs, C., *Histoire de la danse*, trans. from German, Paris, 1938. Has different pictures in the German and American editions (Berlin, 1993; New York, 1937). Cuisinier, J., *Danses magiques de Kelantan*, Paris, 1936. Holt, C., *Dance Quest in Celebes*, Paris, Maisonneuve, 1939.

29. Wallaschek, R., *Primitive Music*, London, 1893; *Anfänge der Tonkunst*, Leipzig, 1903. Stumpf, C., *Die Anfänge der Musik*, Leipzig, 1911. Sachs, C. *Geist und Werden der Musikinstrumente*, Berlin, 1929. Schaeffner, A., *Origine des instruments de musique*, Paris, 1936. Ankermann, B., 'Die afrikanischen Musikinstrumente', *Ethnologischer Notizblatt* 3, Berlin, 1901. Sachs, C., *Les instruments de musique de Madagascar*, Paris, 1938. Kirby, P., *The Musical Instruments of the Native Races of South Africa*, Oxford, 1934. Hornbostel, E. von, 'The Ethnology of African Sound-instruments', *Africa*, 1933: 129–157, 277–311. Lachmann, R., *Musik der Orients*, Breslau, 1929. Marcel-Dubois, C., *Les instruments de musique de l'Inde ancienne*, Paris, 1941. Kolinski, M., 'Die Musik der Primitivstämme auf Malakka', *Anthropos* 25: 585–648. All the studies of J. Kunst concerning Indonesian instruments: *De toonskunst van Java* (The Hague, 1934), *[...] van Bali* (Weltevreden, 1925), *Music in Nias* (Leiden, 1939), *[...] in Flores* (Leiden, 1942). Kaudern, W., *Ethnographical Studies in Celebes, vol. 3: Musical Instruments*, Göteborg, 1927. Best, E. *Games ...* [n. 8]: 105–183. The studies by M.F. Bukofzer, E.G. Burrows, F. Densmore, etc. Izikowitz, K.G., *Musical and Other Sound Instruments of the South American Indians*, Göteborg, 1935. Balfour, H., *The Natural History of the Musical Bow*, Oxford, 1899. See also Stumpf, C., *Tonpsychologie*, Leipzig, 1883. Lalo, C., *Eléments d'une esthétique musicale scientifique*, Paris, 1939. Brelet, G., 'Musiques exotiques et valeurs permanentes de l'art musical', *Revue philosophique*, 1946: 71–96.

30. Preuss, K.Th., 'Der Unterbau des Dramas', *Vorträge der Bibliothek Warburg* 7, 1927–28; 'Phallische Fruchtbarkeitsdämonen als Träger des alt-mexikanischen Dramas', *Archiv f. Anthropologie*, n.s. 1, 1904: 129–188. Ridgeway, W., *The Dramas and Dramatic Dances of Non-European Races, in Special Reference to the Origin of Greek Tragedy*, Cambridge, 1915. Reich, H., *Der Mimus*, Berlin, 1903. Jacob, G., *Geschichte des Schattentheaters ...*, Berlin, 1907. Rassers, W.H., Over den oorsprong van het Javaansche tooneel, *Bijdragen tot de Taal-, Land- en Volkenkunde van Netherlandsch-Indie* 88, 1931. Kats, J., *Het javaansche tooneel*, Weltevreden, 1923. Roussel, L., *Karagheuz ou un théâtre d'ombres à Athènes*, 2 vols, Athens, 1921. Przyluski, J., 'Le théâtre d'ombres et la caverne de Platon', *Byzantion* 13, 1938: 595–603. Péri, N., Préface aux *Cinq nô*, Paris, Bossard, 1921. Beaujard, A., *Le théâtre comique des Japonais*, Paris, 1937. Lévi, S., *Le théâtre indien*, Paris, 1890. Leclère, A., 'Le théâtre cambodgien', *Revue d'ethnographie et de sociologie*, 1910: 257–82. Bacot, J. (ed.), *Trois mystères tibétains*, Paris, Bossard, 1921. See also: Barth, A., 'De l'origine et de la propagation des fables', *Journal des savants*, 1903. Villiers, A., *La Psychologie du comédien*, Paris, 1942.

31. Gummere, F.B. *The Beginning of Poetry*, New York, 1901. Wundt, W., *Sprachgeschichte und Sprachpsychologie*, Leipzig, 1901. Boeckel, D., *Psychologie der Volksdichtung*, Leipzig, 1906. Boas, F., 'The Folklore of the Eskimo', *J. Am. Folklore*, 17, 1904: 1–13. Bogoras, W., 'The Folklore of North Eastern Asia, as Compared with that of North Western America', *Am. Anth.* 4/4, 1902: 577–684. Deloria, E., *Dakota Texts*, Am. Ethnological Society, 14, New York, 1932. Meinhof, C., *Die Dichtung der Afrikaner*, Berlin, 1911. Sapir, E., *Nootka Texts: Tales and Ethnological Narratives*, Philadelphia, 1939. Vieillard, G., 'Poèmes peuls du Fouta Djallon', *Bulletin du Comité d'études historiques et scientifiques de l'Afrique occidentale française*, 20, 1937: 225–311. Walton, E.L. and Waterman, T.T., 'American Indian Poetry', *Am. Anth.* 27, 1925: 25–52. Petsch, R., *Neue Beiträge zur Kenntniss des Volksrätsels*, Berlin, 1899 (a study of the collective psychology of riddles). Werner, A., *Myths and Legends of the Bantu*, London, 1933.

32. See Granet, M., *Fêtes et chansons anciennes de la Chine*, Paris, 1919; *Danses et légendes de la Chine ancienne*, Paris, 1926. Nguyen Van Huyen, *Les chants alternés des garçons et des filles en Annam*, Paris, 1934.

33. Paulhan, J., *Les Hain-Tenys*, Paris, 1938.

34. Beckwith, M.W., *The Hawaïan Romance of Laieikawai*, ARBAE 33 (1911–12), 1919: 285–666. Boas, F., *Kathlamet Texts*, Washington, 1901; *Kutenai Tales*, Washington, 1901. Cosquin, E., *Etudes folkloriques* ..., Paris, 1922. Dupuis-Yakouba, A., *Les Gow, ou chasseurs du Niger* ..., Paris, 1911. Junod, H.A., *Les chants et les contes des Ba-Ronga*, Lausanne, 1897. Leenhardt, M., *Documents néo-calédoniens*, Paris, 1932. Radin, P., 'Literary Aspects of North American Mythology', *Canada Geological Survey Museum Bulletin* 16, Ottawa, 1915. Rattray, R.S., *Ashanti Folk-tales*, Oxford, 1930. Swanton, J.R., 'Haida Texts and Myths (Skidegate Dialect)', *BAE Bull.* 29, 1905 (1906). Thalbitzer, W., *The Ammassalik Eskimo: Language and Folklore*, Copenhagen, 1923.

35. See Werner, H., *Die Ursprünge der Lyrik: eine Entwicklungspsychologie*, Munich, 1924.

6

Economic Phenomena

Of all the moral phenomena, economic ones are those that remain most firmly grounded in matter. They are usually classified among material phenomena, side by side with techniques. But they are not merely material phenomena; they are collective representations governing the attitude of members of a society towards matter.

By definition, an economic phenomenon is a social phenomenon, one governing a whole set of activities concerning objects that may be more or less necessary, but are all commonly called 'goods'. The economic side of these phenomena distinguishes them from purely technical actions: it may be a service that is paid for, or a good that changes hands. Why are economic phenomena qualified as 'political'? Because they are general in a given society, a given *polis*, a given town, as against being simply economic. Until the sixteenth century, economy and political economy were virtually conflated, but since that time economy has been opposed to luxury, and economy and luxury alike have become subjects for study.

According to Bücher, the world's economic life goes through three stages: the closed domestic economy, the open domestic economy, and social economy. In fact, the closed domestic economy, as Bücher conceives of it, corresponds to the economy of an individual family. As he sees it, the house in the Middle Ages would be a typical instance of the closed economy, but he is forgetting that the lady of the house in the Middle Ages already has her maids and serfs, who feed her. Furthermore, as far as noble families are concerned, there is noble spending, that is to say money is spent freely. Among the Australians we find a system of total prestations. The ideal for an Australian clan is to welcome another clan and offer it everything. A maximum of individuation for one part of the year, and a maximum of openness for another part of the year: that sums up the Australian economy.

Stammler[1] defines an economic phenomenon as a phenomenon involving masses that attain mutual equality according to law. But there can be no transmission unless society is to some extent present to sanction the transmission.

For Giddings,[2] economic phenomena are the result of the conflict between jural and technical phenomena. No doubt; but what is involved here is the products of technology, not the techniques themselves. In fact, all these authors forget the economic phenomenon itself.

We shall keep to the definition of Simiand, according to whom 'the economic phenomenon is distinguished by the presence of a market generally, and by the notion of value always'.[3] Economic goods and services are those whose value is fixed by a particular social mass. Where there is no notion of value, there is no economic phenomenon.

Such a definition of economic phenomena has the advantage of dispensing with the notion of need and utility. Undoubtedly, a market is made from the needs and utilities of the mass who engage in it. But those needs are not inherently fixed, for it is sufficient to live, and one can live poorly; they are determined by the mass itself, by its tastes and not by its needs. The elasticity of human needs is such that no logical calculus whatever is capable of fixing its limits. The very notion of need is relative to a particular condition of society, at a particular period; when the social conditions change, needs change. In so far as these notions of needs and utilities operate, they do not do so in a way that is rational, elemental and intellectualist, as they are usually described; they function strictly in statistical fashion. I am referring here to the great Austrian school of political economy and its theory of marginal utility. Marginal utility is defined statistically by the state of the market and the state of civilisation. In all cases, the notion of value for the individual comes into play. These are phenomena involving masses. It is clear that notions of utility and purpose are not the fundamental notions in economic phenomena.

Moreover, phenomena that we take to be specifically economic, such as the division of labour, are not so. The division of labour is not exclusively an economic phenomenon; it is a jural phenomenon, often a metaphysical and religious one, and always a moral one. The main division of labour we observe in most cases is that which distributes tasks according to sex and age. But in some societies, only women can be potters; elsewhere, only men can be weavers. There is no rationality here. Finally, the organisation of a trade, the organisation of the labour itself, while it is indeed an economic phenomenon, is in fact, above all, a technical phenomenon. There can be no division of labour without a definite condition of society, without an assignment of tasks by society itself.

Economic phenomena are defined to some extent by the presence of the notion of value, as aesthetic phenomena are indicated by the presence of the notion of beauty and moral phenomena by that of moral good. Economic value is a matter which one should not try to understand by starting from the philosophy of values. At the most, we can speak of a hierarchy of economic values, but there is no place for speculation on value judgements.

Economic reasoning is a recent type of reasoning. *Homo economicus* already exists in Aristotle, but it really dates only from Mandeville's *Fable of the bees*

[1723]. The great works of the English and the Dutch, particularly the studies by Gresham, had paved the way for Mandeville's theory. The category 'economic' is a modern category. Modern man is always in a market. We have almost reached the absolute end of the closed domestic economy, owing to the primacy of the monetary factors of capital accumulation and credit distribution, to the development of mechanical mass production requiring considerable capital, and to the reduction even of agriculture to economic forms. Moreover, we think on a national scale of values and even an international one. The problem of distribution, which in the past used to take place within the clan and the family according to fixed rules, is now resolved in the public market.

The question of the priority of communism over individualism does not arise. Father Schmidt quotes an Australian song, which he takes as proving that the whole Australian cycle is individualistic. A mother sings to her child: 'You will be rich, you will be strong, you will be tall, you will be master'. But Father Schmidt does not quote the whole text, which says: 'You will be rich, give to your mother, give to your father, give to your brothers, give to everyone' – which is the opposite of individualism. In reality everything happens as if each individual and each social group were in a constant state of endosmosis and exosmosis relative to all the others.

If one really wants, societies can be defined by their communism or individualism, or more precisely by the degree of communism and individualism that they show. Both are always present; the task is to determine their respective proportions.

If it is really desired, we can define the category 'economic' in the thinking of a society as being the whole set of values, and institutions relating to those values, acknowledged by that society. Thus, we shall say that rural property in the neighbourhood of Paris belongs to a capitalist economic regime. Here we have large farms requiring massive financial investments; the work is done by paid employees, not by the owner. But the technology is that of an industrial enterprise, and the organisation also is of an industrial nature.

In primitive societies, the economy is dispersed through all the other activities, and we do not find the individualism of our acquisitive society. Thus economic phenomena have to be studied from a particular angle, namely in their relations with other phenomena. In order to study the economy of a particular society, one should study in turn each value and each institution relating to these values. In very many cases, people pay to dance such and such a dance; the dance is an economic valuable, and one needs to record its nature, the mode of payment, and so on.

The use of the inventory method faces obstacles in this context, since the natives will always be tempted to express value in terms of a currency. Prices are a function of the currency; so the currency ought to be a standard of value, and as such it ought to have a relative permanence; however, this is generally not the case.

In many regions, one will find at least the memory of indigenous currencies: cowrie shells, or iron money in Africa. In Melanesian areas, the notion of money is very clear. Nearly everywhere else, one finds objects which perform the function of a currency. Even when there is no currency in a strict sense, economic phenomena are evaluated quantitatively. The fieldworker should therefore use the method of a quantitative inventory. He or she should enter every house and ask the price of every item, activity and service. Wherever it exists, the institution of the market will be of great help in compiling the inventory. Variations in market value should be carefully recorded. One will see the bard, the poet and the dancer being paid; so there is a notion of recompense or salary. Observe too the relations between those values that have been or will be produced, and the technology as a whole; also relations with techniques and technomorphology, and the location of industries. A particular industry can only be situated in a particular location, given a particular technology: thence arise exchanges and prerogatives.

Study finally the links between markets and meeting places, roads and transportation routes. All of this can be observed quantitatively: the number of things produced in such and such a place, by such and such people. Transport facilities, existence of a waterway, for example), and transport capacity, using porters, or beasts of burden) determine the commercial value of a country.

Observe the livestock; the hunting grounds and the abundance of game, the fishing spots; and the whole array of granaries. A most important notion is that of surplus, the exhibition or display of wealth, studied by Malinowski in the Trobriand Islands. Observation should proceed day by day, noting the seasons, the festivals, the market day, etc.

A certain form of economy consists in unbridled exploitation, which is current in societies of the archaic type. The ideal here is to exhaust an area of land. But the destruction of forests often is a necessity for natives who know of no fertiliser other than ash and are therefore forced to shift their cultivation areas periodically.

Other forms of economy are international. The Arunta practise trade which, linking tribe with tribe, extends as far as the Gulf of Carpentaria. The travels of rock crystal and amber date from the Upper Palaeolithic. Thus from very early on trade was international, often over long distances.

Finally, trade is based on exchanges or prestations. One has on each occasion to study the parties involved: family with family, generation with generation ...

Production

Who produces? Make inventories, by industry and by season; by sex, age, class, caste, clan, village, extended local group; for the village economy, urban economy and inter-urban economy.

Forms of production should be distinguished according to the nature of labour, which may be done collectively or individually. There are times when labour can only be done collectively: clearing forest requires the presence of all the workers. While studying the various phases of labour, distinguish between *corvée*, communal labour, family labour and individual work.

The division of labour is essentially social. If the division is obvious, it is expressed in the form of privilege, hunting as a privilege of the nobility). Does the headman work or not? The work of serfs and of slaves. The division between hunters, fishermen, and farmers often occurs for reasons that are mainly of a technomorphological order. The whole of New Zealand is divided between hunters and fishermen.

The division of labour may be by crafts, sometimes with a special organisation of crafts. Carpenters form a caste in Fiji,[4] and blacksmiths are everywhere grouped into a caste. There are specialisations linked with families, the craft secrets being handed down from father to son or from uncle to nephew. Sorcery is a craft. Consider the general regime of production, and special regimes according to industries, economic classes, and castes; also slavery and serfdom.

Next come the forms of production. A small number of them is typical of the people we wrongly call primitives. Generally, 'primitives' know how to make a great number of objects for personal use. Crafts and financial capital should be observed according to the forms of ownership; these are essentially jural phenomena. The issue of manufacturing will arise in some places. Private production and public production. The issue of ownership and of use, which is distinct from ownership.

The beginnings of higher forms of industry are clearly present in the Sudan, and also in Indo-China among the Moï. Islamic, European and Chinese influences may have played a significant role here. The transformation of Senegal by the cultivation of groundnuts.

Distribution and Consumption

Nothing is more erroneous than the notion of barter. All the speculation by Adam Smith rests on a mistake by Cook concerning Polynesians who climbed aboard ship and offered the Europeans an exchange, not of objects, but of gifts. The notion of barter was born in the 18th and 19th centuries from our utilitarianism.

Originally there was a system which I shall call that of total prestations. When an Australian Kurnai finds himself in the same camp as his parents-in-law, he is not allowed to eat any of the game he brings back; his in-laws take everything and their right is absolute. The reciprocity is total, it is what we call communism, but it is only practised between individuals. From the beginning, *commercium* goes side by side with *connubium*; marriage follows trade and trade follows marriage. Mandatory gift giving, fictitious gifts, and what is called 'legal theft' are in fact communism based on the individual – social and familial. The fundamental mistake is to oppose communism and individualism.

Moreover, these exchanges occur in ways differing from our own: the value of the object changes in the course of exchange. This could be expressed by the notion of interest, but it is not. The Kwakiutl of America have a currency consisting of copper plates that are exchanged in the course of large-scale ceremonies they call 'potlatches'. The value of a particular shield depends on the number of potlatches in which it has already appeared, for the shield is inseparable from the ceremony that is somehow part of it. The same facts can be observed in the Trobriand Islands where noble trade, the *kula*, coexists with common trade where people exchange products of equal value. In the *kula*, the talismans of a clan increase their value as they pass through different hands, since the value remains linked with the family. Something of this state of mind is still present in the way we conceive of crown jewels. I tried to describe this kind of unequal distribution economy in my work on the gift.[5] But that work deals with the religious and moral value of the transmitted objects, while what we are concerned with here is the whole set of gift systems, the whole set of potlatch systems.

The primitive form of all these necessary exchanges, which are neither voluntary nor purely economic, is what I call total prestations. In our Western societies, contracts are strictly determined by the object, the date and the fulfilment of the contractual conditions. I buy a loaf, and my relation with the baker begins and ends there. In contrast, in all non-market societies, exchange occurs between people who are bound more or less permanently, sometimes absolutely and totally; prestations to one's own parents-in-law, for instance.

Total prestations are usually of equivalent value. A owes everything to B, who himself owes everything to C; I owe everything to my parents-in-law, but my sons-in-law owe me everything. It is comparable to the economy of the barracks, where the soldier has everything paid on his behalf, but he no longer belongs to himself. It is what is called primitive communism, but the expression is imprecise – what is involved is total reciprocity. Throughout the Melanesian region, a man who wants a boat has it built by his sisters' husbands. But he builds the boat of his wife's brothers, for in owing them his wife he owes them everything. In our way of life, total reciprocity no longer exists except in marriage, between spouses.

Usually, things are equal: rights of the father-in-law, rights of the brother-in-law, a right to everything, a right to a particular part. Taken to the limit, a system of reciprocities will correspond exactly to what we call communism; but it will always be something strictly individual, the whole set of individual positions constituting the system of total reciprocities.

The form these exchanges take always implies that they are voluntary – obligatory, yet voluntary. It is conceived of in the form of a gift, not in the form of barter or payment; and yet, it is a payment. The worker who comes to weed or thresh grain must be fed throughout the period of his weeding or threshing. In these societies, the sharing of work is at once necessary and obligatory, and yet it is voluntary. There is no method of constraint; the individual is free.

These institutions are very strong throughout the Black world. The whole of the economic life of a Thonga man in South Africa is dominated by the payment of bride-price, the *lobola*. The prestations are equal, complete and reciprocal, but not always between the same individuals. It is what I call alternating reciprocity: I can do for my children what my children cannot do for me. According to an old French saying, 'a father can feed ten children; ten children cannot feed a father'; but I owe to my children what my father gave me. It is not necessarily the same person who gives and who gives back, providing the circle is finally completed. This is alternating and indirect reciprocity, on which our civilisations still proceed, whatever they think to be the case, since in a particular society, the total of assets is necessarily equal to the total of debts.

In addition to this relative equivalence and these total prestations involving complete equivalence, the societies we are studying know of other prestations associated with agonistic values, with rivalries. I am rich, therefore I must spend more than you do. You invite me for dinner and receive me as best you can; I am bound to give you back a dinner still more extravagant. Unequal total prestations, or *potlatch* as the institution is called in North West America, correspond to a system of rivalry between people bound by reciprocity. This regular extreme form of indirect reciprocity can be carried very far, even leading to the destruction of wealth. What happens is that people destroy valuables, for instance in the course of funerary rituals, not only for the dead to carry them off to the netherworld, but also to display the wealth of their group. The notion of the display of wealth leads to extreme forms, for instance at gatherings of Gypsies, who burn thousand-franc notes in sheer ostentation.[6] The destruction of wealth does not mean here that we are dealing with anti-economic phenomena. Pure spending is not an anti-economic phenomenon; it is simply the opposite of private economy. A Kwakiutl chief's ideal is to find himself ruined at the end of his potlatch; in any case, he is sure he will receive twice as much eventually. All these exchanges of unequal values should therefore be studied, for the inequality is still an economic phenomenon. These institutions lead to considerable events, including relative forms of market; they lead to complete circuits. Boas attended potlatches among the Kwakiutl costing 20,000 dollars.

Next comes the market. The beginnings of the market are an important phenomenon. Some societies ignore it (for instance, the Celts) or regard it as an inferior institution. But nearly everywhere, we find at least its elements. The Negroes can be divided into peoples who hold a market every three days, every four days, or every seven days. Whenever there is a market, study the various locations where it is held – a market is often itinerant – market regulations, peace in the market, the rites, and whether it is permanent. Who attends the market? How do people haggle, make contracts, give guarantees? Does the market take place in the town or outside? Are prices fixed beforehand? The notion of a fair price. Prices can become fixed while the value of the currency changes.

In very many cases, international trade takes place between societies belonging to different levels of civilisation: for example, the Malaysians trading with other Indonesian tribes. The reason for silent trade[7] is often the distrust felt by one of the parties, the weaker one, who refuses to allow strangers access to its territory.

Some tribes consist almost exclusively of merchants: the Hausa and Dioula of West Africa are traders, often operating over very long distances. These merchant tribes have often provided sedentary populations with military dynasties: for example, the Hausa in Chad and the Greeks in Cyrenaica.

International trade can take place over very long distances, in Australia for instance, where trade is usually conducted through women. Primitive forms of trade are heavily marked with magical elements: people exchange precious objects and scarce commodities.

Currency

The adjustment of the two economic domains of production and consumption occurs via the notion of value. When there is no simple jural adjustment, as in total prestations, value is measured with currency.[8]

Currency is a phenomenon more widespread than is generally believed. Even in Australia, certain rock crystals regarded as extremely precious can serve to measure value in a certain sense. All these early forms of currency therefore should be studied; they usually correspond to precious raw materials or objects: quartz, amber, jade? ... The inhabitants of Atakpamé in Togo have a god of the exchange rate.

As soon as there is currency, in fact, there is an exchange rate; a dynamic and psychological element comes into play. Social relations are always dynamic by definition; they are only static by convention. Because they bring together people of different sexes and different ages, they create a certain dynamism.

Currency exists throughout North America. Among the Iroquois, *wampum* is pearl work that people lend, but it must be given back augmented by one unit, for the fact of the exchange increases its value. The Eskimos, the whole of Melanesia, and part of Polynesia are familiar with currency; the Maoris practise a cult of jade.

Currency can appear in extremely varied forms: precious stones, polished stone axes, discs of deerskin, paper money as in China ... Certain ornaments of rare feathers can serve as currency. All crystals, all precious stones, cowrie shells which have spread across the whole of Africa and come from the Indian Ocean. Finally, all forms of metal.

Elliot Smith and Perry thought they could prove that Megalithic civilisation as a whole was a civilisation of gold prospectors.[9] Brass, in the form of wires, plates, or bracelets, iron in the shape of knives, in spearheads, or blades for digging tools, are very widespread throughout Africa.

Certain mats, for instance in the Samoa Islands, are used as currency units. Very often, these mats have a coat of arms; people pile them up, like title deeds from a joint stock company. Throughout North West America, the currency unit is a blanket. Even nowadays, the Federal State pays in blankets the indemnities it owes to the Indians who have been expropriated.

One of the strangest currencies is salt, so evidently consumable. The salt bar is legal currency throughout Africa, from Guinea to Abyssinia and the Nile Valley. Tobacco currency; alcohol and palm wine, the beer unit. Currency counted by heads of cattle.

From the moment there is a jural scale of prices, there is a system of currencies forming a single currency. The fair price is the price statistically determined; we cannot deduce it from anything at all. Such a hierarchy of prices constitutes something stable in the midst of things that change.

Finally, from the moment European nations intervene, there appears the problem of the economic clash, of acculturation or colonisation.[10]

Notes

1. Stammler, R., *Theorie der Rechtswissenschaft*, Halle, 1911.
2. Giddings, F.H., *The Principles of Sociology* .... New York, 1896.
3. Simiand, F., *Cours d'économie politique*, first year, 1930–31.
4. Hocart, A.M., *Les Castes*, trans., Paris, 1938 [first English edition 1950!].
5. Mauss, M., 'Essai sur le don, forme et raison de l'échange dans les sociétés archaïques', *AS*, n.s. 1, 1923–24: 30–186. On the *kula*, see Malinowski, B., *Argonauts of the Western Pacific*, London, 1922.
6. See Maunier, R., 'Recherches sur les échanges rituels en Afrique du Nord', *AS*, n.s. 2, 1924–25: 11–97.
7. See Grierson, P.J.H., *The Silent Trade*, Edinburgh, 1903.
8. Ridgeway, W., *The Origins of Metallic Currency and Weight Standards*, Cambridge, 1892. Schurtz, H., *Grundriss einer Entstehungsgeschichte des Geldes*, Weimar, 1898. Simiand, F., 'La monnaie, réalité sociale', *Annales sociologiques*, série D. Sociologie économique, fasc. I, 1934: 1–58; and discussion at the Institut français de sociologie, *ibid*: 59–86. Armstrong, W.E., *Rossell Island, an Ethnological Study*, Cambridge, 1928. Leenhardt, M., *Gens* ... [Chapter 2, n. 6]: 21–30.
9. See notably Perry, W.J., 'The Relationship Between the Geographical Distribution of Megalithic Monuments and Ancient Mines', *Mem. and Proc. of the Manchester Literary and Philosophical Society* 60, 1915–16: 1 ff.; *The Children of the Sun*, London, 1923; *The Growth of Civilization*, London, 1924.
10. Armstrong, W.E., *Rossell Island* ... [n. 8]. Beaglehole, E., *Notes on Hopi Economic Life*, Yale U. Publ. in Anthrop. 15, 1937. Birket-Smith, K., *The Eskimo*, London, 1936. Boas, F., *The Central Eskimo*, ARBAE 6 (1884–85), 1888; *Ethnology of the Kwakiutl*, ARBAE 35 (1913–14), 1921. Bogoras, W., *The Chukchee: Material Culture*, Mem. AMNH (Jesup) 7/1, 1904. Bücher, K., *Die Entstehung der Volkswirtschaft, sechs Vorträge*, Tübingen, 1893. Evans-Pritchard, E.E., 'Economic Life of the Nuer: Cattle', *Sudan Notes and Records*, 20, 1937: 209–245; 21, 1938: 31–78. Firth, R., *Primitive Economics of the New Zealand Maori*, New York, 1929; 'Currency, Primitive', *Encyclopaedia Britannica*, 14th ed., 1929. Grierson, P.J.H., *Silent Trade* [n. 7]. Grosse, E., *Die Formen der Familie und die Formen der Wirtschaft*, Freiburg and Leipzig, 1896. Hewitt, J.N.B., 'Wampum', *BAE Handbook of American Indians*, 1908. Koppers, W., *Die Menschliche Wirtschaft: der Mensch aller Zeiten, III. Völker und Kulturen*, Regensburg, 1924: 377–630. Leenhardt, M., *Gens* ... [Chapter 2, n. 6]. Malinowski, B., *Argonauts* ... [n. 5]. Marshall, A., *Principles of Economics*, 8th ed., London, 1936. Mauss, M., 'Essai sur le don' [n. 5].

Murdock, G.P., *Rank and Potlatch among the Haida*, Yale U. Publ. in Anthrop. 13, 1936. Richards, A.I., *Hunger and Work in a Savage Tribe*, London, 1932. Schurtz, H., *Grundriss* ... [n. 8]. Seligman, E.R.A., *Principles of Economics*, New York, 1905. Thurnwald, R., *L'économie primitive*, trans. from German, Paris, 1937. Tueting, L.T., 'Native Trade in Southeast New Guinea', *Bernice P. Bishop Museum Occas. Papers* 11, 15, 1935. Vierkandt, A., 'Die wirtschaftlichen Verhältnisse der Natur-Völker', *Z. f. Sozialwissenschaft*, 1899: 81–97, 175–185.

7

Jural Phenomena

In the field of ethnology we [in France] understand by law (*droit*) what the Anglo-Saxons call 'social anthropology', which means in fact our jural and moral sociology. As society becomes more and more secular, the role of morality increases. In our society, morality plays a more important role than law. Law remains unconscious among us, and becomes conscious only in situations of conflict (for example, the marriage contract). The opposite is found in primitive societies, where the individual is all the time immersed in a flux of prestations and counter-prestations; here, custom extends into the smallest acts of family life. A certain attitude, consisting in constant awareness of the law, is typical of primitive peoples, who by no means live in a state of nature, such as the first Europeans imagined, especially for the Polynesians.

In the societies pertaining to ethnography, all jural phenomena without exception are moral phenomena, but this does not mean that all moral phenomena are necessarily jural phenomena, in the strict sense. In any case, to separate jural phenomena from religious or economic ones leads to an absurdity.

Social organisation is generally understood to mean political organisation, but the latter only constitutes one part of law, and not the most profound. Law comprises the whole of customs and laws; as such, it forms the framework of society, it is 'the precipitate of a people' (Portalis). What defines a group of people is neither its religion nor its technology, it is quite simply its law. All the other phenomena, including religious ones – no matter what is said about national religions – can stretch beyond the confines of a given society. But what defines us cannot reach beyond our frontiers. Thus the phenomenon of law is the phenomenon that gives specificity to a society. No doubt jural phenomena have travelled, just like all the other elements of civilisation, but in a different way: they travel by leaps.

Law can further be characterised by its intimacy and by the widely felt sentiments of community that accompany it. Throughout the Roman Empire only the position of the *civis romanus* [Roman citizen] was guaranteed;

everyone else was subject only to the *ius gentium*, which means that that they relied on the emperor's indulgence.[1]

Law is generally invested with a well marked religious quality. The word 'responsibility' (*responsabilité*) in the French legal vocabulary dates only from the Revolution. Previously, the term existed only in theology, and incrimination was conflated with indictment.

The various constituent parts of the law can be more or less sacred: Rome knew the law of the *pontifices*, and the teaching of law among the Maori takes place in secret. While the law is essentially a public phenomenon, it nevertheless remains in one respect highly intimate. True legal specialists possess the secrets of the law.

It is often very hard to distinguish between jural and economic phenomena. How can a distinction be made between what is jural and what is economic in communal labour? In Melanesia, the man who wants to have a new boat asks his brothers-in-law, who owe him this gift: it is a way of organising the economy, but one that is essentially bound up with legal phenomena. A son-in-law in respect of his mother-in-law is everywhere obliged to perform multiple economic services. In fact, economic phenomena are generally legal phenomena. The difference lies in the presence of the notion of value in the economic phenomenon and the notion of moral good (*bien moral*) in the jural one.

Jural and moral phenomena cannot be distinguished from religious ones on the basis of their obligatory character, since the latter possess the same character. Initiation is at once a jural and a religious event. It is a matter of making the young man materially, morally and religiously, and perhaps of giving him access to women and property. The distinction between law and religion can be made on the basis of the nature of the obligations. In the one case, it is a matter of sacred things, and not just the individual; in the other, it is a matter of social, moral and jural things. Sanction itself is construed as a matter of law, or of duty. The vendetta is a moral obligation: one has a moral obligation to inflict punishment.

This notion of law and duty is precise in native practices, which all contain the notion of moral good and evil – a notion that makes it possible to recognise the phenomenon of law: 'Law is what is said by the virtuous' (Manu [the Sanskrit law code]). This notion of good and evil applies to the relations between the individual and his fellows. Without this art of moral life, there can be no communal life, whether it be life in groups or sub-groups – clans, families, sexes, classes, etc.

But how can we distinguish law from morality in the societies that concern us? The whole system of moral and legal ideas corresponds to the system of these collective expectations. Law is the means of organising the system of collective expectations and ensuring respect for individuals, for their value, for their groupings; also for their hierarchy. Jural phenomena are moral phenomena that have been organised. This is still the case with our modern law: civil responsibility and criminal responsibility are strictly determined. The formula 'ignorance of the law is no excuse' corresponds to this system of collective expectations. Fundamentally, when we are ignorant of the law we are usually in the wrong, for there is a latent awareness and a latent knowledge in every custom and in every moral precept – and I would add: in every legal system, for not everything can be expressed in black and white. Hence the enormous superiority of so-called customary legal systems over written ones; cases serve as precedents – and the notion of precedent and usage is fundamental in law.

We recognise the presence of morality and religion only from the presence of the notion of moral obligation, and secondarily, from the presence of the notion of infraction and the notion of sanction. There is moral obligation when there is moral sanction, when there is diffuse sanction; there is jural obligation when the obligation is cast in precise terms and likewise for the infraction[2] and for the penalty. There is always morality in law; there is always a notion of moral obligation in law, as there is in morality. The obligation is merely more definite and more jural in the case of the law.

We have another means of discerning moral and legal phenomena. All laws are deemed good by definition. Furthermore, conformity to laws is good, it is necessary for social life. All that conforms to the law is good and all that militates against such conformity is bad. Thus moral and legal phenomena can be recognised by the presence of the notion of good and evil, defined beforehand and always sanctioned. There is no wrong unless either your conscience or that of other people says there is wrong. Here, once again, we should submit to the evaluation of the natives and forget our Western judgements. What the natives say is moral is moral; what they say is good is good, and what they say is the law is the law.

The observer will be faced with legal systems entirely different from our own. An initial difficulty, which derives from the customary nature of the law, can be overcome by familiarising oneself with ancient French law or with English law. Certain legal systems, however, were written down in very ancient times: the oldest is the code of Hammurabi, composed at the start of the second millennium BC and found in Suse. Doubtless, the laws of Manu were already compiled when Athens still had only a few Tables and Rome did not possess any systematic code.

Customary law does not necessary clash with written law. In all legal systems there always exists a customary law. In France, large sections of the law are still only customary law. It is simply a fantasy to claim that everything can be deduced from something constituted by reason. Customaries, where they exist, use exactly the same mode of expression as our legal adages. The model customary is the Adat of the Dutch East Indies. The compilation of customs is an on-going process in West Africa.

Customary law may not be written law, but it nonetheless has its own formulation – in a set of proverbs, legal sayings and etiquette formulae, often in verse, such as may be found for instance in the moral of a fable or in a myth. The whole corpus of the Mahābhārata and the Rāmāyana, India's great epics, constitutes a book of law; one can cite them in a court of law. So one should be on the look-out for law in more or less any context.

Law still can be recorded orally in some cases. The verdicts of the first king of Tahiti have been published. Thus one should not think that oral and customary methods cannot give rise to a strictly articulated legal system. Legal specialists will be found everywhere: heralds and lawyers, familiar with the problems faced by everybody in the context of all the property owned in the area, and equally familiar with genealogies. Law will be observable in the discussion meetings attended by the whole village or the whole society, at which legal sayings take on great importance. Sometimes the administration of the law takes place within a secret society, but the announcement of the verdict is public.

Thus there exist people to whom the law is entrusted, legal specialists and genealogists, who can be observed speaking the law. Furthermore, verdicts are announced publicly except in cases where the punishment is to be inflicted secretly. So there is a means by which the law can be evaluated, namely the people's feelings. Under such circumstances customary law functions normally, with a perfect awareness and a relatively imperfect formulation, since the latter is not deliberately sought.

Custom always has a somewhat diffuse character; it becomes conscious of itself only in the context of particular cases. There is thus in time, as in number and space, a diffuseness in law – even more so than in custom. The observer should above all register the reactions of the crowd. On the basis of such reactions, he or she will discover the law – very easily, so far as criminal law is concerned.

Customary law has still another characteristic: it is not only public, but also private. The distinction between public and private law, which is made by our codes, is a recent one. Private retaliation used to be accepted until the last capitulary [in 884]; private wars were allowed in the Middle Ages between nobles, since two feudal lords of high and low justice stood in relation to each other like two States. Thus there is a constant mixing of public and private law. Individual retaliation exists side by side with public punishment – the general case in Africa. Customary laws are a mix, in a way, of public and private law, of unformulated law and also of formulated law. The only type of law truly absent is that between nations. But the mixing of private and public, of moral and jural sanction, is normal.

Much more could be said on the difficulty of legal studies. Many of our classifications are here of no value. Not only is the legislation to be observed of the customary type; not only does the law appear solely at particular moments, and not only is it divided up differently, but it has different relations with morality and it fulfils other functions than those with which we are familiar. Relations we deem to be private are public and vice versa. Phenomena that we regard as moral are jural elsewhere, and conversely; for instance, the relations between parents and children.

Another difficulty stems from the plurality of rights. Each clan has its own; and in a society made of several tribes, each tribe has its own. The rights of men are not the rights of women. Finally, there is a total inequality among owners and a variety of rights and responsibilities depending on the object that is owned. We had something of the kind before the Revolution: inequality based on social position, and total inequality based on age; variety according to the things appropriated. The house is generally treated as movable property, not immovable property. So, a plurality of rights and responsibilities, and a variety of them: *acceptio personae, acceptio rei, acceptio conditionis.*

Law can also vary over time, under the influence of external phenomena, such as the introduction of money. Customary law is supposed to be rigorously fixed and unchanging, but this idea is a general fiction attaching to all types of law, including customary law. In fact, it is via customary law that changes are made, which end up being written down in the code. This amounts to a fairly slow adaptation of social conditions: it is a fundamental problem of civilisation and colonisation.

Methods of Observation

The first method should be the *case method.* The observer should draw up a statistical inventory of all the cases tried in the archives of the circumscription since the archives were founded. The observer will thus merely be applying the method of the Pandects,[3] noting in each case every legal saying that is cited. It is necessary to note as many cases as possible, for the law always applies globally; a legal specialist must be familiar with the law as a whole.

The *biographical or life-history method* will be most useful here. In this method one has an individual enumerate all the properties he has had, how they were acquired, how they were split up, those he gave to his sons, each of them, when they got married, and so on. This method interrelates with the previous one, which covers only the litigious cases. There are non-litigious cases that belong just as much under the heading of law.

Finally, wherever it is possible, one will turn to *direct observation* of the law. There is no difficulty here in Black countries, where jural assemblies are nearly always public: the chief administers justice surrounded by his court and assisted by his heralds.

Here, professional legal specialists, especially heralds, will be of great help. The diviners and those who administer ordeals will be well worth interviewing. There are also circles of high dignitaries, elders in the society of men or in the secret society. The ideal is to find a native specialist who is trained in our methods and nevertheless capable of interpreting his own legal system; there is at least one instance.[4] In such cases, the legal specialist is also the legislator, for there is no difference between those who formulate the law and those who apply it. Even among us, such a distinction remains somewhat theoretical.

With a little luck, one will be able to obtain a recitation of those sets of formulas, sayings and proverbs which are fundamental. In some cases there exist real native codes – for instance, in Madagascar; and throughout the Berber world people are familiar with their *qānūns* – roughly speaking their written legislative conventions. It will be necessary also to gather all the myths, all the tales and all the epics. Legal phenomena will emerge as the hero's adventures take their course.

The major difficulty will be to identify legal systems of a relatively pure kind, since, very generally, one will be confronted with composite societies where the segmentation is such that some parts are independent of each other. A society is composed of itself, of sub-groups and of individuals. Our plan for studying jural phenomena will therefore unfold naturally as follows:

- Political and social organisation, the State;
- Domestic, politico-familial or politico-domestic organisation: clans, extended family, family; marriage;
- Property law;
- Contract law;
- Criminal law; and
- Procedure.

Social and Political Organisation[5]

As we saw above [at the start of Chapter 3], a society corresponds to a definite group of people usually living on a definite territory with a definite constitution. Once and for all, political society is defined by the number of 'us'. There are 'us' and there are the others.

Straightaway there appears the notion of sub-groups. Political and social organisation coordinates sub-groups and individuals, as is still the case among us. A first difficulty lies in definitions. The words *peuple* or *peuplade* 'people' are best avoided; the word 'tribe' is preferable, a tribe being defined by the protection of its members and by a fact of international private law: we [the French] all stand by the last or least Frenchman who is abroad. In very many cases, the observer will meet with composite societies. In such societies there is always one inferior element, or two, the so-called national minorities. Other difficulties stem from the phenomenon of the name or nomenclatures, and the notion of federation. There were in Athens three other Athens: an Ionic city, a Thracian city, and Pelasgian city. Rome likewise included elements that were Greek, Latin, Etruscan ...

So the task is to compile the history of the various societies that compose the whole society and whose origins can differ fundamentally: the divine Pelasgians were at Athens before the Thracians and before the Ionians. One needs the history of the clans and the history of the royal family.

Once the various elements of the society have been identified, each of them should be studied in turn. Very few societies consist of only a single tribe. The counting should not stop there: a tribe includes several clans, and each clan includes several sub-clans, several phratries. This will bring to light the various forms of political organisation coordinating the whole; it will bring to light also the society of men, the society of warriors, the secret societies, castes and guilds. The list should be drawn up from a historical point of view, backed up if possible by statistical and cartographic documentation.

Primary Forms of Social Organisation: Monarchy, Chiefdoms, Democracy

The political organisation usually corresponds either to a monarchy or a democracy. However, on the one hand, the king is never all-powerful; he is subject to a certain amount of control, if only that of his close relatives. On the other hand, democratic power presents a certain degree of concentration; as a result, monarchies are as unstable as democracies are stable. There are often several royal families for a single throne – for example, in Tahiti.

Monarchy[6]

A study of monarchy should begin with a detailed study of the king's family. The royal family does not necessarily have the same legal constitution as other domestic groups. In many societies, incest between king and queen is the norm; the king marries his sister in order to maintain the purity of the bloodline. The king and queen are the origin of things. In the beginning, there was incest between Earth and Heaven, and this is what must be reproduced. Hence the genealogical study of the royal family; and the detailed history of each king. Within the royal family or royal clan, the king is always chosen; there is never primogeniture, and there is never a line defined by destiny. Royal labour is often divided between two or several individuals: the day king and the night king, the kings of fire and water, of war and peace. Among the Hova [of Madagascar], the prime minister was regularly the husband of the queen.

A study of the *king's figure* should cover the name of his ancestors, his totem (the panther, for example, throughout the Black world), his royal insignia, the talismans, including secret ones. Etiquette and taboos; the isolation of the king often marks his celestial nature. Note what he eats, and the beliefs concerning his words and his soul; also the customs, if any, regarding his killing (if he is weak or unlucky, if he becomes too old ...). Is there an interregnum, a cult of the royal ancestors, etc.?

Record the *king's rights* over his family and his ministers: do his envoys wear a *récade*, as a sign of their messenger status? The king's rights over his subjects: does he have the right of life and death over them? His fiscal rights. The role of the king in criminal law and in civil law: oaths in the name of the king, and ordeals in which he is invoked. The place of the king in international law – for instance, in matters of war and peace. The king's rights in matters of private law; the prestations he receives, and those he owes. Being the treasurer of the tribe, clan, or nation, the king is in this capacity placed under certain obligations. *Rights over the king* can be exercised, for instance, concerning the potlatch. He may be obliged to provide medical and magical services (the king of France heals scrofula[7]). The responsibility attributed to the king can go so far that he may be put to death in case of sustained harvest failure or in the case of his decrepitude, which, according to common belief, corresponds to a weakening of the land; this applies throughout the Black world.

The *organisation of the court*, often very precise, in some cases represents the State as on a map.[8] The rights, the duties and the privileges of each position should be studied. What are the hereditary functions? Make a detailed historical study of each of them. Princes, ministers, priests, griots, heralds, bards, slaves, men and women, guards. Each member of the royal family should be subjected to a detailed enquiry. Chronicle each king.

An inventory of *the king's treasures* should also be made – the royal herds, the royal hunting grounds.

The court can be studied more easily when a general move takes place, at which point the place and the role of each office holder will become apparent. The etiquette will explain clearly the whole organisation that it symbolises.

Chiefdoms

Between monarchy and democracy, which are polar forms of political organisation, chiefs or headmen are to be found everywhere. Chiefs may or may not belong to the royal family, but in relation to their people they are more or less in the same situation as kings. If the chief is in command, it is by virtue of a particular essence emanating from him. Among the Betsileo, all genuine chiefs are called Hovas, which does not mean they all come from the Imerina [Plateau] or that they are all priests; but the tribe cannot do without priests: God is a chief.

Our own ideas about nobility are very weak. There exists no population that is perfectly democratic. In ancient Germany nobility was a regular phenomenon; it existed even in Iceland – that model of democracies – and even in the Swiss cantons. Among the Celts as well as in the Scottish clan, the chief is an eponym: he is at once military chief and civil chief, chief of the family, chief of the clan, and he incarnates its ancestor. The nobles constitute the hierarchy of an empire.

So more or less everywhere there has been some confusion between administrative nobility and nobility of race. And here lies the important issue of administrative tenure and land tenure. An English Law Lord is lord on the grounds of his function, but on those grounds only, and his nobility cannot be transmitted to his children. In the past, the loss of the noble's estate used to entail the loss of the title: the Duke of Bordeaux was duke at Bordeaux. A landed tenure on the other hand is a tenure by birth: the Duke of Norfolk is Earl Marshal at court.

The nobility evolves constantly between a minimum and a maximum. The difference between a petty Breton nobleman living in his manor and a well-to-do peasant was very small.

All the issues concerning feudalism arise here: some hierarchies are entirely of a royal order, such as the *cabécères* of Dahomey.[9] The nobles are the delegates of the Prince; this is the administrative chiefdom, and it is also the origin of part of our own nobility, notably of the whole *noblesse de robe*. Besides administrative chiefdoms, there are also purely military chiefdoms: the war king is not always king of peace.

Study all the prestations to which a particular title of nobility gives the right; all tenures *ex officio*: the noble may be someone who carries the crown.

Democracy

It is very rare for monarchies to exist without any component of democracy, and it is equally rare to come across a pure democracy. Leaders exercise their authority in an assembly where they are confronted by the mass of the people. Among the Germans, as among the Celts, a legend claims that there has never been anything else but democracies. This is a total mistake: nobles are found everywhere. Throughout the Indo-European world there has never been any absolute democracy. Democracy is not generally the condition of a State; it is the condition of a large proportion of the segments of the State, segments based on clans or tribes. But within each of these segments there are noble families, or functions that are to some degree noble. Everywhere, one finds at least the society of men, and within it, the society of elders.

The existence of pure democracies is a myth that became established in the sixteenth century in the confederation of the Swiss cantons. The legend of William Tell only developed in the sixteenth century, relating facts from the thirteenth century. In every democracy there is a stratum of chiefs or nobles. The organisation of the Mongols has been labelled a horde organisation, thus ignoring the fact that the prince of the horde is surrounded by the twelve banners and the twelve princes of the twelve Mongol States; but since the whole troop is mounted, the infantrymen cannot be distinguished from the cavalrymen – whence the impression of a lack of hierarchy.

Usually, democracy boils down to clan democracy. The basic and structural element then becomes a segmented element, a democratic statelet that carries with it a certain fraternity and a certain amorphism.

All Negro villages, all Indonesian villages, all Malagasy villages, the whole of India are acquainted with a kind of municipal council, society of men or council of elders. Maine saw in this feature parallels with the Irish communes.[10] This is indeed the mode of functioning of the Scottish, Irish and Welsh clan, and the whole Indo-European family. The elders constitute the administration of the tribe and the clan. They are grouped according to grades of age and nobility, which often overlap. After the introduction of the horse, all the American Plains Indians instituted the rules that are still called by the

French phrase *compte des coups* ('counting the blows'). Someone who is hit in the fray deems himself beaten, and promotion within the tribe depends on the number of blows struck. This institution goes back in all probability to the first French Canadian trappers. Nearly everywhere, then, one will find hierarchy within the clan and within the tribe; but such hierarchy does not preclude either democracy or tribal unity.

Lets us now consider the main features of democracy. Political organisation exists whenever there is a political entity (*organe*), whenever individuals fulfil a function acknowledged by the community. Nearly everywhere one finds a certain minimum level of organisation; such organisation can be temporary, like the clan council in Australia and in the Andaman Islands. Meetings of the clan council or the tribe council are accompanied by a certain degree of ceremonial. Etiquette is the norm; in Australia, during assemblies people speak a different language from the one spoken in everyday life. The notion of Parliament is a fundamental one.[11] Everywhere, there is a place where people must speak peacefully to each other. There is the right to speak, and the right, not to vote, but to agree or disagree. We find something similar in the councils during the Wars of Religion.

Assemblies of this kind are too often mistaken for wholly popular assemblies. The council of elders gathers separately, but when its meeting is over, it explains to the troops the decisions that have been taken. True, the people are present. In Scotland, a clan council takes place on the day of the clan festival and games. It is the presence of the mass of members that gives the clan this aspect of pure democracy, but the mass is an organised one, sorted into families, clans, sub-clans and localities. When the gathering breaks up, each family recovers its independence.

The democratic form of the State is accompanied by a particular mode of administering justice. Private justice is administered within the family. In the case of collective justice, the clan can in some instances proceed to an enquiry among all the families of the clan, the chief's family excluded.

Clan assemblies, or tribal assemblies, are often gathered to settle quarrels. All Australian tribal assemblies begin with a series of regular fights, or duels without fatal outcome. Weapons are carried to council meetings, for the free man can be recognised by the fact that he carries arms: 'You can tell the Republic', says Aristotle, 'by the fact that the people have not laid down their weapons'. In this respect, a Sioux clan behaves like the tribes of Israel in the Bible.

Also typical of the democratic State are the rites of convening and hospitality: *hostis*, the enemy, is the opposite of *hospes*, the host. The rules of hospitality are fundamental ones. The rules for convening the tribe are highly elaborated in Australia and also in North America; they are at the root of the alliance rituals and communal meals. The guild was essentially a society that organised communal meals.

Secondary Forms of Social Organisation[12]

The secondary forms of exercising power are of no less importance than the primary forms, the sole difference being that, by their very definition, the secondary forms are segmented. The most important form of the socio-political division of labour is the sexual division, which excludes women from politics. The society of men runs part of public affairs.

Society of Men

In order to describe the society of men, let us suppose as a hypothesis that it has nothing to do with secret societies.

The society of men is usually manifested in the Melanesian and Polynesian world by the presence of a house, the men's house, and by the existence of particular sanctuaries. Africa generally has two kinds of meeting places; sacred groves play a major role here. The Papuan world has a men's house for each phratry. Very often, the men's house indicates the existence of a society of men, but also its independence, and sometimes even the challenge it represents. One therefore needs to determine whether there is one men's house per phratry, or locality, or whether there are several.

The men's house is generally divided according to clans, each clan possessing its own cells as well as its own sanctuaries. In the Fiji Islands, the men's house is of considerable size.

In the organisation of the society of men, division according to age can overlap with other divisions. Its internal organisation can regulate the conditions of marriage, initiation, military rank and the position of the head of the family. It can dominate the entire military and civil organisation of the State. It is within the society of men that the real forms of political organisation are to be found. Let us not forget that the guilds were the means of emancipation for the communes.

The society of men is normally divided according to the age grade system. The elders govern, and the others obey with a view to themselves governing later on. Among the Arunta of Australia, initiation lasts about thirty years; only after this will a man be in possession of all the grades. The organisation is often rigid; initiation is the fundamental phenomenon, with the conquest of the grades that it brings. Very often, the adolescent leaves his family to enter the society of men; in particular, he is not initiated by his father or father's brothers, but by his mother's brothers, who are his future fathers-in-law. It is with them that he lives and it is in their men's house that he will be initiated. The institution of pageboys is a survival of this situation; fosterage corresponds to the obligation to be raised by one's future father-in-law. Grades are conquered slowly, after tests of all kinds, ritual and military. Grades can also be lost, their loss corresponding to a kind of forced retirement.

The society of men often plays a major judicial role. Very often, criminal law lies essentially in its hands, executions sometimes taking place in secret. Its religious functions are also most important, whether it be divided into clans or fraternities – the fraternities may themselves be clans or former clans. Besides its secret sessions, the society of men appears publicly on certain occasions, notably when it banishes women from the village for its ceremonies, or on the contrary when it makes only short public appearances. Everything related to the language of the society of men should be noted, its relations with ordinary language, etc.

Even in Australia, the society of men can wield real legislative power: this is where customs are modified, new ones introduced, and old ones abandoned. In some cases, the society of men corresponds to groupings of guilds: for instance, the carpenters' guild in the Fiji Islands and the blacksmiths' guild in Central Africa.

Societies of women, which are very widespread, are far less well known. In a great many cases, women constitute colleges. We are told of 'convents' of priestesses in Dahomey.

Secret Societies

A secret society is secret in the way it functions; but since its function is a public one, it always acts publicly to some degree. Its members belong to various clans, and the grades within the society overlap with the divisions between clans.

The members are members for life, a minimum requirement in a secret society. Very often, a secret society is a fraternity whose members come either from the clans or from the classes, and even from the guilds. The fraternity is secret, extremely so – in regard to everything that is not public. The arrival of masks belonging to the fraternity is public. The question arises of the legality or illegality of secret societies. The way in which we too readily interpret secret societies as hostile to the State is a mistake. We always imagine secret societies from the point of view of our own society. It is true that they are in part societies that plot, but they fulfil a regular function. In the work of P. Hazoumé,[13] a secret society in Dahomey appears to us as a small society engaged in private plots; but the author himself acknowledges that all the secret societies are connected with the great myth of the Hunter, the one who revealed hunting. In any case, the secrecy is only relative; one is secret for others. For whom, for what, where, and in what conditions is one bound to secrecy? The investigation should deal with these various points.

A so-called secret society is reported from Melanesia, but it corresponds in fact to the grouping of the age sets of the men's society by clans and by totems.[14] In his book *La Foi jurée*,[15] Davy describes similar phenomena in North West America. There are ten secret societies, and one is elected to a particular grade of a particular society according to one's clan. No one can accede to a higher grade without having passed through all the lower grades. It is a succession of fraternities, recruited according to age, wealth, potlatches and clans.

It will often be difficult to distinguish between a secret society and the society of men, which itself can be made up of several secret societies with highly hierarchical age sets. In very complex societies such as those of North West America, a person normally has two lives: a winter life and a summer life. In summer the society is grouped by clans and families, in winter by fraternities and secret societies. But the fraternities themselves are ranked by clan and age. Furthermore, there is a system of given names corresponding exactly to the system of animals, gods or ancestors that have to be reincarnated. Throughout Melanesia, clans are divided by age sets; there is neither recruitment nor election, but a son can lose the rank transmitted through his father. It is not enough to belong to such and such clan in order to have access to such and such grade in the secret society. The grades are reached via the ecstatic experiences specified in this ranking in relation to the clan of the postulant. If the candidate has not had his revelation, he cannot gain the grade he aspires to. As to the six family princes of the Kwakiutl, they can only remain princes provided they are cannibals.

A secret society usually possesses significant powers, even terrifying ones. From the civil point of view, it administers the interests of each of its members. There is in Tahiti a society of the *Areoi*, the only secret society that I really know of in Polynesia. The *Areoi*, that is to say the people who eat with the king, the counts, are in the king's pay. They eat from the hand of the king, and they execute his orders. The military role of the secret society appears less important than that of the society of men, because it is in the society of men that ages are normally fixed. In criminal law, the secret society plays an important role.

In a secret society, the rise from a lower to a higher grade is always an occasion for vast expense. One buys the grade; the duties and benefits are for sale. A secret society's treasury is usually made up of a large number of religious objects. This toing and froing between grades and fraternities is a significant phenomenon on which all of Orphism was based. Consider the international character of secret societies. Secret societies play an important role in religious life – a public role and a secret role. Very often, the punishments that are decreed are inflicted by magic. Within the secret society there is normally a fraternity cult. Finally, a secret society has a language of its own, which remains secret for the uninitiated.

These secondary forms of organisation of power are compatible both with democracy and monarchy. They are normally intertwined. To a large extent, we can say that the secret forms are intended to determine leaders; the set-up can already be called the rule of committees.

Castes and Classes[16]

When all these grades are acquired [by birth] and are hereditary, and when in addition there is endogamy within this hereditary category, and one can only marry or procreate[17] within a given social group – then we are dealing with castes. A caste is a strictly endogamous class, itself divided into clans. It is generally believed that castes exist only in India, but in fact they can be encountered more or less anywhere. We have an exact and complete list running from the Vedic clans[18] until today, but caste is also a Polynesian and

Malayan phenomenon. From a linguistic point of view, the extreme cases are presented by Samoa and Japan where, given your particular identity, you cannot speak of a thing with an interlocutor without adjusting your language to take account of these three factors. It is only within a caste that you all use the same language.

Usually, a caste has a special living area in the village or town. It has its headmen. Throughout the Black world, blacksmiths, goldsmiths and griots are grouped in castes. The Dioula traders form a caste in the societies among which they are dispersed. In Chad, Muslims form a caste which is characterised at first glance by the use of horses, in contrast to indigenous people who have to go on foot. Castes of weavers and carpenters exist in the Fiji Islands, the caste of executioners in Western Europe.

Class differs from caste only by the lack of heredity and endogamy; it is simply a social distinction, most often based on wealth. Each class has its own appropriate language.

Study how it is possible to rise from a lower class to the next higher one (usually through wealth or political power). There are also obligations or distributions fixed for each class. Such organisations are still very much alive throughout the Arab world.

Most often, the observer will be confronted with a tangle of classes, castes, chiefdoms, monarchic organisations and democratic ones. If so, it will be necessary to study all of them at the same time. We have no right to ascribe such and such political organisation to some society without having conducted a thorough investigation of the organisation and without having measured the exact position of democratic, monarchic and caste (etc.) institutions in what constitutes its jural system of public law.

Domestic Organisation[19]

All societies in the French colonies are societies based on units that are familial or politico-domestic. Nowhere has the extended family (*la grande famille*) disappeared, nor even for the most part, the clan. The political unit is not the individual, but the family. While in our Western countries the family now has only a private role in fact or in law, in these societies it is the real social unit.

As a political unit the family forms a transition between the political legal system and the strictly familial legal system of these [tribal] societies. In Germanic law – and this remained the case until the end of the Carolingian dynasty – the hunt for the murderer is the prerogative of the family, not the State: it is the family, not the state, that receives the compensation. The murderer must reimburse the relatives, or must reimburse the mother of the victim. The victim's relatives have the right and even the duty to hunt down the murderer: this is the vendetta. Our penal system, and our system of suing for damages, correspond to nothing in these societies. The general state of our knowledge concerning these issues is poor: the proportion of Australian societies that are well studied is not more than one in fifty. For some whole regions (Guyana and much of Madagascar) information is completely lacking.

In our Western society, the family is a matter of fact from which rights derive. Nearly everywhere else the family is a matter of law from which certain facts derive. It has taken fifty years for Durkheim's argument on this matter to become generally accepted. Where descent is reckoned in the mother's line alone, kinship exists only through women; elsewhere descent is reckoned only in the father's line. In Roman law, the mother is related to her children only by means of a legal fiction: she is regarded as the daughter of her husband, *loco filiae* [in the place of a daughter]. It is not matters of fact that create the family, but matters of law. However, families do not exist unless there is at least the fiction of a matter of fact. The matter of fact is not determined by the reality, as among ourselves, it is determined by the phenomenon of law. Even so, then, there are certain underlying facts, notably the notion of descent.

The family links a group of people who share the same blood either naturally or artificially, and who are united by a series of mutual and reciprocal rights and duties deriving from this belief in consanguinity; this belief can be marked by a shared name, or a family name. In the Maori clan, as in the Scottish clan, the only individual who really has a name is the clan chief, but all the clan members partake of his nature up to a certain point. To be precise, surnames are a recent phenomenon, dating from feudalism. More often, we find a series of given names or forenames that are clan property. Such forenames are inherited and often correspond to reincarnations.

It follows from the preceding that in most cases, if not all, the observer will encounter families based on different principles from our own. One finds in the societies of the French colonies nearly all the possible forms of politico-domestic organisation, often quite entangled. One should not, therefore, seek one single organisation in countries where the rule is not the unity of the law but, on the contrary, its plurality. One will find primitive forms mixed with advanced forms. A Dioula trader in West Africa lives isolated and independent throughout the period when he is travelling, but when he returns to his village he places his gold dust in the hands of the patriarch of the joint family; from the day he returns it no longer belongs to him. The same phenomena prevail in Tibetan law. The mixing of forms is a normal mixing and can be explained by the fundamental notion of the plurality of types of relative. The system of inheritance in ancient Roman law, according to the law of the Twelve Tables, recognises three orders of heirs: the *sui heredes*, the agnates and the *gentiles*.

Let us take a couple of examples. China is divided into twelve clans and all the members of a particular clan believe that they are related. In India, there are groupings of considerable importance that both are and are not castes. So the different levels of recognition of kinship need to be distinguished. Life histories and autobiographies can be very useful here. The comparison of several life histories will yield a certain number of forenames and surnames. In fact, the real name is very often kept secret; it will be easier to discover the surname [or family name], the *cognomen.*

The Roman nomenclature: *nomen,* the clan name, *praenomen* [*prénom,* given name or forename] and *cognomen,* can be used here. The forename is a personal and hereditary name. Normally, there is only one individual bearing a particular forename within a particular clan. Each group has its own fixed series of forenames while surnames, attached to the forenames, have inside the clan become the strictly maintained property of the family.

The simplest hypothesis is that which divides a society into two moieties, or two phratries, within each of which descent is reckoned in a single line, male or female. The distinction between generations creates a second division, and that between the sexes a third.

Following this hypothesis, if descent is reckoned in the mother's line, a father belonging to generation 1 in group A will give birth to a son who belongs to generation 2 in group B; the grandson will be A3, belonging to the same moiety, and in the simplest case, belonging to the same age set as his maternal grandfather.[20]

The main difficulty will be to distinguish between alliance and kinship. The As are all allied to the Bs, but they are not all kin with the Bs and in some cases they are even definitely not kin. In order to note this distinction, Morgan, and then Rivers, have distinguished between consanguinity and affinity. In a society where descent is reckoned in the mother's line, my wife's kin are my relatives by alliance and I am related only by alliance to my children. In a society where descent is reckoned only in the father's line, my wife is related only by alliance to my children. On the one hand: kinship properly speaking, or consanguinity; on the other: simply relationship by alliance, or affinity.

A	B
1	1
2	2
3	3

When descent is reckoned only in the father's line, a wife transmits nothing, no totem, and no legacy. When all that counts is filiation via women, the husband is a sort of parasite in the system of descent. The difficulty lies in combining the two kinds of descent. Among the [Australian] Warramunga the problem was solved by deciding that women had no soul, and therefore they did not reincarnate and did not transmit anything. In Swabian law, unlike Saxon law, a woman does not inherit and no one inherits from her.

Generally, both lines, the mother's and the father's, are taken into account, but they are of different significance. It is only in late Indo-European law, and also in Polynesian law, that both lines are counted in exactly the same way. Even among the Latins, only agnation counted. We would not be kin to our mothers if our ancestors had not known the Germanic family.

However, the division into two original moieties is but a hypothesis, the simplest. More often one will be confronted with several clans distributed among several phratries, or with large joint families, recruiting in the mother's line or the father's, each one having at its head a leader who holds all his people in his grasp, *in manu*. The nuclear family (*famille individuelle*), which plays so large a role in our societies, is far less salient here. Hence the existence of *classificatory kinship*, that is to say of a kinship system where a single term refers not to a single individual, but to a whole class of relatives. Classificatory kinship exists among us only with reference to cousins, uncles or aunts; we distinguish between brothers and cousins. But in societies where classificatory kinship prevails, I call 'brothers' all men from the same family and same generation as myself, and I call 'wives' all my wife's sisters, that is to say all the girls belonging to the same family and the same generation. Reciprocally, my wife calls all my brothers 'husbands'. The members of two kinship categories are all of equal rank and of the same kind in their mutual relationships. Classificatory kinship describes symmetrical positions within one group, or within two groups who face each other. This is where all the discussions of group marriage become relevant.

Classificatory kinship is often reciprocal. Grandson and grandfather address each other by the same name; father and son call each other by the same name, or more precisely, there is only a single term to refer to the 'father-son' relationship. Compare the German *Enkel* [grandson], from *avunculus*, 'little uncle', 'little ancestor'. Kinship terms also vary according to the sex of speaker and the sex of the person referred to.

No study of the family can be undertaken until one has observed and described all the legal statuses that are possible in the society.

Classificatory kinship explains a certain number of customs that are widespread in so-called primitive societies. The taboo concerning the mother-in-law that still survives among us, can be very easily explained on the basis of the figure above. An A2 can only marry a B2; the mother-in-law is a B1 and belongs to the forbidden generation of the permitted phratry. On the other hand, the son-in-law owes her his wife's birth and he is thereby in a state of permanent indebtedness towards her. Another curious status is that of the sister's son when descent is in the male line. An A2 necessarily marries a B2, daughter of a B1, so he marries the daughter of his mother's brother. In some societies, the nephew must do whatever he can for his mother's brother and future father-in-law. This goes as far as homosexual relations among the Papuan Kiwai or among the Marind Anim, where the child is brought up entirely at the home of his mother's brother. Elsewhere, in the Fiji Islands, the sister's son, *vasu*, has all rights over his mother's brother and can strip him of everything he possesses.[21]

In each case, an effort must be made to distinguish between actual kinship and jural kinship. This distinction will make it easy to settle the famous question of primitive promiscuity. In fact, primitive promiscuity does not exist, but simply a right to marriage. The contexts in which there is genuine promiscuity are contexts of total sexual licence, which is compulsory, yet restricted to certain very solemn festivals, on certain days of the year. In Australia and in the Malagasy world, the worst forms of incest are prescribed during these festivals; but they are strictly prohibited all the rest of the year.

The study of the family should be made by starting with life histories and autobiographies. These life histories will make it possible to use the genealogical method, which by itself will reveal the exact type of kinship terminology in the society under study. The genealogical method consists in gathering all the kinship terms used by a particular individual to refer to the various members of his family for whom the exact kinship relation to the informant is known. When transcribed onto the family tree of the family being studied, the terms will immediately bring to light the various categories of relatives. The father category will include all the father's brothers; the brother category will group together all the cousins in the father's line or in the mother's line, and so on.[22] The history of several individuals belonging to the same group will then make it possible to reconstruct the history of the group itself. Furthermore, precious information will thus be obtained about property and its modes of transmission, about inheritance, etc.

The starting point should never be marriage which, as will be clear from the preceding, far from creating the family, is most often its consequence; marriage is an effect, not a cause. The nuclear family only becomes the legal family relatively late [in human history]. The clan and the large joint family are far more important. The role of the nuclear family has greatly increased among us recently.

Observing the politico-domestic groups will often form the essence of the observer's task. The important phenomena, in fact, do not happen either at the level of the individual or at the level of the tribe, but above all at the level of the segments that compose the society.

In our Western countries, it would be difficult to amputate a province without seriously affecting the life of the whole society. Elsewhere, however, in some politico-domestic regimes, immense masses can be cut off, but the society still survives. A Malay clan can emigrate as a whole, but the tribe remains; a joint family leaves the clan, but the clan remains. This segmentary character does exist among us too, but only at the level of the individual; it is individuals, not groups, who split off.

Our working hypothesis, which envisages a society divided into two amorphous exogamous clans, rules out Lewis Henry Morgan's horde, which was supposedly characterised by kinship and marriage based on promiscuity.[23] Morgan believed in primitive promiscuity, without any distinction between people of the same generation. According to him, at this stage of society, each man could marry his sister, each man had absolute rights to sexual relations with all his sisters, who were also his wives. In fact, Morgan generalised on the basis of one precise case, that of the *punalua* kinship in the Hawaii Islands, where a man is only the temporary possessor of his wife, and the latter can be abducted by one of her brothers.

The view that exogamy preceded the clan, the society being simply divided into two matrimonial classes, was still maintained by Graebner.

We thought for a long time that we could point to societies divided into two amorphous exogamous clans. Thus all the societies in South-East Australia, we thought, were [internally] divided between 'falcons' and 'crows'. In fact, we now know that no society exists which knows only two amorphous exogamous clans. The society that comes closest to this state of affairs is that of the Todas of South-East India. However, if the Todas are indeed divided into two groups that are strictly exogamous, they represent one of the highest points of what Dravidian civilisation must have been – they speak a Dravidian language; it is therefore impossible here to use the term 'primitive'.[24]

Phratries

Each of these clans is always divided into at least three generations. This is the type of organisation most frequently found both in Australian societies and throughout North and South America, as well as in the greater part of Africa. The whole Aztec grouping functioned phratry to phratry. Potlatches in North America are given phratry to phratry even more than clan to clan. Exogamy is even more the norm within the phratry than within the clan; phratries always remain exogamous. However, in Athens the phratry did not possess this feature, and for that reason its existence has been harder to detect.

We are therefore confronted most of the time with phratries divided into clans, sub-clans and joint families. Within these divisions there operates jural kinship and classificatory kinship, which is kinship *de facto*. An organisation, therefore, that is always fairly complicated.

It was thought for a long time that all the Australian tribes were united by a common language of gestures, a secret language. There is indeed a developed language of gestures in those tribes. But the first concern of an Australian traveller arriving in a new tribe is to state which phratry he belongs to and within it, which is his marriage class [or section]. As soon as he is thus situated, he is entitled to be addressed by the appropriate classificatory kinship terms; this gives all the Australian societies the appearance of being a single family.

All of this can be conceptualised in a manner that is strictly and exclusively jural. Generally [as anthropologists], we shall not speak of exogamy, but of decline (*dégénération*), of a hierarchy of collective forms of the family, in contrast to the individual [nuclear] form that remains the sole one today.

The Clan

The clan can be described as a huge family, egalitarian as regards the various generations composing the clan, but not necessarily egalitarian throughout.

The notion of fraternity is present in the clan, but most important is the notion of the identity of the blood which flows in its members, and flows at different ages. It is the Germanic *Sippe*, corresponding to the Sanskrit word *sabha*, 'the group entitled to an assembly house'.[25] Throughout the Indo-European world, this assembly house is the house of the large joint family, and the *Sippe* is the large joint family in Germanic law.

The clan defines itself through the notion of perfect consanguinity; everybody has the same blood, the same life. In Arabic, the term meaning clan also translates as 'life' or 'blood'. People who belong to the same clan possess the same nature. The expression of this community of life, blood and soul is the name: *gentiles sunt inter se, qui eodem nomine sunt.*[26] All the Fabii are people of the same blood, and all the Julii are suited to becoming Caesar. The clan is life, the clan is blood.

The first sign of the clan is the *name*. Where there is a name, there is at least a family, and very often a clan. One finds clans with names and families without names. The clan implies a common blood, a common life and a common descent. The name is always a generic name rather than an individual one, the individual name being a recent invention. This generic name is usually expressed in a *coat of arms* or *blazon*. The blazon can be altogether elementary, consisting only of a simple tattoo, or it can be of huge dimensions. The entire American North West strictly decorates everything with its blazon.

The clan is also manifested by the belief in a common descent shared by men and by a particular species of animal or plant – a belief which constitutes *totemism*. However, one can find clans without totems, albeit no totems without clans. The link with the totem is a very general link, but it is not absolutely necessary. In some societies, only the phratry totems matter. Totemism is marked by kinship of substance between humans and the animal or plant species that is revered. It is the same life that flows in both. The links are those of cult.[27] Name, blazon, totem: these are three quasi-ideological features of the clan.

The clan manifests itself also by jural links. First of all by a certain fraternity, a certain equality, between its members. It is true that Durkheim perhaps did not sufficiently distinguish the generations within the clan, and somewhat exaggerated its amorphism. But in the final analysis, the amorphism exists, and within the same generation the fraternity is absolute: all brothers are brothers, and all fathers are fathers to some degree. Among the Sioux, everyone is arranged on two sides, by age sets and by sub-totems. Relative fraternity, therefore, and relative equality of the whole clan, and even of the whole phratry. All the sons of the [Arab] *sherif* are *sherif* and brothers.

The clan also often possesses communal land; it always has its sanctuary, shared by all its members. The Berber clan is characterised by the presence of its festival.

The existence of rights, including property rights, held in common by all members of the clan, leads to remarkable results. The clan is a place where there is no public adjudication of conflicts. Blood vengeance does not exist inside the clan, since the clan is the blood – it [a killing] is an accident. The clan has the right of low and high justice over all its members, and no outsider has the right to oversee its judgements.

Blood vengeance operates between clans, and compensations are paid between clans. This is what has been called, though the expression is ill chosen, 'collective responsibility'. In fact, what exists is two collectivities that can be in a state of war, carrying out their vengeance and receiving their compensation.

There are also other features of the clan, less necessary, but fairly specific. We here encounter segmentary societies: each clan enjoys its independence, an independence that is marked by the possibility of becoming a clan member through all the systems of artificial kinship, in particular through adoption. In many cases, the clan contains a fixed number of souls, a fixed number of forenames, and a number of animals living with the clan.

Finally, the question arises of superordinate rights and individual rights.

A clan or clans can be of various kinds. Primary clans, which correspond to phratries, are everywhere more or less obliterated. Furthermore, some clans have extremely definite institutions relating to locality [of residence]: patrilocal clans or matrilocal ones. Depending on whether descent is traced through the father or the mother, the clan will have patrilineal descent or matrilineal. Exogamy is very much the norm and endogamous clans are exceptions. An endogamous clan nearly always corresponds to a caste, like royal families. Normally, a certain degree of kinship is a total impediment to marriage.

The clan also can be *local*, or simply *nominal*, in which case it groups individuals dispersed in various settlements, where they can be recognised by their patronymic. Large totemic clans are always to some degree nominal and not local. But, there also exist local clans that are very large, like the Scottish clan. In other places, a clan contains only a very small number of individuals, for instance among the Arunta of Australia. A clan that seems insignificant today in some regions may have played a significant historical role.

The doctrine claiming that exogamy is a feature of the clan was maintained by Frazer and Durkheim.[28] In fact, exogamy is not necessarily clan exogamy, since very often the clan has degenerated and is no longer anything more than a group of relatives (*parentèle*).

Descent within the clan is generally reckoned in one line only, which raises the issue of descent through the female line (*descendance utérine*) or through the male line. We say that clan has uterine descent when its stock (*souche*) is formed by the women, which does not mean that the women control the clan, but rather that they are its means of propagation. Uterine descent does not mean that the women predominate, but that they form the line and stock of the clan. It is a gross error to confuse matriarchy with uterine descent, given that the person who is in authority in a family based on matrilineal descent is normally the mother's brother. You can recognise uterine descent by the important role of the mother's brother or of the sister's son. Theoreticians from the end of the nineteenth century thought that the world began with uterine kinship; they thought that the primitive form of kinship was kinship through women. This issue, long debated, only presents a purely theoretical interest. In practice, the main divisions rest on sex and generation. My father must not be from the same stock as my mother, and my mother must not belong to the same generation as myself, otherwise I should have the right to be her husband. Hence, in all societies, on the basis of the division between the sexes, there is always simultaneously uterine descent and male descent. However, the two forms of descent are not reckoned in the same way. The problem that was debated over more than thirty years is non-existent. There can be heredity through women and heredity through men, but people do not inherit the same goods in both lines. Among the Ashanti, a child inherits his mother's blood and his father's spirit.[29]

Age differentiation can produce more critical divisions. Age sets cross-cut differences between phratries or between clans.

In a great many cases, one meets with a society divided into a small number of clans distributed across a relatively large area. Because of the rule of exogamy, in each place several clans will be represented, each struggling to maintain preponderance; these are matters of both public and private interest, and fundamental ones. Alliances between clans are very often enduring. It is understood that clan A normally looks for its wives in clan A' of the opposite moiety. Throughout the Iroquois group, a 'bear' marries a 'she-wolf'. When one encounters a majority of bears and bears with uterine descent we can talk of a uterine clan. Here, the men bring the women to live among themselves; elsewhere, the mother's brothers retain their nephews and future sons-in-law.

These rights over persons are expressed by property rights; such and such property becomes extinct with a particular line. The essential things are property and blood vengeance. The question is to know whether the son abandons his mother to fight for his father's clan, or conversely.

The social organisation also finds expression at mourning, through the arrival of the mourners, who are in the one case the uterine relatives, and in the other the patrilineal ones. A uterine grouping, whose significance was previously unsuspected, may thus come to light at funerals.

In these name-based clans, a distinction is also needed between extended family and clan. What matters is not the range of individuals, but the number of references made to people, their reckoning of kinship.

Finally, one very often observes a combination of the two kinds of clan implying a combination of the two sorts of descent. In a single society, Kroeber found two kinds of clan, one transmitting membership through the blood, the other through spirit.[30]

Furthermore, the clans can be articulated or divided into sub-clans, which may themselves be sub-divided. This is what Haddon observed in the Torres Straits, and what he described under the name of 'linked totems' – totems that are associated and form a series: a hierarchy of clans, names and clan divisions, corresponding to a hierarchy of the world, a real cosmology.[31]

Such forms of classification are also found in the Pueblo world, in the Sioux and Iroquois worlds,[32] and almost throughout America. It seems indeed that a similar cosmology existed in Mexico and Peru – the first mention of a totem is in Garcilaso de la Vega.

One may therefore encounter a series of totems, in other words a series of sub-clans. These series can be complex, the sub-clans often being compared to the branches of a tree; it is a matter of situating the bird on the tree. The division into sub-totems can also end up by reproducing the group's mythical animal. Among the Zuñi, 'Right eye of the jaguar' is normally placed behind 'Right nostril' and to the right of 'Left eye'. On the ground the clan members will reproduce the sacred jaguar. The same arrangement recurs at the meetings of the Iroquois council, the ranking being very clear. The division into more or less numerous sub-clans can therefore go so far as to locate a single individual.

Finally, a clan can fade out, for example when all its sub-clans have themselves risen to the dignity of clans. It is always far more difficult for exogamy to disappear than for the totem. The clan often survives only in name, which gives those who use it a vague feeling of kinship. Elsewhere, it survives in the form of military organisation. In Rome, assemblies by century [*comitia centuriata*] and assemblies by tribe [*comitia curiata*] correspond to the *gentes* in the latter case, and to the army in the former. The question of military organisation arises here, and that of the men's society.

The local clan is more often patrilocal than matrilocal. It rather often arises from one of these sub-clans where the men must have remained clustered, as it were excluding descendants through female members. Here, exogamy is exclusively local. One can have a paternal name and local affiliation together with a maternal name.

The system of organisation will clearly appear at meetings of elders, or during assemblies in the men's house, where all the men gather in the house of their phratry. We can then say that Parliament is in permanent session. The Roman Senate and the assembly of *gentes* represented by the *patres* correspond to these sessions. Those who are clan members by blood may have associated with them slaves, whether free or not, clients, prisoners, etc. Very often, the military organisation of the tribe includes divisions based on age grades and clans. This applied to the Polish army until the fifteenth century. Lastly, the question arises of the relations between clan and tribe.

The Family[33]

The extended family or joint family is a concentration of the clan, or more precisely, of the sub-clan. We did not begin with the original couple; we began with more or less large masses that gradually concentrated or contracted. Evolution involved the fixation of concentric circles of kinship that became ever narrower. So we should not explain joint kinship by a multiplication of the household; on the contrary, we should explain the nuclear family by starting from joint kinship.

The extended family consists of a group of blood relatives bearing the same name and living on a particular piece of land. Obedience is owed to the eldest man of the eldest generation, and the younger brother, not the son, is heir; thus the king of Nepal who wanted to leave the kingdom to his son had to massacre all his brothers. It is what used to be called in France the silent community, or the tacit community, where all the members pool everything under the control of the patriarch. Sons receive their dowries from the community, not from their fathers. The patriarch is an administrator of goods, which are usually inalienable.

Maine's description of the joint family in his *Ancient Law*[34] is a landmark in our studies. Maine discovered that the family in the Punjab was identical with that in Ireland. In his wake, we observe the presence of the joint family almost throughout the Indo-European world. The *zadruga* of the Balkans recurs in all the northern Celtic countries. In Rome, the group of agnates was very strong and included all the descendants of a single male ancestor, including women, but not the sons of the latter.

The features of the joint family are the same as those of the clan. We find again the presence of a common name, the association of each generation within the family, and absolute equality within each generation. All those who belong to the same generation in relation to the ancestor are brothers, and everyone is to some degree the son of the ancestor. This shows in marriage, of which an aberrant form, albeit a strong one, is sororal polygyny or fraternal polyandry.[35]

The most important feature in the joint family is the notion of the common ancestor, of whom the patriarch is the living representative. The joint family is in this respect clearly distinct from the clan, within which the cult of ancestors is fairly rare.

Within the joint family inheritance is by generation. Apart from the authority of the patriarch, equality between members of each generation is absolute. There is no division according to the branches of the family, no representation of the branches; there is only per capita division within each generation. Usually, at this stage, the only form of exogamy remaining is that of the joint family. Joint ownership of the property is general; the property remains subsumed in the patrimony. In so far as there is any division, it is equal. In reality, there is no inheritance within the family, for the latter is everlasting, whereas the nuclear family is founded anew in each generation.

Within the joint family, the patriarch distributes the work in the fields, and manages real assets and sometimes the movable property. Sometimes too, one finds individual savings, more or less limited in size. Equality among all does not mean reciprocity among all. What exists is not communism properly speaking, but total reciprocity; members of the group expect not the community of goods, but that of services. Finally, membership in the egalitarian group is relatively free, and members of the family can break their agnatic bond in order to form a new family. The presence of the joint family can be detected on the ground by the existence of the large house enclosed by walls, or by the long house.

While the general features remain the same, these joint families can follow the male or female line, or they can observe both forms of descent. In a Malayan joint family, married daughters remain at home and are visited by their husbands at night: this is 'furtive marriage'. We can therefore distinguish two kinds of joint family. On the one hand, the paternal joint family, the typical Indo-European family where the eldest agnate, the eldest of the men still alive in the stock, is in command. On the other hand, the maternal joint family – for example, part of the Germanic family. Depending on the case, the rights in real assets will be transmitted by the male stock or by the female stock, the movable property being more attached to the individual. But agnation does not necessarily exclude cognation; patrilineal descent does not exclude acknowledging inheritance in the female line.

In a maternal joint family, the patriarch is the representative of the eldest woman of the eldest generation. In Madagascar, this is the prime minister, the queen's husband. Elsewhere, it is her brother, or her mother's eldest brother. But reckoning descent in the mother's line does not mean there is a matriarchal family, a family where women are in charge. It simply means that the recruitment to the male hierarchy is via the female line.

The presence of the maternal family can easily be detected by the position of the mother's brothers. The mother's brother is the protector, and normally the tutor. The position of women is also seen in the interior arrangement of the house. Inside the long house, each household has its quarters. But in the maternal family the husband is not in his own place, and sometimes he even only visits his wife at night by stealth.

The property of children in the maternal family belongs to the maternal grandfather, or to the mother's brother. The husband is a sort of lodger or *locum tenens*, often, of his son. The husband is second-in-command to his son and also to his father-in-law.

Polyandry is regular in some societies with uterine descent, for instance among the Scythians and throughout the Numidian or Libyan world. It still exists in Tibet, where a woman has several brothers as husbands, each family including several women. Usually, the management of property is carried out by the elder brother of one of the women in the house, and not by a husband.

The paternal family does not yield a very different picture, in the sense that in both cases it is always men who are in control. The role of men does not differ, only their position changes. With agnatic descent, it is the wives who are strangers to the family, being only child bearers. The agnatic joint family left them practically nothing but this extended kinship (*parentèle*) in Roman law, while the *genos* in Greece was apparently something intermediate between the clan, the joint family and the patriarchal family, the joint family being predominant. This family of agnates was particularly important in the Indo-Iranian world and throughout the Celtic world, whereas in the original

Germanic law the maternal joint family played a primary role. This agnatic joint family still exists in some societies in North America. In this case, a woman is not kin to her children; she is merely their cognate, purchased by the husband in order to have children. Hence an erroneous conception of the marriage, as if the wife were her husband's slave.

In the agnatic family, a woman only owns her personal possessions, her non-dowry objects (*paraphernaux*), but over these she enjoys the most extensive rights. The mistake consists in thinking that there exists only one legal form applicable to all property and to all owners, whoever they be. On the contrary, the plurality of legal forms is the norm.

Within the paternal family everything happens as in the maternal family with division per capita and not by branch [per stirpes], between individuals of a single generation. There is no communism, but direct or indirect reciprocity.

Within the paternal joint family there may exist sororal polygyny, that is the obligatory general marriage of one family to another family from a different clan or from the other moiety. This sororal polygyny corresponds to polyandry in maternal families. The levirate is a survival of it.

In Icelandic law, the individed joint family is still very clearly marked on the ground by the enclosure, the Norse close. A son has the right to build a house in his father's enclosure, but he has no right to sell this house. The enclosed area has a surrounding wall made of stone or wood; the kraal is a kraal for the clan, village, or joint family, but never for the individual family.

As for livestock, the ownership is joint; livestock belongs to the group of agnates. Estate assets are owned jointly when it is a matter of the subsoil, but not necessarily when it is a matter of what is established on the surface, notably fields, and above all, gardens.

Generally, solidarity is absolute in criminal matters within the joint family. In contract law, potlatches take place between one joint family and another more often than between nuclear families. Such conceptions are also expressed in traditions of hospitality.

We come finally to what appears to us the most ancient form of the family, and is in fact the most recent one from a jural point of view: the NUCLEAR FAMILY ('*famille conjugale*'). It is Rome that recognised the existence in law of the nuclear family, while continuing to ignore kinship through women.

De facto the nuclear family exists everywhere. Individuals always know who are their real father and their real mother, and continue to recognise them as such after the parents are dead. Ties of affection and ties of other sorts are always closer between real parents and children. But in law the nuclear family is rarely acknowledged.

In most cases, one will observe the *de facto* coexistence of nuclear family and joint family. The nuclear family exists *de facto* since [the stage represented by] Australia. It is the family in a legal sense that undergoes the huge variations in scale that we have just described. It will therefore be necessary to observe the nuclear family *de facto* and in its actual activity. Among the Eskimos and in a large part of north Asia, the organisation varies according to the seasons. The nuclear family lives in isolation during summer in order to hunt. In winter, all members of the extended family gather in the large communal house. An Australian group is normally made up of three or four households living in three or four shelters, and moving on gradually as and when the hunting grounds become exhausted. The large gatherings of clans, moieties or tribes occur only at specific times of the year for specific purposes.

When one of the spouses dies, the nuclear family vanishes completely. Relatives on the mother's side come to fetch their people, relatives on the father's side take the others. A wife may be held responsible for the death of her husband.

Is the nuclear family patrilineal or matrilineal? In China, I have no relatives except my paternal ancestors. A wife worships the tablet of her husband's ancestors, and not that of her own. Children are kin in the patriline only. Matriarchy, an equally aberrant form, is found in India, in particular among the high castes of the Brahmins; it is usual in Micronesia.

In the nuclear family, study particularly the role of the father. Does he have the right of life and death over his children? Study infanticide and the exposure of the newborn. In all societies the father has always tended to transmit his rights to his sons while safeguarding for them the rights they hold from their mother. This is the history of all royal families and the history of all marriages. Nearly everywhere one will find conflicts between agnatic and cognatic descent.

Marriage

Marriage is the legal bond uniting two persons with a view to founding a family, *de facto* or *de jure* – in principle a family in the legal sense, but there are all possible degrees between marriage proper and a factual situation which ends up as a legal one so far as concerns the children. It is the sanction for a certain sexual morality. In the societies that concern us, marriage is not the source of the family; it is only a moment in it, an incident. We alone live under the conjugal [nuclear] principle. The whole evolution of domestic law boils down to evolution towards the nuclear family. Marriage starts from virtually nothing and ends up being virtually everything – the *usucapio*[36] in this respect was only abolished in the eighth century.

The problematic issue of primitive promiscuity should be ignored – one should concentrate on distinguishing between facts and law. The idea of marriage practised exclusively by very large groups (groups of brothers and groups of sisters) is wrong. What exists is the possibility of sexual relations that can lead to actual liaisons, but always ones that are sporadic and strictly regulated; it can never lead to a legal state of marriage. Group marriage only ever occurred between small groups restricted by age and sex. In the commonest case, my brothers and I must marry our mother's brother's daughters; the legal condition precedes the actual liaison.

Lewis H. Morgan[37] thought he found group marriage in Hawaii practised on a very large scale. He started from the *punalua* kinship whereby a man can call 'wife' all women of his generation, and whereby sexual relations within the same generation are permitted. Starting from there, Morgan reached the conclusion of primitive promiscuity. In fact, sexual licence is obligatory in Hawaii throughout the first month of the year and during one week at very great festivals; otherwise, it is prohibited. Moreover, there is no distinction in Hawaii between the word 'wife' and the word 'sister'. Finally, mariage implies for the king the obligation to wed his blood sister. Incestuous in essence, the royal dynasty mirrors the image of Heaven and Earth, overriding any question of lineage or heredity. Thus what seemed to Morgan to be proof of group marriage only corresponds to sexual licence limited to particular periods and, in adition, to an incestuous royal marriage.

All marriage rules, and especially the institution of sections, aim at establishing marriage prohibitions between the generations. Nearly all Black societies have at least four sections corresponding to two generations per moiety. In some societies, the classification is more complex and results in restricting marriage options to very narrow groups; the aim is to ensure the reincarnation of a particular ancestor with absolute certainty. In this way there may be as many as eight sections.

The institution of sections is far more widespread than is usually thought. The existence of such classes can be recognised from the very particular position of the mother-in-law and from the joking relationships.[38] Sections are either aligned opposite each other or staggered in order to allow the presence of a gerontocracy whereby the old men keep the young girls for themselves.[39] An important question is whether the organisation of these sections is or is not connected with totemism. Very often, the two moieties have a totem name.[40]

Exogamy (that is to say the incest prohibition) should not be seen as the complete opposite of endogamy; exogamy relating to the family nearly always corresponds to clan endogamy. We [in the West] no longer know anything more than the prohibition on marrying within our own branch of the family. Being a breach of exogamy laws, incest is a public offence; it inspires horror, even when committed unknowingly (Oedipus). Sometimes, however, incest is deliberately sought, for it alone allows absolute purity of the blood (royal family in Hawaii; Pharaohs).

As far as polygamy and monogamy are concerned, absolute monogamy exists only in law. Sororal polygyny (in Tibet), fraternal polyandry (in Africa)[41] can nearly always be explained on economic grounds. Polygyny is a normal practice in regions where husband and wife cannot enjoy sexual intercourse between the birth and the weaning of each child.

The question of the stability of marriage should hold the observer's attention for longer. The bond uniting the spouses is a legal bond; but what is its nature? Is it a contract of sale, of guarantee, or of lease? In the best marriages, children are reserved before their birth. It is really a matter of prestations between moieties. Generally, marriage creates bonds between in-laws on both sides. There are odd inequalities in responsibilities and odd differences both in public law and private law, a husband's rights over his wife being at variance with a wife's rights over her husband. This question of the division of rights, which runs in parallel to the division of labour, reappears regarding children.

Marriage Ceremonies

Marriage is a private act that has no impact on the spouses' civil status. Marriage rites aim at averting the difficulties that can arise when two different human beings live together. The 'purchase price' paid for the bride corresponds more precisely to a contract of lease. A man from one family is granted a wife belonging to another family who will permit him to ensure that he has descendants. The ceremony itself is a moment of crisis that has to be overcome. In certain cases defloration is a ritual act, carried out by the priest publicly – for instance, in Samoa. Elsewhere, the bride is simply transported to the house of the bridegroom. In these cases the betrothal rites are very protracted (e.g. in Southern Africa). The wedding night is not necessarily the night of the marriage, as there are often several attempts. In Melanesia, the girls' promenade corresponds to what explorers used to call 'normal prostitution'. All this does not mean there is no marriage ceremony. The fact of living together, a female presence alongside the man, the birth of children – all this brings a change in the religious status of the spouses, whether the husband comes to live with his wife or the wife is taken away by the husband.

Concerning the engagement, distinctions must be made as to marriage classes, and as to who has the connubium, with whom. Contractual forms in which relatives act as intermediaries occur frequently from Australia onwards (Davy sees here the possible origin of all contracts). Description of the betrothal, which can start before the birth of the spouses. Taboos concerning betrothal, the prestations a husband must supply to his future in-laws constitute the essence of marriage in all the societies that belong to ethnography. It is the principle of the bridegroom's bondage – Jacob in the house of Laban. Jacob was a servant for ten years in order to obtain a contract that would secure him children. In all the sultanates of the Black world, the suitor for the princess royal faces serious ordeals. Taboos concerning the bride, the mother-in-law, and the father-in-law.[42] Marriage is one moment in the process of betrothal, and it often takes place after the first sexual relations. Marriage by capture, or combined with abduction, is frequent. It is found already among the Kurnai in Australia. Wrestling among Best Men, which still takes place in many parts of the French countryside, is a survival of it. The custom of Valentines. These rites symbolise the passage from one family to another and the violence that necessarily accompanies the passage. Record rituals for abduction, and rituals of communion: communal meals and visits back and forth between the two families. All these rites aim at helping the spouses to come gradually into closer contact. Then come taboos on the bridegroom – what is called 'furtive marriage', when the husband can only visit his wife secretly. Finally, all the threshold rites, and rites of introduction to the ancestors. In Madagascar the notion of contract is clear. Note the lack of dowry and avoid using the term. It is better to talk of the guarantees given by the husband to his wife's family, or of the price he pays for the enjoyment of the woman. Religious phenomena here are generally of secondary importance. Note the conditions of place and time. Marriage often takes place with the woman fate intended for you, a woman predestined to be yours.

Married Life

Does married life have an enduring character or a temporary one?[43] Does it take place in the wife's family or in the husband's? Religious rules concerning menstruation, breast-feeding, hunting, warfare, and actions prohibited within the household; husband and wife rarely eat together. Position of the wife in the household, sexual division of labour, existence of masculine goods and feminine goods. Here, a woman owns everything; there, she owns nothing. Avoid the idea of woman as a beast of burden, slave to her husband, but distinguish real women slaves or captives from other women. Studying the position of the first wife raises the issue of concubinage and jealousy between co-wives; infanticide, abortion, etc.

Marriage should be studied in a statistical way: adultery (the institution of the gallant is a regular one in the Black world); wives who are loaned, exchanged, rented out; regulation of adultery and temporary marriage (for instance, in the case of prolonged absence of the husband among the Dioula of Sudan). The host's rights, the prince's rights, etc.; foreseeable cases of infidelity. In criminal and civil law, the solidarity between husband and wife is often very weak. The links between the husband and his in-laws, in particular brothers-in-law (cf. Bluebeard).

Divorce

Who can dissolve the marriage bond? Among Blacks, it is most often the wife; among the Semites, the husband. Under what circumstances? Repudiation is the usual form of divorce. Divorce usually entails repayment of the goods given by the husband to his future parents-in-law. Make a statistical study of divorce cases. The life history method will be useful here. Record the fate of the children.

Bereavement

Widowerhood generally is insignificant; widowhood is far more serious, the wife often being accused of murdering her husband. A wife is more the mourner than she is the person mourned for. Cases where the widow is sacrificed or commits suicide are not rare. Prohibitions affecting the widow. In many cases, the widow remains consecrated to her dead husband throughout the primary burial until the end of mourning.[44] Very often, a wife is something to be inherited: a son inherits his father's wives (his own mother excepted). The usual distinction between masculine and feminine goods nearly always debars a husband from any right to inherit his wife's property, and a wife from any right to inherit her husband's.

Moral Phenomena in Marriage

Strictly jural phenomena are always surrounded by a halo of phenomena that are not strictly sanctioned. This is what we call morality. In our society, morality is conflated with the law, especially in matters of marriage and sexuality; but modesty and morality are all matters of convention. Behaviour that we regard as unseemly is elsewhere, on the contrary, prescribed by tradition; it is morally right for a young girl in the Solomon Islands to choose her gallant. It is therefore essential to abandon from the outset all subjective explanations of a moral order. New Caledonia possesses very violent taboos towards sisters. Almost everywhere, during his initiation, a young man is not allowed to be seen by women; he lives in the bush and takes flight when women approach. In a great many cases, it is forbidden to touch a woman, for it is important that the male and female substance should be put in contact only with due deliberation. This idea of substance was indicated by Durkheim. In contrast with these extreme precepts, certain phenomena of licence can go very far: for instance, the prostitution of priestesses in what are called the 'convents' in Guinea – some of the priests can be of the male gender. Prostitution by way of hospitality is in fact communion by way of hospitality. In some ceremonies, all the boys attempt sex with all the girls.[45] Prostitution in the sense we understand it is quite rare, and probably of Semitic origin. Homosexual relationships among women are exceptional, and fairly rare among men, except in New Guinea where they reach a high point (among the Marind Anim, between the sister's son and his maternal uncle, his future father-in-law). Phallic cults. Finally, military associations, for instance Epaminondas and the Seven against Thebes.

Property[46]

The fundamental distinction between personal property and real assets, dominant in our legal system, is an arbitrary distinction largely ignored by other societies. In the wake of Roman law, we have accomplished a huge effort at synthesis and unification; but law, and property law in particular, *ius utendi et abutendi*, does not proceed from one single principle; it rather leads to it. In Roman law, a slave is still *res mancipi*, he is not a man, not a person.[47] Everywhere, the observer will face a plurality of property rights, and very many things that are not directly palpable may be susceptible to ownership in just the same way as tangible things – real property, not fictions. I am the owner of the tree where I have deposited my soul; also, the totem owns me; an Australian tribe can be the owner of a *corroboree*. Furthermore, women's property is not the same as men's; ownership of movables is not ownership of immovables, and so on. Ownership by the king, the tribe, the clan, the village, the neighbourhood, the joint family can all be superimposed on the same object. One should therefore study things as they present themselves, without preconceptions, without trying to relate indigenous rights to our Civil Code, and without using European terminology. Never speak in terms of lease, securities, movables, or immovables.

The issue of individual versus collective property should be totally ignored. The terms we apply to things have no significance whatsoever. In a joint family, one will find collective property administered by a single individual, the patriarch. The fact that the patriarch is only the manager – in one place a sovereign manager, in another subject to strict control – entails no contradiction.

Nearly everywhere we find a distinction between property and possession. The *usucapio* is a fairly common mode of access to property, found in Madagascar, for example. The right of use is often distinguished from the law of landownership, and occupation is distinct from possession. It will be necessary, as far as real rights are concerned, to give up numerous associations of ideas that are specific to our society, for instance in matters of leasing (hiring of objects and services ...).

One should proceed by making an inventory of all the things subject to ownership within the domain, persuading the elders and legal experts to provide all possible explanations. Observers should limit themselves to describing what they see, or what they are told, in the native terminology, and distinguishing between situations of law and situations of fact. Look out for legal headings or the notions that correspond to headings but are not always formulated consciously. In Black countries, nearly everywhere one finds a most acute sense of the notion of custom or prescription, similar to the notions found in ancient French law. Again, call on the method of case histories. The history of a plot of land or of a movable object will allow the detailed study of modes of acquiring, sharing out and transmitting property, and of ownership or usufruct.

The analysis of the legal system should be carried out by bringing together the information thus obtained. One will find a very general conflation of real law and private law, rights and obligations being closely interlinked. The right to a dance or to a song is more hereditary than the right to a plot of land. The notion of a legal matter and a legal case is both very different from our own conception in some respects and very similar to it in others.

There is also a widespread conflation of law bearing on movables and on immovables, things that are immovable by nature being the more important, as they are for us.

Nearly everywhere property has a religious character that is very strongly marked. It is even protected by a system of taboos – the same sanctions prohibit the approach to sacred objects. Hence theft is relatively rare. The linking of property rights with mourning, with the cult of ancestors, etc.

To repeat the point, one should refrain from understanding communal property and individual property as absolute opposites. Thus the game the hunter kills does not belong to him; such and such a noble part of the animal belongs by law to the head of the family, this other part belongs to the hunter's mother-in-law, etc.

Finally, property does not follow a theoretical line; it follows all the lines of social structure, varying according to the objects involved *and* according to the persons – according to the owner's sex, age, section, etc.

Immovables

According to our legal system, together with the land, we own the air, the light and the sub-soil. Throughout the Black world these notions are carefully distinguished. The owner of a plot of land does not necessarily own a tree planted on that land, and the owner of a tree does not always own its fruits. One should therefore study this series of ranked rights. Prior knowledge of early French law or English law will prove very useful here. In England, there is only one owner: the king – all tenures are his. Some are complete land tenures: tenures of the manor or the lord, which includes ownership of the soil and sub-soil, the land being untransferable as long as there are legitimate heirs. Mines are the lord's property, unlike France, where they are state concessions.

One often meets a form of ownership called the long lease (*bail emphytéotique*), a lease for a very long period. Forms of ownership in Madagascar are very remarkable from this point of view.[48]

Land law is the most developed form of law, even among nomads, who own the territories on which they practise transhumance. Though it is firmly rooted in the soil, this kind of law is subject to many qualifications. Land law is above all a right to use that can be encumbered (e.g., throughout Guinea) by easements such as hunting, which is the privilege of the king and nobles. Ownership of the sub-soil is different from ownership of the surface; one can simply own the produce from seedtime to harvesting: *arva per annos mutant* [they change the arable land yearly], says Tacitus of the Germans [26.2]. Ownership of the land, on the other hand, is untransferable. Linked to the family, clan and tribe, far more than to the individual, it cannot leave the family and be yielded to a stranger. Survivals of a similar situation can be seen in Norman law; sale with right of repurchase (*réméré*) and high lineage rights are still in force in Jersey.

The observer should study with particular care the nature of the bond linking the group who own something with the object owned. In Ashantiland, it is the blood of women that circulates in the soil.[49] Throughout the Sudan one finds the institution of the Master of the Earth, the representative of the first inhabitants; ownership is linked with the myth of Mother Earth, of the earth as dwelling place of the ancestors, who have the power to grant abundance or inflict famine. Observe the feelings that each possession evokes in its owner:[50]

the feelings of the chief towards his shrines and his deities. Note all the rules ensuring that such and such a thing is transmitted to a particular individual or is managed by a particular individual. Depending on the year or the season, the rights can vary from individual to collective according to their nature: pasture rights are governed by the system of crop rotation and fallowing. So ownership varies not only according to the nature of the object and the owner, but also over time.

A distinction will normally be made between the following: collective ownership by the family ([the Germanic] *hof* or [Roman] *curia*), patriarchal ownership of the house (*haus*), individual ownership of trees and orchards (*gaard*), the rights of the tenant farmer over his field while he cultivates it (*akker*), eminent ownership rights over the quarter, and temporary ownership rights over the field; finally, ownership of common land (*wald*), to which there applies a right of common grazing – an individual right, yet one possessed by everybody. Double morphology is the rule in Black countries, where fields are owned by the agnatic family and gardens by individuals, and the same plot can be field or garden according to the time of year.[51]

An easement is not necessarily a fragmentation of ownership; it can be, in its origin, a manifestation of the superior rights of (for instance) the chief. Moreover, there is normally a right of way across all holdings for the benefit of all the holdings. Easements of the street, of the rubbish heap, easements of irrigation (very important) and manure are general.

Modes of acquiring property. In our societies, everything is for sale, but this has only been the case recently, for roughly 150 years. Elsewhere, the normal way of transmitting property is by succession. In Ashantiland, as throughout Guinea, women inherit from women, and men from men. The land being strictly female property, there can be no real estate sold outside the matrilineal family without a real *detestatio sacrorum* [solemn renunciation]. The gods have to give permission for property to be transferred to another line. Restriction within the lineage is a widespread institution, but it is generally found in the form of a prohibition on selling outside the family. Lease and sale are rare, and donation is often provisional, as a lieutenantcy. In the Malagasy world, one still finds property granted for services to the public, and the share of the conqueror, as in Germanic law. The Hova soldier in non-Hova country is entitled to a field on which he lives, *hetra*, from the Sanskrit word *kshatriya*, which refers to the warrior caste.[52]

Securities and mortages mean a hold on the individual, not on his property. A debtor will give as security his son, not his land. The family buys back the individual who has been pledged, since the family is the true owner.

Dispossession from land following the arrival of Europeans in colonial territories is a fundamental phenomenon that leads in many cases to a redistribution of property, with the introduction of land ownership where it was previously unknown. But imposing a new system of land tenure without a profound knowledge of the previous system has serious disadvantages.

Movables

Movables are far fewer than immovables. In our society, movables correspond to only one form of ownership, always the same. This is not the case everywhere, and the house may be the prime instance of movables, not immovables. The legal status of the owner affects the nature of ownership, and here we come back to the major division mentioned above between masculine and feminine goods. In France, even today, the bride's wardrobe is excluded from the joint property of the family, even though this has not been specified by contract. There is nothing resembling capital in the societies pertaining to ethnography, except the harvests, tools and bride's *paraphernaux*. The chest is shared by the whole of Asia and North West America. In this chest are kept masks, magic swords and ceremonial clothing – in short, the main movables. Among the Kwakiutl, the loss of a chest led to the demotion of the owner, who lost face.

One very often encounters feudal rights: the right of the lord to the first sheaf, or to a tithe of the harvest. This situation corresponds to titular ownership rather than to obligations. A single object can be subject to rights possessed by the prince, the chief, the priests, the ancestors, the various members of the family, and finally fellow tribesmen. Possession normally implies the obligation to share; possession is shared possession, the joint ownership of movables being the general rule. To own a particular object is also to be accountable for it.

The nature of the rights varies also according to the nature of what is possessed. The whole of Southern Africa is familiar with the *lobola*, a nearly infinite debt owed by the husband to his parents-in-law, never involving anything but cattle. Hunting and fishing rights correspond to rights of individual or collective consumption.

The link between the owner and the object owned is characteristic of a certain type of ownership. Very often, the soul of the owner is located in the object, by the application of a mark or blazon, or by magical connections. Study rights over found objects (which rarely remain in the hands of the finder); also the conditions applying to borrowing, restrictions on the right of use, and that strange institution, so widespread, the right to destroy things legally (*muru, potlatch*).

Payments to settle vendettas entail enormous exchanges of goods, the head of the family being not the absolute owner but simply the treasurer of family assets. The position is the same for the clan chief or tribal chief.

Money, which is commonly found, is always individual to some degree. It circulates between particular clans and particular people, corresponding to a title deed for the things it represents.[53]

Finally, relationships in law are normally everlasting, since the legal bond generally connects not an individual to a thing or another person, but a family to some property or to another family. All the classificatory sons are bound to pay the debts of all their classificatory fathers.

Another type of ownership is that possessed over slaves. Outside European societies, a slave is an individual adopted by the family, whether it be in Black Africa or among the Iroquois, where it was common practice for an old man to adopt the murderer of his son. Slaves proper should be distinguished from serfs and captives.

In *serfdom*, an entire population is dominated by a conquering people who have become owners of the land. The former occupants must therefore cultivate the land on behalf of their masters; this is the origin of tenant farming and sharecropping. Such a situation can be recognised by the reduced independence in the cults of the subjugated population, and by the lack of blazon, sometimes also by the lack of a soul, where only the nobles have a right to a personal soul. Throughout the Nilotic world, one finds the distinction noted by Roscoe between Bahima, conqueror pastoralists who do not cultivate, and Bahera, conquered agriculturalists who work for their masters.[54] The large dynasties of sultans who settled on the Niger installed a social order of this kind. The relations between masters and serfs must be studied both from an individual perspective and a collective one.

Captives are prisoners of war or individuals imprisoned for debt. Normally, a prisoner of war becomes what is called a hut captive, being incorporated into the family and marrying a woman who is also a captive. Usually, a captive cannot be sold, but he has lost his honour. This is the ordinary form of slavery in Africa where Semitic influence has not penetrated, and where white slave traders were not recruiting manpower for the plantations in America.

Finally, slavery as generally understood does not appear to be a primitive institution. The purchase of an individual and his reduction to the status of object is a consequence of the Asiatic law current in towns and large kingdoms – law attested since the oldest Sumerian legal texts. Like prostitution, slavery seems to have its centre between Egypt and China.[55]

One should note that slaves are better treated in so-called primitive societies than in Egypt or Ancient Greece. The rights of slaves were non-existent in Rome, where they were regarded as things, *res mancipi*. In Black countries, a slave has rights and obligations: among the Mossi, a slave is free if he manages to escape. A slave is entitled to the fruit of his labour, to personal savings and to food; he has a wife (a child born of the master and a captive woman sets its mother free); he has rights in regard to third parties, he can inherit, be emancipated, adopted, etc.

Contract Law[56]

At the base of the issues concerning contract we find the theory of Henry Sumner Maine, which was adopted by Durkheim: the societies that preceded our own are societies where the source of a contract is not to be found in the consent of the two parties, but in their civil status; where contract not only involves things or services, but also the civil, political or family status of the contracting parties. Contracts are made on the basis of social position, not of individual decision, and the individual who does not return a potlatch is crushed by the burden of shame and loses his status as noble. It is only in our society that contracts are made without reference to the social position of the contracting party, who merely has to be capable of undertaking a commitment. In order to understand primitive contract law, one can think of the situation in our law of a minor or, in the past, of a married woman, who could not commit herself without her husband's authorisation.

Moreover, one notes an obvious evolution from public and collective obligation towards private and individual obligation. Nearly everywhere, it is not only the contracting parties who are responsible for the commitment, but also all the individuals they represent. The chief who makes a contract is the treasurer and representative of his clan. Even nowadays, a Scottish clan would be dishonoured if it were not to participate in the feasts given by its chief. A contract, even when it is made between individuals, tacitly commits collectivities according to their status. A common mistake is to think that the condition of being under contract is alien to societies other than our own. In fact, it is impossible to conceive of legal systems being entirely non-contractual. We make the opposite error in thinking that all our actions are contractual, that marriage for instance is a contract, whereas the marriage contract comes up on the margins of the act of marriage, strictly speaking. Marriage has all the aspects of a contract, but it is not one; it is an act of public law at the same time as an act of private law.

Our contracts are made in relation to the object or service required, without assuming any other bond between the contracting parties. Elsewhere, normally, a contract implies an alliance: I make a contract with you because I am in some way your ally. At the base of any contract there is alliance through blood, threshold agreement or marriage ... The notion of alliance is still very clear in Semitic law. The biblical theory of the covenant (*alliance*) is well known: the word 'circumcision', imperfectly translated as 'sign', really means 'seal': circumcision is the seal of God. The people of the covenant are those who bear the seal of God; it is between them and God that the contract exists. The alliance within which a contract should be made corresponds to a fundamental notion of very early Roman law.

Moreover, a contract is always an undertaking to *praestare*, that is to hand over or supply an object or service. One possibility is that the prestation is total: I shall owe you everything I possess and all possible services, I am bound to you for life – this is a consequence of the alliance. The other possibility is that the prestation is partial: you owe as much as I give. Far more widespread originally, the total prestation still exists among us between spouses, unless it is specified otherwise in the marriage contract.

In order to study obligations, one should refer to the definitions in Roman law. Paul's definition in the Digest: '*obligationum substantia non in eo consistit, ut aliquid corpus nostrum vel aliquam servitutem nostram faciat, sed ut alium nobis obstringat ad dandum aliquid vel faciendum vel praestandum'.*[57] Note that it is not only the object that matters, but also the obligation to deliver it; this was a major invention of Roman law. Furthermore, a huge revolution was created by the formula of Justinian in his *Institutes*, III, 13: '*Obligatio est iuris vinculum, quo necessitate astringimur alicuius solvendae rei secundum nostrae civitatis iura'.*[58] '*Secundum nostrae civitatis iura*': it is no longer religious or military condition that determines the law, but civil condition. Hence the possibility of making a judge assess the injury caused, even if the injury was fatal. The theory of obligation developed to a considerable degree in Rome, and we are still not through with it. While the German and Swiss codes devote two whole sections to civil responsibility, each with more than sixty articles, we are restricted in this matter to the jurisprudence of the Supreme Court (*Cour de Cassation*), based entirely on article 1384 of the Civil Code.

Principles of observation. In the societies under study one should not look for any of the classical contracts of Western law: purchase, sale, lease ... Among us, a purchase implies a sale that is final; elsewhere, the rule will be sale subject to right of repurchase. We know that even today, in English law, family assets are not for sale. Sales on the market, in public, are impossible in a society ignoring markets; and the Celts apparently only took up markets towards the third century BC, the Germans only towards the fourth or fifth century of our era. Many contracts, for instance the hiring out of services, remain unknown in the form in which we conceive of them; the notion of paid work is alien to these issues, as it was in Rome. Thus contracts are not to be looked for where we make them, but need to be looked for where we lack them. As was said above, a contract is a manifestation of alliance. One should look for contracts in friendship, in marriage (marriage is a contract of alliance involving the concession of a woman or of children), and in hospitality. In Nordic lands, the contract of hospitality involved a right of access to women until a very recent period. A dance or a mask can be the object of contracts. Personal contracts, such as the contract of hospitality, are of the essence, and material contracts are only accessory to them.

Contracts also have an enduring and collective character. They are made between tribes or clans more often than between individuals. It follows from this that a contract is most often the equivalent of a treaty. This is the theory propounded by Davy in his work *La foi jurée*.

Finally, the contract always includes the idea of order: to pay, [Latin] *pagare*, pacify. This notion of the peace that results from fulfilling a contract and from the pact that binds the contracting parties – in other words, the promise of peace inherent in carrying out the contract – is a fundamental notion even in our own customs. The notion of a breach of contract is above all the notion of a disturbance that is public, not only private.

In order to study contracts, one should turn to the case method, making an effort to study all types of contract. This is often difficult, since law applies globally, not article by article. One should describe the mood, words, gestures and prestations of each of the parties.

A certain number of principles are common to all contracts. A contract always has as object a thing or a cause, *res, causa*; and it always has a legitimate cause. But, unlike what we are used to, a contract may vary according to the contracting parties; a contract is made between families, classes or clans, and the internal contract is intended only to make the external contract possible. I am obliged to provide my chief with everything I can, in return for which he spends everything he has on the war in which I fight for him. The public responsibility of a clan chief, for instance among the Betsileo, is unlimited, and so is the subservience of the clan as a whole to the chief. There is no way of doing otherwise, we cannot all be standard bearers; one person will carry the standard and the others will follow. Moreover, the non-fulfilment of a contract nearly everywhere leads to criminal proceedings against the defaulting party. The evolution of Roman law on this point is well known. In most cases, failure to fulfil the contract amounts to giving someone a hold over oneself, the obligation always arising *ex delicto*, and never *ex pacto*. Note the very general absence of the notion of fault (*culpa*), and the general absence of criminal negligence (*quasi-délit*). One is held accountable whether or not there is intent to cause harm. Criminal negligence, committed without harmful intent, implies the acceptance of compensation instead of vendetta.

Finally, contract law has a customary character, which does not prevent contracts from being attested in one way or another. For instance, we observe the use of a tally as early as the Australian aborigines. Deriving from the status of the contracting parties, contracts do not need to be written. I know what I owe to my clan chief and I know what he owes me. Within the family, contracts are not needed, each member being by virtue of membership in permanent contract with all the other members. Being consequences of a particular condition, some obligations do not need to be formulated as such; it is what even today is called the moral situation of the family, or the moral situation of marriage. There is no need for an explicit contract within the family, where the contract is the natural state of things. Finally, the exchange of promises unaccompanied by external formalities is not sanctioned (compare the evolution of Roman law on this point[59]). We usually think that the consent of the two parties is the sufficient generating cause of a contract, and that a contract can be entered into tacitly without even a start on the process of fulfilment, which would give proof of its existence. But this notion of a voluntary bond completely ignores the question of the capacity of the contracting party: a child lacks the right to commit himself. Only contracts entered into publicly, on the Stock Exchange for example, are made orally with a minimum of formalities.

Contracts should be distinguished into those of total prestation and those where the prestation is only partial. The former appear as early as Australia, and are found in much of the Polynesian world (despite its being very advanced), as well as throughout North America. Total prestation is manifested, for two clans, by the fact of their being in a state of permanent contract; each individual owes everything to everyone else in his clan and to everyone in the opposite clan. The permanent and collective character of such a contract makes it a genuine treaty, with the necessary display of wealth vis-à-vis the other party. Services extend to everything and to everyone at any moment; it is what is in hospitality called generosity (*largesse*). Such a contract can also be purely individual, and have remarkable forms: Australia is already acquainted with the market, carried on via women as intermediaries; it is women who go and exchange the most precious goods, and to that end they cross the territories of other tribes. If they were armed, the men could cross these territories, but usually they prefer to send their women, who are wives of the marriage class of the contracting parties and have sexual relations with them. In other cases, two men belonging to different groups have exchanged their umbilical cords. They can make a contract provided that they never see each other. Such emphatic prohibitions on intimacy towards people joined by the closest of bonds are altogether remarkable.

Usually, maximal contracts are made between brothers-in-law. This is the case, for example, in the Sioux world, where everything happens within these themes of total prestation. I initiate all my sisters' sons or all my nephews, or all my sons-in-law by marriage class. The contract is here connected with marriage, initiation, hospitality, post-marriage rights, etc. To pay is to make peace. Thus one becomes aware of a curious notion, that of the unselfish circulation of wealth. *Res* comes from [Sanskrit] *ra(tih)*, what gives pleasure. The interest is here aesthetic and culinary; we are present at a permanent village festival (*frairie*).

For each contract, note who are the contracting parties: individuals, collectivities, or individuals representing a collectivity ... The capacity varies according to the object of the contract. It is very rare for an individual, in his own personal name, to be able to make a contract concerning his immovables. Note the provisions of the contract; whether or not it is obligatory, whether or not transferable, and if so, how. The nature, formalism and publicity of the contract. Formalism is the rule; a contract is altogether solemn, with frightening commitments in the potlatch, where all the members of the clan commit themselves as a group.

Note also the role of currency and securities. The gift is the normal form of commitment; the gift is security against the receiver.[60] We read in the *Digest*: '*dona naturaliter ad remunerandum*' – gifts are by nature made in the hope that they will be repaid. Ingratitude is still a legitimate cause for revoking a donation in French law.

Finally, the modes of acquiring contracts. Contracts are transmissible by right of succession: when my father dies, I inherit all his potlatches.

Criminal Law[61]

Criminal law has a double object: the study of breaches of social duties and the study of reactions to such breaches.[62] It is one instance of the theory of sanctions. Society reacts against everything that offends it. As a group reaction, criminal law does not correspond to a phenomenon of social structure, but to a functional phenomenon: the jury is a functional element, in contrast to judges and prisons, which are structural elements. Crime is to be defined as a violation of law that provokes this reaction, and punishment is society's *public* reaction to those breaches. We thus find in the vendetta, or private war, which manifests this reaction, a mixing of public and private that is difficult to analyse. The indictment is public, the carrying out of punishment more often private. Note again the complete absence of the element of intention; a public crime often corresponds to a private fault (an example can be found in conjugal solidarity).

French legal systems and primitive ones show remarkable differences on this point. Neither the methods of indictment, nor the methods of imputing blame, nor the methods of inflicting punishment – none of these are similar. Notice the lack of an authority established to administer punishment. The judges will be clan elders or religious leaders. No one fulfils just this one function. Note too the general lack of a penal code, except in Madagascar, the lack of a notion of responsibility as we conceive it, the automatic character of the punishment – the culprit often punishes himself (the murderer kills himself or flees); and finally the automatic character of the punishment:[63] without the punishment being announced, the process is set in motion publicly; it is the action of society as a whole – for example, in the case of stoning.

Principles of observation. First of all, an effort should be made to find legal specialists and authorities in matters relating to penal procedure: animist priests (*féticheurs*), those who administer ordeals, etc. Here too, proceed by drawing up a list of cases and scrutinising the judicial archives, in which the natives may have been induced to lay out their customs. It may happen that trials before the European authorities are trials directed against the sanctions inflicted by native judges (the secret society in most cases) for a crime of which the administration was unaware.[64] The study of public discussions in Black countries is an excellent method of investigation. The study of proverbs, sayings, legends and tales will provide further useful examples of crimes and reactions to these crimes. Note the methods of inflicting punishment. The majority of crimes pertain to magic, so the punishments are often prescribed by secret societies.

Criminal law is public law. All crimes are of a religious nature and correspond to the breaking of prohibitions. A murder is a violation of a blood taboo. Hence the religious nature of the corresponding punishment.

Since they correspond to different concepts from ours, the breaches of law are not the same as ours. Thus a woman stepping over a man or an inferior stepping over a superior, or the like, is always a serious crime. Consider crimes committed against animals. On the crimes of kings, see Frazer.[65]

Furthermore, there are possibilities of negotiation and compensation between different aspects of law. In the case of vendetta for instance, the killing of the murderer in retaliation can be replaced by his adoption, so that the victim's father adopts the murderer of his son and treats him as his own son. In addition, the mixing of public and private is a constant feature, being very clear, for instance, in judicial duels.

Finally, one should distinguish at all times between internal law and external law. The law applied within the family or clan is not the same as the law applying to an outsider.

Infractions can be classified according to how serious they are from the natives' point of view. The notion of fault and the search for intent to harm are nearly always absent. The objective, material element in the infraction is all that counts here. Crime committed inside the group will be treated differently from crime committed outside. Here, religious notions become relevant, the crime being related to beliefs about the spirits of the dead, to exogamy, and so on. Theft is generally assessed far more severely if it is inside the village.

The crime will vary also according to the criminal and according to the victim. There are crimes of etiquette, crimes of magic, and simple breaches of rules. A stranger is as such a suspect and is normally regarded as a criminal.

Private crimes committed within the family often incur no sanction at all. On the other hand, the notion of natural death remains unknown, a death being blamed on a witch or enemy; a widow is often held responsible for her husband's death by the close relatives of the husband.

Punishment everywhere has a character that is religious, automatic, violent and unreasoning. It is inflicted in contexts where we would not look for it, for example, in the mutilation of the body of a man struck by lightning – lightning being an expression of celestial wrath. Very often, punishment is not pronounced by a judge, but is applied by the crowd even before the judgement is delivered: stoning, lynching, etc. Since crime is an offence against the gods, punishment takes on the character of an expiatory offering.[66]

Public punishment is essentially variable, both as regards how it is inflicted (who inflicts it, where, when, against whom is it announced ...) and as regards its nature. The death penalty can be replaced by exile – which is scarcely less severe – or by financial compensation. Fines seem to be as rare as financial compensation is common. Moreover, compensation can be replaced by the offer of a woman; from her a child will be born in the offended group and in this child the breath of the victim will be revived. Note the punishments inflicted on animals.

As for private punishment or vendetta, study the avenger, the avenged, the victim and their relationships. Private punishment does not involve the bringing of a charge. At the origin of civil responsibility we find all possible types of compensation. Formal armed combat, which is often the outcome of inflicting private punishment, can degenerate into an ordeal, but in that case the punishment is inflicted publicly.

Study also the procedures for remission of punishment: laws regarding asylum, or pardon or forgetting; the period of testing imposed in the infliction of a particular punishment, and so on.

Responsibility is a late notion. First comes the pursuit of vengeance, the desire to inflict suffering equal to what one has undergone; the search for the real culprit comes only later. What matters is the moral person, the family or clan, to which the murderer belongs. Hence the first step is to determine which clan or tribe is guilty. Divinatory procedures are already used for this purpose among the Australian Arunta, while torture is a recent custom, belonging in the domain of procedure. Furthermore, if responsibility is originally very weak in civil law, this is because it admits of division into equal parts, for instance between brothers, in cases of enslavement for debt in Sudan. In religious law, on the other hand, collective responsibility is very strong and can go up the line of ascendants or weigh down indefinitely all the descendants of the culprit. The seconds in a duel often themselves fight duels.

Finally, the application of criminal law is complicated by the fact that a society does not recognise only a single legal system but applies different levels of law superimposed on each other. The law of the village headman is subordinated to the law of the district head, which itself is lower than the law of the king.

The mixing of public and private law is the rule everywhere in the infliction of punishment. A typical example of such mixing is the case of a thief in ancient Roman law. Acting as a judicial body, the secret society will sometimes seek revenge for one of its members, and will sometimes act under the influence of public opinion.

Judicial Organisation and Procedure[67]

Judicial organisation studies the means that law puts at the disposal of individuals in order to ensure that their just rights are acknowledged and respected. The public-private mixing is here fundamental.

Etiquette plays an essential role throughout judicial organisation. The course of a trial is dominated by the use of certain established words and gestures. Formalism is absolute. In a Germanic trial, not a single gesture was insignificant; a party who by mistake touched one of the magistrates in the course of the sitting lost his case by that very act. The Ewe in Togo have a procedure for taking oaths that reproduces exactly the procedure of the Roman *sacramentum*.

The debate generally takes a different form from the one we are accustomed to. The question is not whether in committing murder you acted with intent or inadvertently; the question is whether *your* clan killed *my* son. Ideally, one wants to identify the murderer in order to kill *his* son: this is what we still find in [the novel] *Colomba*.[68] The search for the truth and the search for intent are not in the foreground – which does not mean that they are totally ignored.

Furthermore, the outcome is not reached by means of investigation, as with us. If a man dies, it is because his wife poisoned him or betrayed him. A poison ordeal is administered to the widow; if she dies as a result, it shows that she was indeed guilty. But people do not investigate the exact circumstances of the husband's death. This is still the principle that dominates the application of the military code, the early Roman rule of decimation. The punishment is intended to frighten the guilty; the fate of the true culprit is far less important.

Procedure will most often appear to be dominated by custom. People will refer to precedents, or to principles that are invariably concrete. Moreover, the procedure will show very marked variations depending on the resources available to each of the parties involved.

The fieldworker should attempt to work case by case, recording directly the phenomena observed. If one lacks prior knowledge of the principles of customary law, it is best to avoid native legal specialists since their explanations could well contribute unnecessary confusion.

Distinguish between entirely public procedures and relatively private ones. Public procedure will show a different aspect depending on whether fieldwork is carried out among peoples with kings, with chiefdoms, or with a hierarchy of secret societies. But even where the organisation is based on kings, the old popular organisation will persist alongside organisation by clan or village. Thus three levels of judicial organisation are superimposed: the people, the chiefs and jural fraternities, and the royal court. The whole Black world is familiar with the jural assembly, where the circle is formed by the whole population or by representatives of the whole population. The sessions of these assemblies are always solemn. Such organisations are wholly comparable to those that preceded the Greek and Roman organisations: this is the agora or the forum. Everything is done in public. This assembly of the people, found in Africa, in Malaysia, among the Annamese, and so on, might make one believe in popular justice, but it does not mean that the population is present in its entirety, nor that it here possesses power.[69]

The judicial assembly is held in a sacred place, or in one that becomes sacred. The holding of the assembly is accompanied by a sacrifice, which attracts spirits. Study everything about this sacred location; note its orientation, the division of the assembly according to clans, villages and families; the presence or absence of women, the rites of divination, the sacrifices, etc. The court assembles on a given day (but the Malagasy *fokonolona* operates every day), and its arrival is solemn; it can be itinerant. Study the summons to a trial, the assembly for it, the sessions of the tribunal that may or may not coincide with market days. Are there auspicious and inauspicious days for administering justice? Observe the plaintiffs, the counsel for the defence, the accused, the herald, the judges, the assessors. If possible, have the speeches in native language taken down in shorthand and translate them in full. Study carefully the eloquence of each speaker. Throughout Polynesia and in Melanesia, eloquence very often consists in speaking a lot; the litigant who speaks most and fastest wins his case.

Who administers justice? In the whole Ewe grouping, in Togo, the king is only the head of the debate, probably in imitation of the Portuguese or maybe, even before the Portuguese, the Normans. In the whole Ashanti grouping, there are delegates of the king; the king is above all head of this popular justice.[70] This was still the function of the Germanic king. One often finds the royal power split in two: the war king and the peace king, the day king and the night king.

Finally, judicial organisation can involve genuine officials. Much of Black Africa is familiar with priests who administer poison for tests, special priests who preside over ordeals; the master of Earth; lawyers, heralds (research their expenses and perquisites). Study the comments on the trial. Very often, proverbs and legal maxims are cited as jural precedents. Record the proverbs and maxims.

Private justice can be administered in public, within secret societies. The secret society delivers its sentence; the public carrying out of this sentence is a jural act, and not simply a murder. It is often the society of men that carries out the sentence. In Melanesia, the sentence can even be carried out by a secret society within the society of men. So the action is secret, but simultaneously private and public within an assembly that one should know about and describe.

The vendetta, which is often carried out in conjunction with others who have sworn to participate, constitutes a transaction that lies between the political form of a fight and the judicial form. A fight: it is still under this form that judicial argument takes place among us. The word quarrel comes from *querela*, 'complaint'. One should study the parties and their complaints. Here two major possibilities present themselves: either a court is set up or there is an instant reaction, such as Durkheim and Fauconnet described – the offended party launches war against the clan of the culprit, or stones him right away without discriminating. In Australia, no death is regarded as natural. The corpse is questioned using some method of divination, and it is the deceased himself who is supposed to lead his relatives in the direction of the guilty tribe. On this point, major differences separate African law or even Asian law from the set of institutions found in North America. In North West America, trials take the form of private quarrels. Normally, there is a fairly high level of peace within the tribe, but conflicts break out between tribes or between moieties. When a member of a tribe feels himself injured by an individual belonging to a clan from the opposite moiety, it is not only the clan or the family of the injured party that sets off, but the whole moiety. Here a constant mixing is found of public and private punishment, of immediate and deferred punishment.

The judgement that follows this debate, where there is a judgement, consists in defining the loser. If I lose, it is because I am guilty. The ordeal is conflated with the pre-trial investigation and with the punishment; the widow who succumbs to the poison test has killed her husband. It is a mode of reasoning, and not a particularly mystical one.

Divination methods are also a method of testing: the plaintiff takes his runes with him to try to put a spell on the judges, on the people, and most especially on his opponent.[71]

He dedicates the culprit to the infernal powers. It is the Latin *devotio* ritual.

The judgement and the infliction of punishment are often conflated. It is far more precise and speedy than among us. If deliberation takes place, try to be present. In any case, observe the carrying out of judgements, even in civil cases. Once the amount of compensation has been agreed, the case is buried, and the public authorities no longer have to intervene.

In all of this, the mixing of civil and criminal and of public and private seems a constant feature, and it is very difficult to assess their relative importance.[72]

Notes

1. [Mauss, in fact, here writes of the ancient Romans in the present tense.]
2. [Taking the French *infliction* as a mistake for *infraction*.]
3. [Compilations of Roman law made under the sixth-century emperor Justinian.]
4. Ajisafe, A.K., *Laws and Customs of the Yoruba*, London and Lagos, 1924.
5. Baden-Powell, B.H., *The Indian Village Community*, London, 1896; *The Origin and Growth of Village Communities in India*, London, 1899. Delafosse, M., *Les civilisations disparues: civilisations négro-africaines*, Paris, 1925. Fletcher, A.C. and La Flesche, F., *The Omaha Tribe*, ARBAE 27 (1905–06), 1911: 15–672. Fortes, M. and Evans-Pritchard, E.E. (eds), *African Political Systems*, Oxford, 1942. Hodge F.W. (ed), *Handbook of American Indians North of Mexico*, BAE Bulletin 27, 1907. Jobbe-Duval, E. 'La commune annamite', *Nouvelle revue historique de droit français et étranger*, 1896: 613–674. Labouret, H., *Paysans d'Afrique occidentale*, Paris, 1941. Lévi-Strauss, C., 'Contribution à l'étude de l'organisation sociale des Indiens Bororo', *JSA* 38, 1936: 269–304. Moret, A. and Davy, G., *Des clans aux empires: l'organisation sociale chez les primitifs et dans l'Orient ancien*, Paris, 1923. Nadel, S.F., *A Black Byzantium: the Kingdom of Nupe in Nigeria*, London, 1942. Rattray, R.S., *Ashanti Law and Constitution*, Oxford, 1929. Swanton, J.R., *Contributions to the Ethnology of the Haida*, Leiden, 1905–09; *Social Condition, Beliefs and Linguistic Relationships of the Tlingit Indians*, ARBAE 26 (1905–06), 1908: 391–512. Wundt, W., 'Die Anfänge der Gesellschaft', *Psychologische Studien* 1, 1905.
6. See Hocart, A.M., *Kingship*, Oxford, 1927; *Kings and Councillors*, London, 1936.
7. Bloch, M., *Les rois thaumaturges*, Strasbourg and Paris, 1924.
8. See Dennett, R.E., *At the Back of the Black Man's Mind*, London, 1926.
9. See Herskovits, M.J., *Dahomey, an Ancient West African Kingdom*. 2 vols, New York, 1938.
10. Maine, Sir H.J.S., *Ancient Law*, London, 1861.
11. [Mauss has in mind that 'parliament' is cognate with French *parler* 'to speak'.]
12. Boas, F., *The Social Organization and Secret Societies of the Kwakiutl Indians*, Washington, 1898. Briem, O.E., *Les sociétés secrètes de mystères*, trans. from Swedish, Paris, 1941. Butt-Thompson, F.W., *West African Secret Societies*, London, 1929. Jeanmaire, H., *Couroi et courètes*, Lille, 1939 (interesting parallel between societies of men in Ancient Greece and modern Black Africa). Schurtz, H., *Altersklassen und Männerbünde*, Berlin, 1902. Webster, H., *Primitive Secret Societies*, New York, 1908.
13. Hazoumé, P., *Le pacte de sang au Dahomey*, Paris, 1937.
14. Rivers, W.H.R., *The History of Melanesian Society*, 2 vols, Cambridge, 1914.

15. Davy, G., *La foi jurée: étude sociologique du problème du contrat: la formation du lien contractuel*, Paris, 1922.
16. See Hocart, A.M., *Les castes* [Chapter 6 n. 4]. Bouglé, C., *Essai sur le régime des castes*, Paris, 1908.
17. [Taking *procéder* 'proceed' as a mistake for *procréer*.]
18. [Mistake for Vedic castes?]
19. Bachofen, J.J., *Das Mutterrecht*, Basle, 1898 (very out-dated, but remains the starting point of our current studies on the family). Best, E., 'Maori nomenclature', *JAI* 22, 1902: 182–202. Boas, F. (based on the data collected by George Hunt), *Ethnology of the Kwakiutl*, ARBAE 35 (1913–14), 1921: 43–1481. Dorsey, J.O., *Siouan Sociology*, ARBAE 15 (1893–94), 1897: 205–245. Frazer, J.G., *Les origines de la famille et du clan*, trans., Paris, 1923. Grosse, E., *Die Formen der Familie and die Formen der Wirtschaft*, Freiburg in Breisgau, 1896. Granet, M., *Catégories matrimoniales et relations de proximité dans la Chine ancienne*, Paris, 1939. Junod, H.A., *Mœurs et coutumes des Bantous*, 2 vols, Paris, 1936. Kohler, J., *Zur Urgeschichte der Ehe: Totemismus, Gruppenehe, Mutterrecht*, Stuttgart, 1896; mainly of historical interest. Lévi-Strauss, C., 'L'analyse structurale en linguistique et en anthropologie', *Word* 1, 1945: 33–53. Lowie, R.H., *Traité de sociologie primitive*, trans., Paris, 1936. Malinowski, B., *The Family among the Australian Aborigines*, London, 1913; *La vie sexuelle des sauvages du nord-ouest de la Mélanésie*, trans., Paris, 1930. Moore, L., *Malabar Law and Custom*, Madras, 1905. Morgan, L.H., *Systems of Consanguinity and Affinity of the Human Family*, Smithsonian Contributions to Knowledge 17, Washington, 1871. Paulme, Denise, *Organisation sociale des Dogons, Soudan français*, Paris, 1940. Haddon, A.C., ed., *Reports of the Cambridge Anthropological Expedition to Torres Straits*, vols. 5–6, Cambridge, 1904–08. Radin, P., *The Social Organization of the Winnebago Indians: an Interpretation*, National Museum of Canada Bulletin 10, 1915. Rivers, W.H.R., *Kinship and Social Organization*, London, 1914. Seligman, B.Z., 'Studies in Semitic kinship', *Bulletin of the School of Oriental and African Studies*, 3/1, 1923: 51–58; 3/2, 1924: 264–280. Starcke, C.N., *Die Primitive Familie in ihrer Entstehung und Entwickelung*, Leipzig, 1888.
20. See M. Leenhardt's charts in *Notes d'ethnologie* ... and *Gens* ... [Chapter 2, n. 6].
21. See Mauss, M., 'Parentés à plaisanterie', *Annuaire de l'EPHE, Ve section*, 1927–28, Melun, 1928.
22. See Rivers, W.H.R., *Kinship* ... [n. 19]. Richards, A.I, 'The Village Census in the Study of Culture Contact', *Africa*, 1935: 20–33.
23. Morgan, L.H., *Systems* ... [n. 19].
24. On the Todas, see Rivers, W.H.R., *The Todas*, London, 1906. [In fact the Todas live in the South-West of India.]
25. [The *Zippe* and *sapa* in the French text are mistakes made by the note-takers.]
26. Cicero, *Top.*, 6.29. ['People of the same *gens*, i.e. clan, are those who share a name.']
27. On totemism as a cult, see below.
28. Frazer, Sir J.G., *Totemism and Exogamy*, London, 1910. Durkheim, E., 'Sur l'organisation matrimoniale des sociétés australiennes', *AS*, 1903–04: 118–147.
29. See Rattray, R.S., *Ashanti*, Oxford, 1923.
30. Kroeber, A., 'The Arapaho', *AMNH Bulletin* 18, 1904: 1–229, 279–454.
31. Haddon, A.C., ed., *Reports* ... [n. 19].
32. Hewitt, J.N.B., *Iroquoian Cosmology, 1st part*, ARBAE 21 (1899–1900), 1903: 133–360.
33. Aginsky, B.W., *Kinship Systems and the Forms of Marriage*, Mem. AAA 45, Menasha, Wisconsin, 1935. Crawley, E., *The Mystic Rose: a Study of Primitive Marriage*, London, 1902. Evans-Pritchard, E.E., 'The Study of Kinship in Primitive Society', *Man* 29, no. 148, 1929. Firth, R., *We, the Tikopia: a Sociological Study of Kinship in Primitive Polynesia*, London, 1936. Frazer, Sir J.G., *Les Origines* ... [n. 19]; *Totemism* ... [n. 28]. Hartland, E.S., *Primitive Paternity*, London, 2 vols, 1909. Howitt, A.W., *The Native Tribes of South-East Australia*, London, 1904. Hutchinson, Rev. H.N., *Marriage Customs in Many Lands*, London, 1897. Kohler, J., 'Zur Urgeschichte der Ehe', *Z. f. vergleichende Rechtswissenschaft* 17, 1904–05: 256–280 [but Mauss probably meant *ibid*. 12, 1895–97: 187–353]. Malinowski, B., *Vie sexuelle* ... [Chapter 2, n. 13]. Morgan, L.H., *Systems* ... [n. 19]. Thurnwald, R., *Banaro Society: Social Organization and Kinship System of a Tribe in the Interior of New Guinea*, Mem. AAA 3/4, 1916. Westermarck, E., *Histoire du mariage humain*, trans. Paris, 1895; *Les cérémonies du mariage au Maroc*, trans. Paris, 1921.
34. Maine, Sir H.J.S., *Ancient Law* [n. 10].

35. See Granet, M., *La polygynie sororale et le sororat dans la Chine féodale*, Paris, 1920.
36. Acquisition of ownership by continued possession for a certain time.
37. Morgan, L.H., *Systems* ... [n. 19]; *Ancient Society*, London, 1877.
38. On joking relationships, see Mauss, M., 'Parentés à plaisanterie' [n. 21].
39. See Brown, A.R., 'The Mother's Brother in South Africa', *SAJS*, 1925, and his articles in *Man* and *JRAI*.
40. See Frazer, Sir J.G., *Totemism* ... [n. 28]; Junod, H.A., *Mœurs et coutumes des Bantous*, Paris, 1927.
41. [Tibet and Africa should probably be transposed.]
42. See Crawley, E., *Mystic Rose* ...[n. 33].
43. See Yates, T.J.A., 'Bantu Marriage and the Birth of the First Child', *Man* 32, no. 159, 1932. Among the Dogon of the French Sudan a wife could formerly only move to her husband's home following the birth of a third child (Paulme, D., *Organisation* ... [n. 19]).
44. See Hertz, R., 'Contribution à une étude sur la représentation collective de la mort', in *Mélanges de sociologie religieuse et de folklore*, Paris, 1928.
45. See Malinowski, B., *Vie sexuelle* ...[Chapter 2, n. 13].
46. Boas, F., Property Marks of Alaskan Eskimo, *Am. Anth.* 1/4: 601–614. Kruyt, A.C., 'Koopen in Midden Celebes', *Mededeelingen der Koninklijke Akademie van Wetenschappen, Afdeeling Letterkunde* 56, ser. B/5, 1923: 149–178. Van Ossenbruggen, E., 'Over het primitief Begrip van Grondeigerdom', *Indische gids*, 1905: 161–192, 360–392. Schapera, I., *A Handbook of Tswana Law and Custom*, Oxford, 1938. Schurtz, I., 'Die Anfänge des Landbesitzes', *Z. f. Sozialwissenschaft*, 1900: 244–255, 352–361. Tschuprow, A.A., *Die Feldgemeinschaft: eine morphologische Untersuchung*, Strasbourg, 1902 (studies agrarian communities; Russian sources). See also *Bulletin du Comité d'études historiques et scientifiques de l'Afrique occidentale française* 18/4, 1935 (dealing mainly with the study of landed property in Senegal). *Coutumiers juridiques de l'Afrique occidentale française*, vol. I, Senegal; vol. II, Sudan; vol. III, miscellaneous, Publ. du Comité d'études historiques et scientifiques de l'A.O.F., Paris, 1936–39. Consult also all the works already cited on social and political organisation and on domestic organisation.
47. [Ownership of *res mancipi* (as distinct from *res nec mancipi*) could only be transferred by solemn procedures.]
48. Julien, G., *Institutions politiques et sociales de Madagascar* ..., Paris, 1909.
49. Rattray, R.S., *Ashanti Law* ... [n. 5].
50. Firth, R., *We, the Tikopia* ...[n. 33].
51. Paulme, D., *Organisation* ... [n. 19].
52. [Sanskrit *kshetra*, 'land, field', does not in fact derive from *kshatriya*.]
53. See Chapter 6 ('Currency').
54. Roscoe, J., *The Soul of Central Africa*, London, 1922.
55. See Nieboer, H.J., *Slavery as an Industrial System*, The Hague, 1900.
56. Davy, G., *La foi jurée* ... [n. 15]. Grierson, P.J.H., *The Silent Trade*, Edinburgh, 1903. Huvelin, P., 'Les tablettes magiques et le droit romain', *Annales internationales d'histoire*, Paris, 1901–02. Lasch, R., 'Das Marktwesen auf den primitiven Kulturstufen', *Z. f. Sozialwissenschaft*, 1906: 617–627, 700–715, 764–782. Maine, Sir H.J.S., *Ancient Law*... [n. 34]. Maunier, R., 'Recherches sur les échanges rituels en Afrique du Nord', *AS*, n.s. 2, 1924–25: 11–97. Mauss, M., 'Essai sur le don ...' [Chapter 6, n. 5]. Sapir, E., 'Some Aspects of Nootka Language and Culture', *Am. Anth.* 13, 1911: 15–29. Schmidt, W. and Koppers, W., *Völker und Kulturen 1: Gesellschaft und Wirtschaft der Völker*, Regensberg, 1924.
57. *Digest*, 44, 7. [The essence of obligations consists not in the fact that it makes ours some object or some service, but in the fact that it binds another person to give or do or perform something for us.]
58. [Obligation is a bond of law whereby we are placed under the necessity of discharging something according to the laws of our state.]
59. On formalism in general and in Roman law in particular, see Jhering, R. von, *Esprit du droit romain* ..., 2nd ed., 4 vols, trans. from German, Paris, 1880.
60. See Mauss, M., 'Gift, Gift', *Mélanges Charles Andler*, Strasbourg, 1924.

61. Glotz, G., *La solidarité de la famille dans le droit criminel en Grèce*, Paris, 1904. Huvelin, P., *La notion de l'injuria dans le très ancient droit romain*, Lyon, 1903. Kulischer, E., 'Untersuchungen über das primitive Strafrecht', Z. f. *vergleichende Rechtswissenschaft*, 16/3: 417 and 469, 1903; 17: 1–22, 1904. Steinmetz, S.R., *Ethnologische Studien zur ersten Entwicklung der Strafe* ..., 2 vols, Groningen, 1928. Westermarck, E., 'Der Ursprung der Strafe ...', Z. f. *Sozialwissenschaft*, Oct-Nov. 1900. *Zum ältesten Strafrecht der Kulturvölker*, Leipzig, 1905 (questions about criminal law put by Mommsen to various jurists).

62. On the religious origin of criminal law, see Mauss, M., 'La religion et les origines du droit pénal', *RHR* 34, 1896: 269–295. *RHR* 35, 1997: 31–60.

63. [The repetition is in the French.]

64. See Talbot, P.A., *The Peoples of Southern Nigeria*, 4 vols, London, 1926.

65. Frazer, Sir J.G., *Lectures on the Early History of Kingship*, London, 1905.

66. See Westermarck, E., *L'origine et le développement des idées morales*, trans., Paris, 1928.

67. Harrison, J.E., *Themis: a Study of the Social Origins of Greek Religion*, Cambridge, 1912. Glotz, G., *L'ordalie dans la Grèce primitive*, Paris, 1904. Meyer, F., *Wirtschaft und Recht der Herero*, Berlin, 1905. Pechuël-Loesche, E., *Die Loango-Expedition*, Stuttgart, 1907. Rattray, R.S., *Ashanti Law* ... [n. 5]. Spieth, J., *Die Ewe-Stämme* ..., Berlin, 1906; *Die Religion der Eweer in Süd-Togo*, Göttingen and Leipzig, 1911. Ubach, E. and Rackow, E., *Sitte und Recht in Nordafrika*, Stuttgart, 1923. See also: *Reports of the Cambridge Anthropological Expedition to Torres Straits*, Cambridge, 1904–09.

68. [By Prosper Mérimée, 1840, about a Corsican vendetta.]

69. See Rattray, R.S., *Ashanti Law* ... [n. 5].

70. *Ibid.*

71. See Spieth, J., *Die Ewe* ... [n. 67].

72. **Chapter Bibliography.** Kohler, J., *Einführung in die Rechtswissenschaft*, Leipzig, 1902. Idem: many articles in the Z. f. *Rechtswissenschaft*. Post, A., *Afrikanische Jurisprudenz* ..., vol. 1, Oldenburg, 1887; *Die Geschlechtsgenossenschaft der Urzeit und die Entstehung der Ehe* ... Oldenburg, 1875; *Die Grundlagen des Rechts und die Grundzüge seiner Entwickelungsgeschichte* ..., Oldenburg, 1884; *Grundriss der ethnologischen Jurisprudenz* ..., 2 vols, Oldenburg, 1894–95. Schultz-Ewerth, E. and Adam, L. (eds), *Das Eingeborenrecht* ... vol. 2, *Ostafrika*, by Ankermann, B., Stuttgart 1929. Steinmetz, S.R., *Rechtsverhältnisse von eingeborenen Völkern in Afrika und Ozeanien*, Berlin 1903. Van Vollenhoven, C., *Het adatrecht van Nederlandsch-Indië*, The Hague, 1931 (corpus of Indonesian law; the investigation into *adat* law in the Indonesian Archipelago runs to thirty volumes). Maunier, R. (dir.), *Études de sociologie et d'ethnologie juridiques*, Paris (33 volumes so far).

8

Moral Phenomena

All legal systems are moral phenomena, but morality is not wholly included in the law.[1] Being a matter of which people are clearly and organically aware, involving precise reactions, law corresponds to expectations that are defined in advance by the whole community, including the guilty and those who lose their cases. Just like the phenomena of religion, esthetics, and so on, jural phenomena are enveloped in a diffuse, amorphous mass of phenomena related to law without actually being law in the strict sense. Around religion there is magic, divination and above all popular superstitions; around law, there is morality.

Law is not conflated with morality, even among us. To study law is not to study morality. Morality is the art of living together, and it can be recognised by the presence of the notion of good. This presence of the notion of good, of duty, of fault can be very clear in many cases, but morality nonetheless remains something that is relatively diffuse. It contains many feelings and actions that are regularly predictable and expected and have useful effects, but that are only formulated occasionally and are not applied with any particular solemnity. In our society morality is internal; we are engaged in debate with our conscience; we question it, it blames us, or more often, gives us its approval. This is the examination of conscience.

This interiorisation of morality hardly exists in so-called primitive societies, where morality appears just as established and just as public as our law. There are people who die from an insult they have not been able to avenge. After they die, their children avenge the insult inflicted on their forebear. The whole of Malaysia, of Malayan and non-Malayan Indo-China, of Madagascar, are familiar with the phenomenon of running *amok*; also with collective states of panic in which the village shuts itself up and forbids anyone from entering. This means either that a villager has committed a sin, or that others have done so, or that they are expecting an attack.

Some societies are essentially warrior societies: in the headhunting world (Malaysia and part of Indo-China), it is impossible for a young man to marry until he has brought his prospective parents-in-law a human head. Elsewhere, other societies appear as peace-loving.[2] Much of Polynesia practises the *muru*, a revenge expedition expressing the maternal relatives' right of inspection over the children of a fellow clanswoman who has married into another clan. In the Admiralty Islands, the Manus explain the *ngang* as follows: 'After her marriage, a woman from group A goes to live in a house of group B; this house is haunted by the ghosts of that group. She gives these ghosts a child. Through carelessness, they allow this child, now grown into a man, to die. The men from group A – the group of the deceased's mother – feel insulted and come to destroy the house and the drinking vessels made from the skulls of these ghosts who let one of their people die, i.e. the child of a woman of their group'.[3]

The essence of the observer's work will here consist in compiling moral and judicial statistics. Thurnwald was able to show in the Solomon Islands that the number of violent deaths was equal to the number of deaths by natural causes.[4] These statistics should for instance cover slavery; the number of divorces, dismissals and separations ... Record the granaries that are full, those that are empty, those that are emptied on the occasion of an initiation or at the end of mourning.

The morality of a society can also be studied by studying its literature and more especially its proverbs. The study of Sanskrit always begins with proverbs; the student who knows his proverbs knows a concrete language and possesses a concrete morality and wisdom. Each proverb calls for a commentary.[5] Record in full the stories concerning this particular proverb, and the narratives in which it is included ... There are often links between proverbs and what is said by diviners, e.g. in the cult of the Fa in Dahomey.[6] These proverbs are often in verse, and may relate to an epic or a lyric poem. Throughout Black Africa, people speak in proverbs. Morality is a form of wisdom, *sophia* [in Greek]. The study of these proverbs will lead to an endless list of questions: the tales, epics, dramas and comedies constitute an unlimited repertoire.

Proverbs often treat of relations between generations and between sexes, and of relations between things and people. The observer should choose any convenient principle of classification, simply trying to be as thorough as possible.

Having completed an investigation of this kind, one will be able to define the moral tone of the society under study, making an effort to remain within the ethos of the society: it is good to practise the vendetta, it is good to be able to offer a human head to your fiancée. The notion of moral uprightness or rectitude is clear in Polynesia, where the word *tika* is the same as in Bengali.

Notions of morality are very often mixed with notions of happiness, virtue, good luck, glory or infamy. If I am lucky, it is because I am within my rights; and I am within my rights since I am lucky. Such reasoning is reversible and by no means self-contradictory; these methods of reasoning are as good as our own.

Note the moral differences between social environments: court morality and popular morality. Women's morality is not men's; the morality of the old is not that of the young, and sexual morality is not general morality. All these various forms of morality interrelate by age, generation, clan, moiety, secret society, class, and so on. All this can be studied in collections of [sayings on] etiquette. This approach will bring to light the characteristics of urbanity, culture, delicacy and gentleness; or on the contrary, features of violence and brutality. It is the whole set of cases that will make it possible to practise a little collective ethology.[7]

The observer should study reactions that are simply moral, without being criminal or civil, i.e. moral punishments. Sending to Coventry is a severe form of punishment. To refuse an initiation can lead to disaster. Nearly everywhere, to lose face is tantamount to losing life, since the person concerned lets himself die out of despair.

The notions of good and bad are generally very clear. Today we know how sensitive children in our societies are to such notions. The child has his own notions of good and bad. The notion of justice or moral law is clear in the Ewe world where the very name of Mahou, the Great God, means 'law'.

Note also all the language taboos, and those displays of respect or familiarity that both seem equally excessive to us. In the Sioux group it is impossible to utter the name of any relative of one's wife; the husband, when speaking of his father- or mother-in-law, will use a circumlocution such as 'those allies who live over there on the other side'.

Finally, distinguish public morality from private morality. Note the attachment to soil and the love of homeland. Very often, the individual severed from his village dies. In the past, homesickness was a regular reason for military discharge in France.

This study of morality will serve as the genuine foundation for a good collective ethology: what we call morality is very often ethology.[8]

Notes

1. No general works to cite on this subject. Nevertheless, see Benedict, R., *Patterns of Culture*, London, 1935, which studies from this angle three societies: the Pueblos of New Mexico, the Melanesians of Dobu Island, and the Kwakiutl of Vancouver.
2. Such as the Gagous studied by Tauxier, L., *Nègres Gouros et Gagou*, Paris, 1924.
3. Mead, M., *Kinship in the Admiralty Islands*, AMNH Anthrop. Papers 34/2, New York, 1934: 314.
4. Thurnwald, R., *Forschungen auf den Salomo-Inseln und dem Bismark-Archipel*, Berlin, 1912.
5. On African proverbs, see Delafosse. M., *L'âme nègre*, Paris, 1922.
6. See Maupoil, B., *La géomancie à l'ancienne Côte des Esclaves*, Paris, 1943 (1946).
7. See Brinton, D.G., *The Basis of Social Relations: a Study in Ethnic Psychology*, New York and London, 1902.
8. [Taking *trop souvent* 'too often' as a mistake for *très souvent*.]

9

Religious Phenomena

The whole series of lectures published in this book starts off from the study of material phenomena and ends up with the study of ideal phenomena. Thus the chapter on law precedes this chapter on religion. Since it involves objects, persons and actions – *res, personae, actiones* – law still contains an element of the material. Indeed, the fundamental mistake of mentalist sociology is to forget that collective life involves objects, that some of its phenomena are material. A philosophy that conceives of cognition (*mentalité*) as something given in itself forgets that it is given only in relation to material phenomena. Law itself remains engaged in the management of objects and persons. Certainly, in its moral aspect, law is already a matter of cognition; if I am the owner of a house, it is because you recognise that I am its owner: this is a moral phenomenon – but the house is standing there. Moreover, a great many jural phenomena concern not only objects, but the relations between men and objects. Thus both in law and in morality there exists, alongside actions bearing on material objects, an administration of bodily movements. This administration is still present in religion where, however, the mass of mental phenomena appears relatively pure – only relatively, for cognition is never really 'pure'; but ultimately it is always worth separating mind and body as far as this is possible. That is why the study of religion comes last. Admittedly, a religious idea is always expressed first in linguistic form, and only thereafter in rituals, which very often belong to the material realm; but ultimately, there is here a tendency towards purity.

We need not dwell at length on the importance of religious phenomena. In most human societies, the fieldworker will be in the presence of *homo religiosus*, religious man, for this is how the members of societies outside the European world define themselves: they themselves are searchers on themselves.[1] In our own society where religion has become just one category among others, *homo religiosus* has given way, not to *homo faber*, but to *homo economicus*: what matters is not making things, but being paid to make them – or not to make them. *Homo economicus* is in any case a recent creation, dating probably from Mandeville and his *Fable of the bees* [1723], in the wake of Gresham and Pepys:

homo economicus comes to us from England. Compare, in France, those who live in towns with those who live in the country. The peasants are preoccupied with their cows, which are the essential precondition for their income, but they retain a concern for their cows as cows, while the dominant preoccupation of the townspeople is of an economic nature, even in their aesthetic activity. Conversely, I recall a Hopi, chief of the Fire Fraternity, whom I met in Washington. A long-distance record-holder, he told me: 'I can run like this because I never stop singing my fire song'; he was convinced that a fire was burning inside him. Similar facts have been recorded in Australia. Beliefs of this kind by no means preclude exact knowledge. Palaeolithic man chose with great care the stones he would use for making arrowheads; contemporary 'primitives' possess precise knowledge of ethnobotany and ethnozoology. In all their actions, in addition to a technical and scientific component, there is a superadded religious component, in contexts where we do not involve religion. Admittedly, their technical activity is also imbued with moral activity. A man hunts to feed his children, but the two aspects are distinct in his mind, and since he distinguishes them, we must keep them separate. In any case, his technical activity is not accompanied by any economic activity. Such superimposition of economic value, or of religious or moral value, onto purely technical activity is a major phenomenon in human societies. It permits one to assess the relative importance of different components in human activities.

Such an assessment constitutes the essence of the work of the observer, who should make a particular effort to record the relations between religion and all other social phenomena. This should be done without presupposing that the people under observation are ignorant of the principle of contradiction, that they are animists or naturists, or that they are familiar with the genitive because they reckon kinship in the male line. Such ideas may be true, but the observations will always be far more valuable than the observer's interpretations.

Some have denied the existence of the principle of contradiction among 'primitives'. It appears rather that the categories work in strange ways in the human mind: where we, as Westerners, see contradiction, others do not – and that is all there is to it. Let us not forget that until the sixteenth century, following Plato, people believed that the reason humans could see was that the eye had the capacity to cast a luminous ray onto the objects seen, that the source of light was internal to the body. Only recently, established scientists were rejecting the thesis of Louis de Broglie on the grounds that it was 'impossible' for a theory of physics to be simultaneously based on particles and waves. The theory of colours has changed completely at least twice in the last sixty years. Many other concepts that we still deem contradictory will become reconcilable in the future. In fact, the play of the categories makes it possible to posit concepts, and everything comes down to the elaboration of concepts.[2] The notions of 'primitives', those on the basis of which their minds work, are intended, like our own, to frame concepts of force: an Australian aboriginal will never try to run down an emu without holding in his mouth a rock crystal. We regard the concept as wrong, but the Australian is convinced he is right: he has run down the emu *because* he had his rock crystal. Aristotle was wrong in thinking that his logical analysis of the Greek language could on its own constitute the analysis of a universal logic; but his vision was right when he said that the purpose of judgement was to form concepts. The study of a single society, however thorough, will never allow anyone to draw general conclusions on human cognition. Nevertheless, the discovery of new concepts and new categories makes a precious contribution to the history of human thought.

A really 'primitive' religion is nowhere to be found. The Australoid elements in the languages of Tierra del Fuego seem well established, and the [biological] anthropology of the inhabitants apparently also shows Australoid elements. The case of the Pygmies seems very complex. Certainly the Malacca Pygmies present nothing primitive; those from Gabon and the Ogooué [River] are problematic, for they display an astonishing mixture of primitive and non-primitive elements; the Ituri Pygmies [North-east Congo] dance true Australian *corroborees*. The Veddas speak Sinhalese, which immediately rules out any idea of 'primitiveness'. That leaves the Andaman Islands Pygmies studied by Radcliffe-Brown.[3] The Pygmies appear to be far more advanced than the Australian aborigines, who remain fairly primitive, though they are strung out between Aurignacian and Neolithic. The Australians possess polished stone tools, and their flaked stone tools belong to a microlithic or Neolithic type. Tylor thought he found Pre-Chellean tools among the Tasmanians, but they were tools in the process of manufacture. The excavations of Miss Bates in South-West Australia yield precise results: Upper Palaeolithic, almost Neolithic. Undoubtedly, phenomena can be found in those areas that are more elementary than in the great mass of humanity, but their 'primitive' character remains altogether relative. The Australian aborigines are as old as Europeans in relation to *Pithecanthropus*, and all peoples living today are equally old. Therefore, do not look for the primitive. Excavations carried out among the Todas in India, who for a long time were deemed the most primitive of men, have revealed a very fine bronze.

A civilisation can be defined by its greater or lesser wealth in objects, tools and ideas. A poor society keeps to the small number of tools and ideas that suffice for it. Above all, do not ask the question on a theoretical level, do not try to know whether the idea appears before the rite or the rite before the idea, or whether animism predates naturism or vice versa. Is totemism a universal phenomenon? The fact seems likely, but can everything be deduced from it? Certainly not. New problems and new concepts have gradually come to light. People ask whether the individual has priority over the collective. But how can we conceive of a society that is not made up of individuals? And on the other hand, how can we imagine a person who does not speak at least one language, or who does not have his ideas, which he believes to be highly original – while in fact they are those of everyone around him.

On the other hand, the study of the relationship between the individual and the collective should claim the sustained attention of the observer. In the case of shamanism for instance, the fieldworker will try to find out whether the shaman knows in advance the animal he will find on his journey to the other world, or the ancestral spirit who will choose him. If so, the implication is that the shaman obeys rules imposed upon him by a particular totem.[4]

In the same way as aesthetics can be defined by the notion of beauty, techniques defined by technical efficacy, economics by the notion of value, and law by the notion of property, *religious or magico-religious phenomena can be defined by the notion of the sacred.* Among all the forces that are called mystical – we shall say *mana* – a certain number are *mana* to such a degree that they are sacred; these constitute religion in the strict sense (*stricto sensu*) as opposed to the others which constitute religion in the broad sense (*lato sensu*). My neighbour sneezes and I say to him politely: 'Bless you'; this is religion in the broad sense. If I truly believe in the seriousness of the effect, that is in the danger caused by sneezing (which would signify the departure of the soul), then to say these words is equivalent to an insult: this is religion in the strict sense. The difference is comparable to that which separates light (*le clair*) and chiaroscuro (*clair-obscur*).

The notion of *mana* appears to be entirely universal. The *nkisi* of the inhabitants of Angola, described by Dapper,[5] is by no means different, nor is the *orenda* of the American Indians. It was Codrington who first reported the existence of the notion of *mana* among the Melanesians. But the word itself is a Polynesian technical term borrowed by the Melanesians of Banks Island. *Mana* means authority at the same time as it means a spiritual thing:[6] a thing or spirit is *mana* if it wields power over the individual, but this spirit is conceived of as somewhat material. The idea may seem to us contradictory, since we have arrived at the notion of a contradiction between mind and matter; but we should ponder the fact that the concept of matter has not always existed.

The *difficulties of observation* seem enormous. They arise firstly from the customary character of very many religious phenomena. Entire ceremonies can take place before the eyes of a foreigner, and he does not see them. In his book on the Betsileo[7] [of Madagascar] Father Dubois shows how the moment the native gets near his house everything becomes religious. Nothing inside the house is purely secular. Each object occupies a specific place; the father always sits at the back, on the right; the whole house is orientated. Likewise in the Chukchi hut, where everything is rigorously ordered. The observer should picture in his mind people who live all the year round like Polish Jews on the day of Yom Kippur: not a single action inside the house is religiously insignificant. The Roman house with its *penetralia* had a rather similar aspect. The simplest societies can be at the same time the most complex.

The importance of religious phenomena varies greatly from one society to another. Some societies who are very little given to religion can nevertheless display many religious scruples ([Latin] *religiones*). According to Festus (the text was probably borrowed from the Book of the Pontifices), *religiones stramenta erant* ('religions used to be bundles of straw') – they were taboos, and no doubt also the knots made of straw which tied together the parts of the Sublician bridge, i.e. the bridge the pontifices had to maintain across the Tiber river. *Religio* is linked to the same root as *religare*, 'to connect, bind': and it was a matter of bundles of straw.

In spite of the customary character of religion, it is nevertheless what is uppermost in the awareness of those who follow its practices. This is especially so among the lower classes, where a sense of the concrete counterbalances that sense of abstract notions. *Substantia*, 'substance', does not differ etymologically from *subsistentia*, 'subsistence, commissariat'.

The best *method of observation* is the philological method, which consists in gathering as many texts as possible. To this end one should acquire a good knowledge of the language, so as to be able to record its nuances. In general, observers of primitive religions fancy that in societies other than their own there are no nuances. In fact, everything consists in nuances – misunderstandings, innuendos, and word play crop up at every moment ('*You are Petrus ...*').[8] Religion is the area where the greatest gaps will be found depending on whether the inquiry has been conducted by means of extensive survey or in-depth local study.[9]

A method similar to the philological one consists of in-depth study of figurative documents. A study of symbolism can lead a very long way.[10]

Preferably, the researcher will proceed without using a questionnaire. When a native has sung in front of him or recited a text, he will go over the text eliciting from the informant an explanation of each word and each verse, asking for a complete exegesis of the text. It is a very long job. A myth contains legal, economic and technical matters. Let us not forget that the Iliad begins with a description of Achilles' shield.[11]

In the course of a local ceremony, study all those who participate; the ideal would be to obtain from each one an account of his action, the story that he sings or the role that he plays. If one does not know the language, the observations may still be interesting, but they will remain fragmentary. On the other hand, the knowledge of the language by itself will remain insufficient if the observer is unable to recognise the rhythmic formulae or verses, which serve as a mnemonic device.

Once all this public material has been gathered, one needs to find a magician who will provide a collection of his formulas, accompanied by the necessary commentary. Rather than by the foreign researcher, this work should be carried out by the recognised local technical expert. Ultimately, the ideal would be to transform the natives into authors rather than informants. Thus La Flesche, a pure Iroquois and member of the Bureau of American Ethnology for forty years, was assigned by the Osage Indians to publish the entire Osage rituals. Hewitt, who revealed to us the notion of *orenda*, is an Iroquois.[12]

In matters of religion, more than in any other field of study, certain types of information can be obtained only after a long period of intimate contact. Hence the need for fieldwork that is lengthy and often very demanding when large tribes or nations are concerned.

Material records call for as many comments as possible, each such record should never be anything but the occasion and the starting point for psychological enquiry. Thus, no painting should ever be collected without requesting the myths to which it relates, and without asking the essential questions about technique and aesthetics. One of the effects of the religious phenomenon is that it always carries with it an aesthetic phenomenon. The investigation should of course be supported by drawings, photographs, films, etc.

Do not be afraid of repetitions, intersections and overlaps. The same story will appear repeatedly in myths, objects and divination. But it is from this very repetition that the characteristic aspect of the society under scrutiny will slowly emerge. The spirit of a civilisation constitutes a whole made up of functions; it is an integration which is different from adding together the whole set of the parts; this integration can be approached only through multiple overlaps.

The fieldworker should study each of the special religious groups – magicians, diviners, high-ranking officials in the society of men – as well as the various religious classes. Among the Maori, the people are divided into the people of three 'baskets' (the same expression is found in Buddhism): at the top, the *warekura* or house of secrets, the house of *ariki* or aristocrats, 'those who know the secrets'; their inferiors, the simple *tohunga* who know fewer secrets, and the common people who know even fewer still. When one establishes the presence of several levels of initiation, each level needs to be studied.

The catechism is perhaps one of the best written books in French, but it is not the whole religion. It will be interesting to gather the text of the catechism, from the mouth of an initiate; it will be even more interesting to find the authors of the catechism.

From another point of view, the researcher may have happened to be present at a certain ritual held by a certain clan; the task is then to find out whether or not in the neighbouring clan another ritual took place, perhaps complementary to the first. The observer should strive to be thorough, to see all the actors, to know all the rituals and all the myths. To achieve this, he should work through the groups, the ages, the sexes and the classes; through private cults and public ones; and through locations. A good catalogue of sacred locations will provide solid foundations for subsequent research. A religious calendar is indispensable. Thus the cult of the Pleiades is very widespread in the southern tropics, where the ascent of the Pleiades marks changes of season. Buddhism is divided into two seasons. Among the Eskimo, the winter religion differs from the summer religion.

Only when the investigation is complete, when a general catalogue has been drawn up, when all the texts, objects and files describing the various rituals have been brought together – only then will the observer be in a position to speak of the religiosity, the soul, the gods, the relations between these, or of superstitions, contradictions, the absence or presence of a sense of religion.

Some of the finest words concerning religion come from the mouth of the last but one of the Moriori, who used to live on Chatham Island west of New Zealand. The Moriori population was decimated by the influenza epidemics brought to them from outside. In order to look after them better, the Governor of New Zealand took the survivors onto the main island where they could be fed more easily. The last but one was a priest. 'My fellow countrymen are all dead,' he said, 'because we were all very *tapu*; and once in exile, we could no longer observe our *tapu*.' This is the state of mind of the martyr who lets himself be tortured rather than renounce his faith.

Religious phenomena can be divided into three groups: religion in the strict sense, religion in the broad sense, with magic and divination; and lastly, superstititions. Religion in the strict sense is characterised by the presence of notions of the sacred, properly speaking, and of obligations, exactly as jural phenomena are characterised: one is not a man before one has been circumcised. The notion of obligation does not enter into religion in the broad sense that includes magic and divination: you are not obliged to have your cards read. However, you expect a certain number of rites; you know that the queen of hearts and the knave of clubs each have a precise role. All this is fixed. Magic and divination can have their codes. Lastly, like a big halo surrounding the nuclei formed by magic and religion, we find folklore, or popular beliefs. Popular beliefs exist even among the Australian aborigines. They are what are called superstitions – a term that is not always apt; an example is carrying a potato about one's person so that joint disease makes a mistake and enters the potato rather than one's knee. This kind of popular magic is not the magic of magicians.

There are other ways of dividing up religious phenomena: into rites and practices as against myths and representations; and finally into structures and organisation. There is religious organisation everywhere, in the same way as there is jural organisation. Further divisions include those into age categories; into secret societies; into priests and laymen; into clans, and into totems.

Be that as it may, for every category of social phenomena one always finds a group of people with their practices and representations. The description is complete when the three orders [group, behaviour, ideas] have been observed exhaustively and when the relations between the three stand out clearly.

Finally, thanks to these divisions and by studying the organisation of the group that carries out a particular rite, one can determine the intensity and spread of each religion: tribal cults; national cults, when the society is made up of several tribes – for instance, the festivals arranged by rota in the Sudan; likewise, among the Pueblo everything happens as in our own countryside where fairs pass from one place to the next. Lastly, international religions.

It has also been possible to record the adaptation of Christianity to shamanic religions and its adoption by the Shoshone and Sioux clans.[13] The spread, which took place instantaneously, led to massacres all the way from the border of New Mexico to the Canadian border and beyond, and in the Missouri valley.

Special cults can spread over considerable distances.

Finally, one should distinguish private cults and public ones, and among private cults, those that are strictly individual. Private cults are often as obligatory as the others.

Religious Phenomena in the Strict Sense

Starting from external facts that can be seen and recorded, we proceed to the study of mental and moral phenomena. Let us hasten to add that, although it is the most mental of all [social] phenomena, religion is not only mental. Quite the opposite, in fact, since the obligatory nature of religious facts is expressed above all by the observance of rites, both positive and negative. The fieldworker should record these rites and ask for their explanation. Thus the first step in the enquiry consists in recording phenomena that are obvious – namely, social practices. Later, an attempt should be made to trace the relations that bring together different rites and thereby correspond to cults. One of the commonest errors, in fact, is to separate religious practices one from another in order to study them in isolation, whereas all the rites are components of one cult, just as all the myths are components of one mythology. The existence of particular cults will come to light via study of the various groups that carry out specific rites at different moments of the year and in different places.

Two methods should be used for observing religious cults: the religious calendar (recording the various rituals occurring during the year[14]), and the history of each group of individuals. The life histories that the fieldworker will have sought from each informant will now serve as useful guides. As far as possible, interviews should be held not only with old and young, but also with women; the sociology of women is practically uncharted territory, in spite of efforts in this direction by Malinowski and his pupils.

All these religious phenomena have a more or less obligatory character: thus a young boy will not be admitted to the adult category before his initiation. But this obligatory character does not lead to constant uniformity; families are more or less large, clans are more or less segmented, hence the [religious] societies are more or less obvious and more or less permanent.

An initial distinction allows one to separate public cults from private ones, such as that of the family or individual. Individual cults are numerous; in particular, part of the life of the young people during their initiation rites is dedicated to them. However, it should not be forgotten that a great number of essentially public cults, for instance the worship of the king, are often at the same time extraordinarily secret. We don't know all the secrets of the court of Abomey, nor those of the Chinese court, the most ancient in the world. Moreover, very many private cults are rigorously mandatory. The Hindus used to distinguish between domestic and public cults – the division adopted here in fact repeats a division in the Sanskrit ritual codes, but they regarded the private cults as no less obligatory than the public ones. All Hindus must have their head shaven, leaving only one tuft of hair; otherwise they lose caste membership and cease to be Hindu. Lastly, some cults are public-private while others are private-public. Each morning, the ordinary Hindu is required to make offerings to his domestic fire, and similarly the Brahmin each day is obliged to make more significant offerings to the public fire. The division nevertheless remains a useful one, for it immediately brings the observer into contact with the performers of the ritual.

Public Cults

The totality of the public cults of a tribe is constituted by the sum of the cults practised by the various clans that compose the tribe. Within this first division into public and private, we classify cults according to their more or less elementary character. The most elementary form of public cult does indeed seem to be totemism.

Totemism[15]

We cannot go back to anything that is more elementary. This does not mean totemism is elementary in essence. The North American Indians have a very developed totemism; while reaching great religious heights, it has nonetheless retained forms that are still very elementary. In South America, each day researchers find new totems that are very advanced.

We shall not debate the issue of whether or not all humanity began with totemism. It is impossible to establish whether or not the Chelleans, and above all the pre-Chelleans, knew any such cult. From the Aurignacians onwards its presence appears more likely, for the very many pictures of animals dating from that era certainly relate to cults. The Australian aborigines were no doubt Aurignacians and to some extent Neolithic; the Tasmanians were Aurignacians.

Normally, totemism is not a cult practised by the whole tribe, but one practised by at least two moieties and generally by several phratries, or even by simple clans which are no longer organised into phratries. Totemism is a *segmentary* cult. We belong to the same tribe; I am wolf and you are bear. The cult of the tribe includes a cult of the wolf and a cult of the bear. Rome had a cult that was clearly totemic: it was the cult of wolves and of the mother she-wolf. As an element of the public cult totemism remains segmentary and *relatively amorphous*: the species is equally consubstantial with all the individuals. Exactly as we are all men, within the phratry we are all wolves and equal as such. A tribe in the Sudan follows a totemic cult of crocodiles: if a crocodile dies, a member of the clan will die, but no one knows who it will be.

Totemism can take very varied forms, and sometimes very complicated ones. Some of the documents by Rivers on Melanesia, where the author believed totemism to be absent, prove on the contrary the presence of this cult: totemism was linked with social organisation on the one hand, and on the other with the form of certain butterflies corresponding to the souls of initiates from different age grades.

Even in cases where it seems as well integrated into general cults as it is for instance among the Pueblo, the totemic cult retains aspects which appear to us very elementary.

The question of the distribution of totemism will not detain us any longer [than that of its primordiality].[16] It is impossible to prove that societies where totemism is now found to be absent did not practise this cult in the past. Moreover, to find totemism does not eliminate the possibility that it was introduced from outside, in one form or another, coming from such and such a place. Following Frazer's study, the number of societies belonging to the domain of ethnography who know nothing of totemism grows smaller every day. One of the few large homogeneous groups who perhaps have very little totemism is the Eskimo, whose level of civilisation corresponds to Upper Palaeolithic. The whole of North America knows totemism. South America seems deeply impregnated with totemism, as does a large part of Africa. Delafosse's discussion of African totemism seems to be one of his few mistakes; when it is expressed in the form of an alliance, totemism is not thereby eliminated. According to Father Trilles,[17] the Pygmies are apparently not without this cult. In Madagascar, there is no totemism among the Malagasy, but there is among the Sakalava who are very close to the Malagasy. We know for certain of the presence of totemism among the Sakai and the Semang of Malacca. The Andaman Islanders have only one public cult, and it is the worship of two animals. In New Caledonia totemism was for a long time searched for in vain, but the documentation of M. Leenhardt brings us proof of its existence. In Indo-China a certain number of instances are known. In Polynesia, the cult scarcely exists except in Samoa and a few other places, but there is no reason to suppose that it did not exist in the past; the Polynesians apparently belong to the same level of civilisation as European Neolithic, and it is possible that, once having reached this stage, they abandoned a certain number of their practices.

While the distribution of totemism remains an issue of secondary importance, the study of the various forms the cult can take appears, in contrast, to be very important. It seems in fact that it should allow us to establish a certain number of civilisational areas. Thus the altogether remarkable presence of the bird totem in Melanesia, where it is the leading totem, would explain a certain Polynesian totemism: the term *manou* attached to the Melanesian totem corresponds to a Polynesian term meaning 'bird', as well as 'kite'.

Nearly always totemism appears in the form of prohibitions. The oldest records we possess on this topic are those on Egyptian totemism;[18] Herodotus notes the kinship of the people of the *nomē* [administrative division] with the animals of a certain species.

Elsewhere, the totem is revealed. The whole of North America and North Asia follow shamanistic customs whereby everyone goes in quest of his totem;

whether it be a collective or individual quest matters little – the North American Indians know which animal can be their totem and go to look for it.

Let us now discuss totemism as such. *Totemism is the cult of a species*, usually animal (but there exist aberrant totems), of an *animal or vegetal species homonymous to the group*, that is to say bearing the same name. One group, one species, one name: and this name is a name for kinsfolk; that is to say, all the members of the clan or phratry believe themselves to be of the same nature as the totemic animals. For instance, among the Cherokee Indians, in the bear phratry there is a tortoise sub-clan: if I belong to this sub-clan, I have all the qualities of the tortoise and all the qualities of the bear; I am tortoise-bear; all the clans of the bear phratry have the quality of bear in addition to their own specific quality.

The totem is generally the object of a cult; in the case of totemic religion, it is necessarily the object of a cult. There is no totem without a cult corresponding at once to a name and to a clan. In the absence of a clan, the observer is confronted with a theriomorphic cult, an animal cult. For example, the prohibition on pork observed by Jews does not mean that they worship the pig; it does not mean that the pig was once a totem for them, or even that it was the totem of their neighbours. In contrast, the cult of the she-wolf at Rome is a totemic cult, since a clan bears the name.

This being clear, the observer could be faced with tribal totems (albeit this is fairly rare), or with totems corresponding to age classes (in the Slavic world, the falcon was the emblem of an age class, not a clan); but the commonest situation is that of phratry or clan totems. An effort should be made to draw up a list of the totems: tribal ones (when relevant), phratry ones and clan ones. Throughout North America, clans are very often strictly numbered and follow each other in order; and within the clan numbers are given to each individual, exactly as in a mobilised regiment. The list of totems cannot be completed without an exhaustive visit to the tribe.

Then come the sub-totems: family totems and even individual totems, which often form unbroken chains. Observing something like this in New Guinea, Haddon spoke of 'linked totems'. Thus it becomes possible in some cases to construct a whole cosmology by starting from each individual. Among the Australian Arunta, the matter is even more complicated: there is a totem for the living person, a totem for his departed soul, and a totem for his reincarnating essence, each with a distinct name determined by myth, location and cult.[19]

Totemism therefore can reach down to the level of the individual; such is the case in Melanesia for instance, where the youths, according to the stages of their initiation, conquer various forms of butterfly. In North America individual totems are widespread. Radin says that among the Winnebago, a grandmother orders her grandson to go into the forest where he will find such and such a totem. If he does not find it, it is because the grandmother, or the grandson, has made a mistake.[20]

Totems conferred at the time of initiation and corresponding to age classes may or may not be integrated in the clans. In Africa, the leopard is the emblem of the kings. Some totems remain the emblems of large societies of aristocrats, or of secret societies; the lion is the emblem of the Negus [Ethiopian sovereign].

Finally, there are caste totems, which we have already met while investigating social morphology [see Chapter 3]. The fieldworker will meet them again in the present context, which will allow further progress in the previous study.

In each case, the observer should study the cult both in its positive and negative aspects, noting whether the women have totems. Among the Ashanti of the Gold Coast, where women are part of a totemic clan, there can sometimes be a real opposition between the matriline and the patriline. Since land is transmitted in the matriline only, a man cannot sell property belonging to the mother's side. At most he could cede it to his mother's uterine nephew. The researcher should seek out objects specially linked to the cult, such as the penis sheath in New Caledonia, recording drawings and tattoos. Such special objects, marked with the totem, are often numerous and very significant – for example the *churinga* throughout Northern Australia. They can be renewed in the course of successive initiations.

At the same time the fieldworker should try to collect the *myth* attached to the totem, as completely as possible, for all the locations traversed by the totem or the troop – for it was already a troop that formed the totem (many examples can be found in Arunta mythology and in Kakadu mythology[21]). Very often, the myth is a geographical one, mentioning all the features of the landscape. Often, the countryside was prefigured by the ancestors. One should study in detail the sacred places where the troops gave rise to swarms of souls or animals. In this way the positive rites are firmly attached to the land and to individuals.

The researcher should next observe the *negative rites*: prohibitions on eating or killing the totem; special customs, even for outsiders, who have killed an animal whose body may have sheltered your external soul. In many cases there is such respect for the totem that only the people of the totem can give the authorisation to eat it. Thus in Australia it is the clan elders who initiate the youth to the food constituting their totems. The problem of the reincarnation of the soul in the totem implies a prohibition on breaking the bones of the animal being eaten – or it may oblige one to do so. Certain parts of the animal's body may be edible to some, but completely prohibited to others.

Respect for blood is very generally observed: a man cannot have sexual intercourse with a woman belonging to the same totem. The father is usually responsible for the blood of the child vis-à-vis his wife's relatives.

Next comes the study of the power of individuals over the totem: yearly ceremonies for the multiplication of the totem, what Frazer calls 'the division of magical labour'. The study of the spatial distribution of the totem also arises in this context.

The totem can play a major part in bodily decoration. It is often the real equivalent of an emblem, for example among the Masai of East Africa, where the emblem is a property mark; it is also the sign of a special power.[22] Study the ritual of ceremonies involving marking with an emblem.

Among the Marind Anim [of New Guinea] one can observe something rare, namely the totemic sacrifice, from which Robertson Smith thought he could deduce the whole theory of sacrifice.[23]

Next come oral rites and dances representing the totem's incarnations, which are often distinctive. Thus, among the Papuans, each individual is precisely located.

The essential element in totemic rituals nearly always consists in *initiation*. The study of initiation will lead to a study of masks and of the hierarchy of totems. An Arunta man reaches full initiation into his own totem only towards the age of forty. Initiation can be conducted by the people of the totem for the benefit of outsiders – I belong to the bear totem and you will not be allowed to eat bear meat until I have authorised you to do so – and also for the benefit of the younger members of the same totem. Generally, the great positive rites of initiation occur at fixed times in the year. These rites are not one-day festivals; they are sessions at which the various clans gather together. Once the whole tribe is assembled, each clan, i.e. each totem, does for all the others what the others do for each one. Sometimes the ritual assumes a private character, but generally all this activity takes on the form of totemic representation or totemic drama. Among the Zuñi of Central America totemic masks parade. The initiation ritual usually corresponds to a repetition of the myth, showing two aspects: one is more or less secret, the other more or less public. Some representations are strictly prohibited to women and children, while others are organised specifically for them. Such spectacles will normally point the researcher in the direction of the myth. To represent something is to represent oneself as being such and such; one represents (*vorstellen* in German) the totem's adventures. Very often, initiation entails processions that are real pilgrimages. Thus all the stories about the caterpillar clan are rigorously acted out by the Arunta on the patch of ground used for the drama.

The question of the external soul will prompt the study of the animals in which the individual's soul resides, the study of the trees related to the animal species, and the study of the various sanctuaries. Record also how totemism relates to the notion of food; to artistic ideas; to dance, to war, and to social organisation in general. The king has his personal totem, which is often the sun. (Solar rajas and lunar rajas in India).

Finally, study the relations between the various tribal myths. Thus in Central America, throughout the Pueblo-Hopi-Zuñi group, the totemic myth is always the history of the origin of the world. It tells of the emergence of the clans from a hole in the Earth, and fixes the order in which they appeared. The totemic ancestor may finally be identified with the civilising hero and, eventually, with the High God.

Major Tribal Cults[24]

The French school of sociology has been criticised for exaggerating the importance of totemism, thereby being led to ignore the existence of any other form of public cult. This criticism is unwarranted. Totemism simply appeared to us as a convenient means to study a certain number of issues. In fact, all the societies we know of have a tribal cult. To determine whether this cult derives from totemism or the other way round is a question on which the researcher engaged in direct observation does not have to reach a verdict during fieldwork.

Initiation rites rank among the most important tribal rituals. A clan cannot initiate its members on its own, for mixed in with initiation are other rituals that go far beyond the scope of clan cults and require the participation of the whole tribe. Thus mixed in with circumcision there is the cult of puberty and also the ritual that gives access to women; initiation to manhood coincides with initiation to marriageability. Part of these rites consists in segregating the youths, often for months on end, from the women of their clans, and especially from their mothers. They are then introduced to the women from other clans whom they can marry, first at a distance, then closer, and finally very closely. But there is one woman they are never introduced to, namely their future mother-in-law.

Initiation is made up of three distinct moments: separation, introduction to masculine life, return to ordinary social existence (*rentrée*). The central part of the ritual nearly always corresponds to a representation of the myth of death and rebirth; the children are swallowed by a monster whose voice is symbolised by the bull-roarer; they are born again as men, and clan members.

Initiation begins with a period of isolation imposed on the whole group of boys; this is how the age classes in the society of men are formed. The duration of isolation varies from a few weeks to several years. Initiation can even last throughout life, for instance in the case of secret societies. On Malekula [New Hebrides] there are about seventeen or eighteen grades; each of them takes three to four years to attain, and each step involves vast expenditure.[25]

Relations with the dead play an important part in initiation rites. Very often, the young man's soul becomes complete at this point. The Australian term for initiation is translated into English as 'making young men'; they are literally made, almost manufactured. The purpose of one ceremony among the Kurnai is to open their fists and to untie their feet; they are taught how to breathe; once the ceremony is over, the youths are men. An Arunta myth describes the same process: this is what the Ancestors did before they were men.

Initiation is often marked by bodily mutilations: tattoos, removal of the lower incisors (which in some cases is linked to a cult of water); insertion of labrets in the lips; circumcision, infibulation, and so on.

The observer should study in detail who it is that applies the tattoos and deformations. This raises the fundamental notion of godparenthood. It is well known that in canon law kinship by baptism is seen as equal to kinship by blood; a godfather is not allowed to marry his goddaughter. The same applies here: there exists kinship based on godparenthood and kinship based on initiation. All the youths initiated at the same time are regularly brothers, at least in Black Africa. In Papua, a real institution of fosterage obliges the young man to live with his uncle – his mother's brother, who is father of his future wife; he serves as wife to his mother's brother.[26]

The initiates' camp is situated away from the village, following the usual rule that sacred places are normally situated in the bush (except in North America where the sacred place is nearly always the public square in the village). The village, the camp and the bush form distinct worlds. The whole of Africa has its sacred woods, which are often mere copses. Any Guinean landscape consists of these woods and these caves.

In the camp, the youths are gradually initiated by their elders into the tribal rites; true representations are staged for their benefit, accompanied by all the revelations they involve. Things that were taboo for them become less and less so, while they themselves become more and more taboo for the non-initiates; they cannot be seen by the women and must not speak to them. Food prohibitions correspond to each period [of the initiation].

The youths learn a secret language. They are taught the comedy of things (*la comédie des choses*). In Australia, certain very curious tests consist in putting to death an individual who laughs in front of certain hilarious things; one must keep a straight face in front of the most comical things, as well as in front of the most tragic ones. The rite of the blanket (the young man is swung, thrown into the air, and caught back in a blanket) corresponds to a real ascent to heaven. Initiation involves one whole component of mystifications and ordeals, and a whole aspect of ragging which Durkheim describes well in *The Elementary Forms of Religious Life*. In the course of their retreat, the youths also receive moral and technical education; military and civic education; and aesthetic education; they learn how to dance.

Initiation into the society of the living is accompanied by initiation into the society of the dead, an initiation into the future life. Measures are taken at this point to insure the youths for and against death. One of the aims of initiation is often to constitute an external soul for the individual; his teeth are deposited in a sanctuary, or in a particular tree, where his external soul will henceforth reside. Finally, the exit from the initiation ritual, or from part of it, is generally crowned by the initiate's marriage.

Where matriarchy is present, *the initiation of girls* is more salient than the initiation of youths. Phallic rites here play an important role, and the crowning of the ritual is often a public defloration – an element belonging at once to religion and to marriage.

When initiation rites are performed without distinction for all the young people of one sex or both sexes, they normally correspond to initiation into the *cult of a high god* – just as circumcision, among the Jews, is a sign of the covenant with God ever since Moses. During fieldwork researchers should not ask themselves about the relative antiquity of this cult. Some peoples may have known it and then forgotten it, while others may have adopted it at a certain point. These phenomena could only be dated with the aid of precise texts.

A hierarchy of the gods is to be found, for example in Australia, corresponding to the hierarchy of phratries: among the Warramunga, Volonga is so to speak half a high god, the god of the cold moiety, and there is a complementary god of heat, who is less known. The cult of the High God is found in a number of so-called primitive societies – which in fact are not in the least primitive – for instance in Polynesian societies. The Polynesians, however, separated from the Asian world at a period probably later than the Bronze Age. The question that arises here concerns national cults and national secrets. For example, some have said that Yo, the high god of Polynesia, corresponds to Yahveh. In fact, Yo can be identified with the cult of the house of secrets, the *warekura*. This is the cult of the final initiation, which teaches that beyond all the gods there is still Yo, in the same way as after the highest grade in the society of men there is still one more.

The cult of Yo is probably a caste cult, and may predate the *cult of kings*. The cult of the High God is often conflated with the royal cult. Where there exists an institution of kingship, one will nearly always find a cult of the High God: in Dahomey, Mahou, god of justice, is also the god of Heaven. In Polynesia, this identity between the Prince and Heaven seems to be complete. In many cases, the king cannot touch the ground; he is carried in a palanquin or he wears special shoes (the queen of Madagascar, the kinglets of Guinea). Frazer spoke of the relations between the cult of the king and the cult of the spirit of vegetation; this is true, but the relations between the cult of Heaven and the cult of the king seem even more important. A king is always the king of somebody; thus the observer will sometimes record a whole series of kings. The cult of Nyankompon in Gold Coast, which offers some parallels with the cult of Christ, is above all the cult of the king as a person.

The study of the cult of the High God will often be more difficult than the study of initiation rituals, in which a large part of the population is involved. In this case, a few isolated priests hold on to their secrets, and the ceremonies are private. It will be necessary to persuade the great court diviner, the high priest, or the leader of the eunuchs to grant an interview.

Very often, the cult of the High God is weak; the god is adored, but people only pay him a distant homage. Thus in Rome, where Jupiter was the Father God, people sacrificed far more to the lesser gods.

In studying the royal cult, one should note the following: the royal totems (leopard, lion); the various royal insignia (headwear, shoes, sceptre); all the prohibitions the king must obey (the food he cannot eat, the places he cannot enter, etc.); and all the prohibitions surrounding the king. Very often the king cannot be wounded; no one may see his blood flowing; he cannot be ill and cannot age, for the strength of the whole nation is incarnated in him. This accounts for the putting to death of the king, or for his obligatory suicide.[27] The name of the king can be conflated with that of the great gods. Finally, the women of the royal family generally have a place apart in society. Particular efforts should be made to define the role of the queen mother, which is often very important.

However small the society under scrutiny, it may nevertheless be linked to a fairly large number of other societies, which have in common an *international cult*. Such a cult moves in rotation from one village to the next, and festivals return at fixed intervals to specific locations. Examples are the Dogon in French Sudan and the Pueblos in Central America. Among the Kwakiutl of North America, the god presiding over initiation is a high god of rock crystal and thunder, who lives at the bottom of the sea and who is in addition the god of the congregation of cannibal princes; for in order to be a prince, one has to eat human flesh regularly.

The observation of these phenomena, which are often quite complex, will not be unproblematic. Consider a series of totemic rituals observed during initiation, noting the order in which they unfold; this order normally reproduces the whole history of the totems. The clan may also move so as to go and celebrate its ceremonies in each of its sanctuaries; in that case note all the movements and the order in which they take place. Study therefore on the one hand the festivals and their sequence, and on the other the sanctuaries. The information thus gathered may overlap, but it will never be superfluous.

Besides the cults of clans, totems, age classes and social classes, all of them having precise locations, there are *cults of places (lieux)* as places. A list should be made of the sanctuaries, including even the simple stone marking the crossing of paths: sanctuaries of town or village, sanctuaries of spirits; places haunted by a dead person, which may or may not be abandoned when the memory of that person has vanished. Sanctuaries of clans; the external souls of the living, and the souls of the dead who as yet have not reincarnated dwell in some particular mysterious corner of a wood.[28] Then there is the soul of the forest, in which the souls of the dead find refuge; erected stones; great rocks to which regular sacrifice is made; drum-trees: in certain forests, several sanctuaries are formed by large trees split from top to bottom and hollowed so as to form drums. River spirits, bush animals, spirits of the directions at sea or in the lagoon ...

Agrarian cults imply agriculture, or, more precisely, horticulture. Their presence will be detected by the study of the agrarian calendar and the sequence of tasks in the fields. Record, with commentaries, all the formulas accompanying the various moments of the agricultural year:[29] sowing, germination, ripening, harvest (the last sheaf); the consumption of grain, the making of fermented drinks, the cult of beer ... The study of activities such as these is endless. There are also cults of wild animals associated with agriculture. The Middle Ages still knew of the hound of rye and the wolf of wheat.

Close to the agrarian cults are the *cults of domesticated animals*, which are the norm among all pastoral peoples. Examples are the cult of the cow among the

Peul or among the Toda in India.[30] In ancient Egypt, some major theriomorphic cults were local cults at the same time. This can often be the case.

One will also find great *nature cults*: cults of the rain and sun, of the wind, of day and night, of cold and heat. Here there is a very significant play on oppositions.

Astronomical cults are very rare except for one, which is universal: the cult of the Pleiades. The whole of Polynesia and the whole of North America possess excellent knowledge of astronomy. The Maya of Central America, as is well known, had solved considerable astronomical problems; the positioning of the Astronomers' Tower in Chichén Itzá [in Yucatan] is perfect.

Finally, among the public cults are to be classified the cult of men and the cult of the law (Mahou among the Ewe of Togo); the cult of kings and chiefs; the cult of peace and war; the rites of alliance; and the rites of the assembly. In actual fact things are more complicated: all public cults are to some extent private cults, and all private cults are to some extent obligatory. A Brahmin who does not light his fire every morning will soon be stoned by the villagers, for it is his role to worship privately his own private fire and not only to honour the communal fire. An individual who does not practise his private cult is blamed by the community; and the society that requires the strictest observance of private cults will be the most liberal one when it comes to public cults.

Private Cults

The distinction between public and private cults is a useful one for the observer, who is thereby enabled to classify and to understand better some of the occasions that have been witnessed. However, it should not prevent one from noting the public and obligatory character of certain private cults: the Midsummer's Day's knot that the peasant hangs over his door after harvest is part of a private ritual, but the gesture is a public one. It is similar for Palm Sunday. Throughout the Ewe world (Togo, Dahomey), the cult of *legba* is obligatory. Everyone must offer sacrifices at fixed dates on the phallic altar incarnating his guardian spirit, which is also his soul, etc. The cult of these minor gods, and of individual totems, corresponds to the cult of the *genius* at Rome. We are still familiar with the cult of the guardian angel or of the patron saint; they are cults that one may or may not practise, but which one is not free to reject. The same applies for all the deified dead, for the cult of the male genius and the female genius. Finally, many private cults are carried out in public. Examples are the cult of fountains, rocks, crossroads and precipices; marriages with trees, life pledges; all greetings, prostrations, etc.

Domestic Cults

Among private cults the most essentially private ones are domestic cults. To study them, follow precisely the plan of the manuals of Sanskrit domestic ritual. The relevant documents are very complete in the *sūtra* text that we possess, and go back to the third century BC:[31] the rituals of birth, initiation, marriage and death. In this connection, the autobiographical method will prove really useful. Ten or so native autobiographies will give a fairly complete picture of these rites.

Birth. Note beliefs concerning conception, sterility, impregnation, and reincarnation; the whole ritual of childbirth, and the taboos that everyone must observe at that time. The couvade is mentioned as late as [the thirteenth-century French prose romance] *Aucassin et Nicolette*: 'the king was lying with child'. Description of the birth ritual: the role of the mother-in-law, and of the mother; what is done with the placenta and the umbilical cord? Are knots untied and fires relighted? What are the taboos surrounding the birth? Do not omit the study of stillbirth; what is done with the dead body? How is the mother purified? Beliefs concerning stillborn babies, and women who die in childbirth. Recognising reincarnated children: people often know beforehand that it is so and so's turn to be reborn. (Reincarnation is generally far less frequent for women than for men; very frequently, women are not reincarnated at all.) The lifting of taboos on the mother, and on the father.[32] The introduction of the child into the family often forms part of the ceremonies during which a name is given to the newborn baby. Who gives the name? In Egypt, the father's family gives the names to girls and the mother's family imposes their names on boys. The whole question of reincarnation and the person is raised by the forename: how the name is chosen; the involvement of divination (the *Fa* in Dahomey); the study of the whole corpus of names: nicknames, names intended to trick spirits, secret names.[33]

The child's *education.* Prohibitions concerning the father and mother up to weaning; the wearing of amulets, etc. Usually, the little boy stays with his mother, impregnated with feminine substance, until initiation, when he makes the transition from a mixed being to a male being. From the moment the child can eat by himself, what are the prohibitions on what he eats, on what he does, etc.? The male child often observes no taboo whatever concerning any female until initiation, which will make him an extremely chaste being, so to speak; the necessary revelations are introduced at the time of puberty.

The obligatory division of the sexes can go as far as the observance of very strict taboos with respect to all older persons of the opposite sex. In New Caledonia, a young man cannot speak with any older woman, including his sisters, but he can speak to younger ones. Initiation can bring about changes of name for men – either a new public name, or even a new nickname.

The position of *twins* varies fundamentally between societies. In one, they are killed; in another, they are deified. They may be more or less identified with the misdeeds of the sun or other gods. The American North West takes them as species of salmon-gods on account of the extreme fertility of salmon.

When pursued on the biographical level and applied to women, this study can point one towards those women's societies, of which we know so little, apart from their existence.

Marriage rites will already have been studied when dealing with matrimonial ceremonies. These rites, as in our own societies, have a legal value; it is only the Civil Code that distinguishes between civil and religious marriage. One knows that this distinction does not yet exist in England, where a purely religious marriage is valid for the State. Let us recall here the importance of betrothal, for which the ritual can be considerable. Societies that practise ritual defloration will require that the fiancée be a virgin. In Samoa the public defloration of the bride is obligatory. At the time of marriage, it can happen that the husband is taboo to his wife; the taboo can endure in some cases, for instance in the myth of Psyche, and to some degree in the myth of Lohengrin.[34] Rites of appropriation of the husband by the wife and of the wife by the husband.

The *ritual of family life* very often merges with the ritual of the sexes: if a war party has failed, it is blamed on the women who have stayed in the village, who are deemed to have been unfaithful. In the American North West and in Polynesia, when the husbands go to sea on expeditions, the wives go and use paddles on the shore. One can here gauge the relative importance of religious phenomena within the family cults. In some cases the husband may have to carry out cults which benefit his son, but which do not belong to the father's clan; who will carry them out? The study of the relations between generations raises problems that are often complicated. Relations with the parents-in-law. The most powerful generation is not necessarily the oldest, for instance in the institution of *vasu* in the Fiji Islands. *Vasu* means 'the rich one' and refers here to the sister's son, who has a right to the riches of all his mother's brothers. In the eyes of the mother's brother, the nephew is a kind of god. Elsewhere, it is the mother's brother who is a kind of god for his nephew. One therefore has to record the position of everyone relative to everyone else within the household.

The ritual of marriage break-up: through divorce, or through death ... (position of the widow or widower). Certain occasional rites will be held to expiate sins, or for the fulfilment of wishes, for instance on recovery from an illness, or in the course of pilgrimages, etc.

Death ritual[35] has already been mentioned while discussing public cults, but it needs to be studied equally in the present context. The fieldworker should distinguish clearly between the various stages of the death ceremony proper and ancestral rituals. Some societies have an ancestor cult while others neglect this, but all societies have death rituals. The great mistake of the euhemerism latent in the science of religions is to think that all the souls of the dead are deified. In fact, there is no god who has not been imaged in the guise of a man, but this is a way of representing him. The Greeks knew of seventeen tombs for Jupiter [Zeus], who is however the nature god par excellence, Father god, god of Heaven and husband of Juno [Hera]. Preoccupation with doctrines should never affect the observation of rituals. The named or unnamed ancestors are the recipients of more or less public cults, while death rituals correspond to a taking leave of the deceased. Undoubtedly, many men from the past have become gods, but many gods have been represented as men, and many have also been represented in the shape of animals, plants, and so on.

When recording death ceremonies, distinguish three phases: the provisional departure of the soul; the first burial; the second burial or funerary service, and sometimes even the third.

Death corresponds to the departure of the soul. The soul escapes. Record the position of the dying person, and the lamentations (which are obligatory) and often begin well before the moment of death. Sometimes, one of those present, chosen from among the eldest, inhales the soul at the moment of its departure. The washing of the corpse, vigils, macerations [of the mourners], etc. The Bible contains long descriptions of such rituals. Death can be the occasion for ransacking and totally destroying everything contained in the deceased's house, even when the death did not occur in it; all the belongings of the deceased must accompany him, for they contain his soul. This accounts for the wealth of grave goods from the Neolithic era onwards. The prohibitions falling immediately on close relatives will indicate the exact structure of the family: those who mourn are the relatives from the two clans in their entirety, not the nation.

The body is buried inside the house or in the courtyard, or else it is carried to the cemetery. Sometimes the corpse is exposed on a platform and dried out by the sun or by fire. The funerary meal can go as far as endocannibalism, which allows the merging of the first and second funerary services.[36]

Then come the rites carried out between the death and the second burial. Australia, Melanesia and Papua practise the cult of the corpse: it is obligatory for the widow to stay beside the corpse throughout the interval between the first and second funerary services. In parts of the world practising headhunting (Eastern India and Burma) one will find the obligation to practise the vendetta before the second burial; the second burial cannot be celebrated until one can place a hunted head beside that of the deceased.

The second funerary service usually corresponds to the final leave-taking of the soul of the deceased, which has been transformed. The rites that now take place repeat those of the first service, but they have a definitive character. In Sanskrit, the soul is first a ghost (in India, those who have not been given a double burial, or those who were so evil while alive that it was impossible to transform them into protective ancestors, form a separate class). The delay between the first and second burial can last one to three years. Until the second burial the deceased is still present and may haunt the living. During the course of the second burial relics are kept separate. In princely Bantu families, only the skulls are conserved. Melanesia and Papua have sanctuaries made of skulls. Our ossuaries contain hardly anything but skulls. Study rites for the conservation of such body parts: rites of cremation and destruction; the breaking open of bones or the refusal to do this. Study all the rites that say farewell to the soul, which describe its journey, which help it to enter the land of the dead; all the rites that put the survivors in touch with the soul; and all the offerings made to it. The rites of coming out of mourning, the return after celebration of the second burial, which often takes place in very distant sanctuaries. Finally, some societies hold a festival for the Dead at fixed dates. All Saints' Day is a Celtic festival.

The various forms of burial are fundamental features which correspond to layers of civilisation and civilisational areas. The phenomenon is particularly clear in prehistory: people appear who practise burials; then people who practise cremation; and then scattered burial grounds; the cemetery arranged in rows corresponds to the Merovingian cemetery. Similarly, headhunting can offer scope for studying questions of distribution; it is practised on the occasion of birth or death. Use of cartographic methods will prove fruitful in such matters, especially when supported by archaeological data.

The cult of the dead, intended to transform the deceased into a particular ancestor, is very different from the *cult of ancestors*, which deals with the relations of the ancestor thus produced with local spirits, gods of the soil, great ancestors and lesser ones, guardian spirits, etc. In some cases, the reincarnation of the ancestor puts an end to his cult, since he is alive again.

Study the ancestors' sanctuary and its location: it may be inside the house, in a cave, in a sacred wood. Are the ancestors worshipped individually or collectively? Their relations with the clans and with the various totems. Distinguish carefully between male and female ancestors; very few female ancestors receive a cult, except in Micronesia, which is a matriarchal region.

Studying the cult of the dead will make it possible to situate the soul, especially if it is complemented by studying the cult of birth. Study the links between the soul and life. Generally, the land of the dead is situated in the beyond: it may be dark or not dark, it is very often a nether world, it may or may not be unpleasant. The division between heaven and hell is uncommon: Hades is by no means a place of punishment in Antiquity – the Elysian Fields are in Hades. Do these ancestors get reincarnated? Do they reappear? Usually, in the fifth generation the ancestors merge into the collectivity of souls and individual memory of them vanishes.

Individual Private Cults

The aim of all social classifications – sections, age classes, etc. – is to bring about by purely ordinal means the allocation of each individual to a specific position within the collectivity. Tylor compares the way in which in East Australia seven or eight individuals are enumerated when being given individual names with the way in which at Rome an individual was called *Quintus* 'the fifth': I am the bear's 'right paw', not its 'left paw'. The distinction between private and public cults is definitely established, but it is one that reduces to unity. We saw above the obligation incumbent on each individual to maintain his own specific cult. Such individual cults are related to actions which, to our eyes, are purely secular: in order to hunt, an Australian aborigine is obliged to hold a piece of rock crystal in his mouth and to murmur constantly a certain formula. An old native woman crossing the streets of Rabat wards off bad fate by tracing a hand of Fatima.[37] All this corresponds to individual cults. In the final analysis, anyone can construct his own personal religion.

Distinguish the *cults* attaching to various *techniques* and arts. Some rituals are purely linguistic: a particular individual must not utter a particular word, while another individual is obliged to utter a specific formula again and again. All of this is strictly individual, forming a mix of mystical and useful elements, which should not be confused with formality and etiquette, and it constitutes the tone of collective life. Thus the North American Indians are all of them very ceremonial in their interactions.

Techniques of walking can be religious; consider techniques of cleanliness (people are clean for religious reasons, or they are dirty for similar reasons); there is an order of Carmelite friars who wear shoes, and another who do not. The ritual of bathing, or of not bathing; the ritual of spitting, the ritual of gaze.

Individual hunting gives rise to complex preparations: casting a spell on the weapons, setting off, casting a spell on the hunting ground, cult of the prey ... Likewise for fishing ritual: in Polynesia no one is allowed to fish before offering the first fruits to the king – a responsibility bearing on the whole shoal of fish. In the Bible, Isaiah's curse weighs upon all those who 'put a spell on their nets'; depending on context, the same individual is not allowed to put a spell on his fishing nets, or conversely he has the duty to do so. The ritual of livestock. Agrarian ritual. The ritual of meals, which can become truly obsessive: some peoples wash their hands three or four times before, during and after the meal; others never wash. The properties of particular waters. People who wash only with sand. Rites involving food prohibitions, which may vary between individuals. I kill an animal: you eat it – and reciprocally.

Rites concerning craft specialisms are widespread, especially for women: the rites of the female or potter. A Berber man, like a Maori man, cannot weave in the presence of a woman: a breach of the rule means an immediate fine.

Rites involved in house building: orientation, foundations; the hearth; the beams, door, threshold, arrangement of the latrines, etc.

Aesthetic rituals can also be classified here. The study of aesthetics by itself does not guarantee discovering all the related religious phenomena, and vice versa. The fieldworker should make a practice of systematically rupturing all the divisions that I am expounding here from a didactic point of view. Things are no more divided than is a living being. We are beings who constitute wholes, collectively and individually.

Individual rituals seen in certain games, which relate to solar or lunar myths: children playing hopscotch 'go up to heaven'.

Rituals of adornment: wearing earrings is meant to protect the ear against any intrusion, not only by evil sounds, but against any evil intrusion whatever its nature. The trade in amber jewellery is above all a magic trade.

Rituals of musical invention, of poetical and dramatic invention. Until Plato, and including him, the poet does not extract things from his own self: it is his

Muse who extracts his work from him. Moreover, the aesthetic product is often revealed: the spirits have come to the poet or musician; the genies made 'his drum dance' for him. Each movement in the dance, each moment in poetry has a religious character: 'melody *and* dance' says Homer. Very often dance is private; the individual dances for his religious pleasure to attain ecstasy. An Eskimo man spends hours on end in wintertime inventing poems for the drum competitions that will take place during summer between remote groups. He recites an incantation against his enemy and he manages to find the verses, music and dance that will get him proclaimed victor in the tournament.

Jural ritual is found, for example, in the runes of Germanic trials. Contracts, oaths, etc., which among us are no longer ritual but belong to the realm of private morality, elsewhere belong in the religious realm.

The ritual of the communal meal, the Last Supper. Eating together is a means of realising a community.

The ritual of the kiss, which is very important. In some societies, nobody kisses children, and nobody speaks to them; elsewhere people speak to them constantly. There can be many different reasons for this. Between the generations and the sexes, relationships that seem to belong to the private sphere also belong in fact to the public sphere and have to be strictly respected. A menstruating woman is not allowed to be in certain parts of the house.

The ritual of absence and return: the recognition of the traveller after a long absence. The crossing of borders (the man who adds a stone to the cairn marking the frontier of a country thereby leaves his sins behind him). The Latins did not cross a river without offering a sacrifice or saying a prayer.

Lastly, *economic rituals*. Mahou Soglo, the high god of Heaven and god of justice among the Ewe of Togo is also the great god of money, the god of the cowrie shells. The natives cast spells on their cowries and on their merchandise; Mahou, the High God, is here a kind of god of exchange. Something of this is still with us: someone purchasing a ticket (*dizième*) for the National Lottery will not take his ticket without surrounding himself with all the precautions he deems necessary.

Rites[38]

We have been examining cults, that is to say groupings of ritual. A second mode of observation consists in studying the various parts of ritual, that is to say rites as such, dividing them into major categories.

Every rite corresponds to a religious representation; there is always a religious representation behind a religious action, i.e. behind a rite; and this action is carried out by a specific individual, by a priest or a college of priests. The ensemble – rites, religious representations and religious organisation – provides an overview of the religious institutions of the society under study. We say representation, not idea, since all phenomena of consciousness, including actions, are representations. Every rite corresponds to a representation.

To make it easier to study them, we shall divide rites into positive and negative. Not to do something is still an action, an act of inhibition is still an act; it is not a negative phenomenon. Pavlov has now provided solid evidence for this assertion; we now know that acts of inhibition are localised in the midbrain, not in the cortex. You cannot do such and such a thing outside certain conditions; an act of inhibition is first of all an act.

Another division separates manual rites from oral ones, 'manual' being taken here in the most general sense of 'bodily'. The two divisions intersect. Thus we have oral taboos and oral prescriptions, and manual rites, both positive and negative.

We are not yet sufficiently habituated to this double division. In his *Taboo and the Perils of the Soul*,[39] Frazer puts all taboos in the same category, and Malinowski does the same. But a positive rite normally has a negative form, and conversely a negative rite is always positive to some degree. To step aside and give way to a superior is a negative gesture, but it expresses the recognition of superiority and it therefore has a positive meaning. In Honolulu, no one may eat fish before the king eats the first fruits of the new shoal; this is a positive rite, since its aim is to allow the king to be the first to desacralise the fish. A raw catalogue of taboos is of no interest. One should always give the motives for a rite, which is a collective act but an intentional one; an effort must always be made to find out the intentions. The fieldworker will only feel satisfied when he has recorded the myth explaining the negative rite.

Manual Rites[40]

The study of rites should start from the phenomena that are easiest to observe: one should undertake the description of everything that can be described. This is a complicated task and often very difficult. A young boy who dances has prepared himself under certain conditions, dances under certain conditions, and stops doing so under certain conditions. All this must be studied from a positive and negative point of view at the same time: whom did he personify, and by what right? With whom did he dance, etc.? This is essential for all public cults and for private cults as well. Describe all the objects involved in ritual, all the public ceremonies, and all the individuals attending them. When describing a religious gathering or a public rite, and especially a major ritual, never forget to mention the names of the spectators, the names of the actors and their role (*qualité*). To give the proper name without indicating the role of each individual is not enough. When the Pope appears in the loggia and addresses the community of the faithful, it is not a matter of Mgr Pacelli talking to the people of Rome. It is therefore necessary to know who is acting, in what role, and in what the role consists. All rites are to some degree functional. Sacrifice has a nature and a function;[41] social things are by definition functional things.

The difficulties in observing rites arise from the fact that they are secret and *simultaneous*. In a major ritual, at a single moment, fifteen or twenty people are doing different things. In order to describe and transcribe, help should be sought from sketches, photographs and filming. Do not neglect the preparations for ritual, which can be extremely lengthy; preparations for the ball game among the Cherokee Indians last several weeks. Finally, every detail must be observed. The officiant used his right hand and not his left hand: why? The spectators stand up, sit down, or hold their breath. Everything has meaning; even silence is a sign. There is no need to distinguish between popular ritual and other rituals, for such distinctions will emerge spontaneously.

Study the rites also according to the material objects used in the cult and the location of the cult.[42] Note the preparation of all the religious objects, their production and their consecration; in India, putting in the eyes of an idol can entail extraordinary sacrifices. Religious museology yields interesting results. Note the religious nature of the raw materials, and the state of mind of the craftsman. Record all the religious sculptures and paintings, and especially the temporary paintings, which are usually overlooked; feather ornamentation, and body painting, and finally all the symbols, classifying the objects according to their nature and function. Do not describe a sacrifice without providing a complete list of the equipment that is used. If the sacrifice is followed by a meal, list the apparatus used to cook such meals. *Leviticus* provides models for such descriptions. For each object note all the uses to which it can be put, and if possible, the limits that are set on these uses – for instance, the vessels of the Jews at Passover, or distinctions between summer vessels and winter vessels. Record all the paraphernalia for consecration, lustration, and initiation. Record everything, including the funeral rites that accompany the killing of large or small animals, the ritual of tying or untying knots, and so on.

Most societies do not practise their cults indifferently in any old location, but rather in places hallowed by a myth, which explains why such and such a sacrifice takes place at this particular location.[43] Sacred places form part of the sacred objects, which themselves are permanent rites. So one should locate all these places, all standing stones, all sacred woods, all *penetralia*: the magician does not act just anywhere. Studying the places will enable one to see who is there and what happens there. Melanesians practise a cult of fish that correspond to funeral totems; these are not just any fish, but fish of a particular type which are found in a particular region of the sea.[44] Rites can therefore be divided both according to objects and to places.

Objects and rites can also be classified according to time.[45] The notion of the festival, of sacred time, of the consecration of the year by a sacred time – the *ver sacrum* of the Romans. The Romans waged war in spring, the Germans engaged in it after harvest. The festival is at once a period of sacred time and a moment of sacred activity. All sorts of things are accomplished at a festival. [Latin] *feria* yields two words: *foire* (fair) and *fête* (festival).[46] The location and date of the festival, etc. Drawing up the religious calendar very often brings to light the whole system of the rhythms of collective life or of the religion under study; a particular rite takes place on a particular day, at a particular time, in a particular place.

Once this is clear, manual rites can also be distinguished more precisely into simple and complex rites: simple rites are very numerous and are generally integrated into complex rites. Simple rites can easily be divided into simple positive rites (e.g., the act of consecration: the laying on of hands, the blessing, the Latin rite of *mancipium* [formal purchase] ...) and negative rites. However, a positive rite can result in a negation: breaking an egg to consecrate an oath is a negative action – with the breaking of the egg the soul of the oath departs. And similarly for all rites involving blood, skin and hair.

Multiple consecrations, accompanied by partial destruction of objects, the part in question communicating directly with sacred objects and beings in the other world: this is the definition of *sacrifice*, which can also be called a system of consecrations.[47] It is not a matter of interpreting sacrifice, of knowing whether it is primarily an offering or a negotiation (*do ut des* [I give in order that you may give]: the formula is attested much earlier in Sanskrit than in Latin); in fact, I have no other means of communicating with God, who is super-celestial, than to send him the smoke – smoke which in any case he does not need to smell: it is idols who actively smell the odour of sacrifice, while God detests it; what matters to him is the purity of Israel. Hence all the sacrificial rituals, starting with the blood alliance, the sacrifices for marking accords, sacrifices of communion, of expiation, etc.

Oral Rites

Another grouping of rituals consists of oral rites. It is a serious mistake to attach the label 'prayer' to all oral rites, to all those sets of words, very often rhythmic and poetic, that accompany a rite or that are rites in themselves: ritual is always formulaic. The greatest formula of Buddhism, which the Tibetans endlessly repeat and make their prayer wheels repeat, is an oral rite.

Oral rites include musical instruments, just as manual rites include all the cult objects, including the sacrificial knife, even when the knife is of stone. Formulaic ritual is always endowed with a certain amount of magical effectiveness; no formula exists without being to some degree theurgic. It is a mistake to distinguish magic from religion by seeing the former as prelogical, as Frazer did. The major doctrine of the Church, accepted by Catholics and Protestants alike, holds that God hears all prayers; he has the freedom not to answer them all, but he is not free not to hear them: to hear is not to answer. Even the powers of Evil, like those of Good, are relatively free vis-à-vis the believer. The devil himself can be prayed to and can make contracts; Mephistopheles is not necessarily attached to Faust.

Prayers[48] can be divided into simple and complex. The invention of prayers, their revelation and formulation. Very often the language is archaic or secret; the Australian aborigines themselves 'say mass in Latin'; in the Arunta formulas one finds archaisms almost two times out of three, and borrowings of archaic forms from the neighbouring languages at least one time out of four. There is a deliberate search for secret language; special languages are the rule rather than the exception. Christ spoke Aramaic; already by then Hebrew had long ceased to be spoken; the Bible was translated into Aramaic; yet people read it aloud in Hebrew; it was chanted while reading in Syriac from the Talmud.

Sanskrit distinguishes formulas into sung formulas, chanted formulas and ritual formulas that consist of the various commands given during the sacrifice. The observer should use a similar distinction, without forgetting commentaries on each prayer. The commentary may be more lengthy than the formula, for a very short formula may sum up a huge mass of material: the Buddhist formula *om mane padme hum* sums up the eighty books of Tibetan Buddhism. The observer should record the formulas on disk, accompanying the recording with a philological study. Note how each formula is used – the use can evolve and become personalised, or it can become a solemn custom. Mention repetitions, which can be indefinite in number. Let us not forget that the rosary comes from Tibet; the Tibetans live in a kind of sound world (*sonorité*) made up of ritual formulas.

Very often, the formula describes what the officiant is aiming to achieve; the act [of uttering it] is at once a consecration, invocation, curse and conjuration. The aim of the sacrifice is to send things back, especially the most sacred things: to say goodbye to the Gods who, without the sacrifice, would exert endless pressure on the sacrificer; to turn away the gods by doing one's duty to them. Here is the whole notion of the Greek *apotropaion*, also found in Sanskrit: the individual is discharging an obligation, is sacrificing so that the god will go away. It is impossible to eat the new grain before the first fruits have been offered to the Gods.

Sounds, breath and gestures can be prayer, in the same way as words. The mythology of the voice is important. Each time you note a prayer, make sure that you note the manual ritual that accompanies it, together with its symbolism. Note, too, rites concerning individual names, surnames, common names, secret names; the obligation to use such and such word; metaphors, and linguistic taboos.[49]

Most forms of symbolism are written: if I write a symbol, it is so that you can understand me; it is the result of a convention agreed between us. Thus one should study the whole range of messages transmitted by message sticks, the symbolism of Sioux blankets made of bison skin, and the like.

Negative Rites[50]

I come now to the taboos I have already mentioned. We encountered them when discussing the religious calendar and religious objects. We already know that the negative character of religion is as important as its positive character; the two complement each other. A religion consists of an ensemble of prohibitions. The first task should therefore be to draw up a catalogue of these prohibitions, taking each taboo in turn along with all possible native commentaries; why can people do such and such a thing, or not do it? Note all the linguistic taboos and all the manual taboos; a soldier is not allowed to salute by raising his kepi.

For each taboo study its nature, its object, and more especially its sanction, which may be inflicted by humans or by gods; it may even not be physically inflicted by the gods. The individual will himself impose the sanction, sometimes to the point of death – this is a form of martyrdom. The man believes himself doomed because he has violated his taboo: this is the notion of the scruple, which plays a major role in religion, perhaps even a fundamental one, as Reinach maintained; he called all scruples taboos and then defined religion by means of scruples. Together with scruples, the other fundamental notion is that of fear and respect – *awe* in English. Fear and respect such as one feels before certain natural phenomena, before the king, or before the gods. The man who has violated his taboo feels shame as a result; the Bantu word for taboo is *hlanipa*, 'to be ashamed'. A feeling of scruple and also a feeling of shame; shame is the sanction for taboos.

At this point one can study the whole notion of pure and impure, good and bad, sacred and profane. The pursuit of such classifications can yield bizarre results. Herodotus felt this very clearly in his description of Egypt: some men feel respect for such and such a thing while others do not – and vice versa. Nothing is more arbitrary, more variable or more extraordinary than classifications; there is nothing more stupid in our language than grammatical gender.

Taboos should be treated as ritual prohibitions. Taboos are above all circumstantial: if a Christian fasts during Lent, it is in order to eat plenty at Easter; fasting on Fridays is a positive ritual as much as a negative one. We always imagine prohibitions in the strict form of the Ten Commandments: thou shalt not kill, thou shalt not covet thy neighbour's wife, nor his ass – we regard ritual prohibitions as strictly categorical. They are so quite often, but the word 'strictly' is nearly always an exaggeration. To fast in Lent so as not to fast the rest of the time – this is a localised imperative. Only those who seek total sanctity surround themselves with strict discipline, imitated from the Buddhist monks. But purely psychological interpretations of asceticism are as erroneous as solely sociological interpretations of the same phenomenon.

Taboos can be divided into simple and complex, such as the great complexes of festivals or initiation. A young Arunta is only cleared of all his taboos when he is about thirty. Taboos can also be classified according to their object. To draw up a catalogue, it is necessary to adopt a classification of taboos, and to follow some principle for classifying them, but this principle should not merely lead to establishing a list; it must not hide the true nature of the taboos. Do not forget that taboos may be not only manual and oral, but also mental: 'Thou shalt not covet'. The notion of sin and expiation is an important one that can only be mentioned here.[51] Rituals of expiation are common, and they are always very important.

Finally, note all the bodily taboos – rules governing snoring, sneezing, etc.

Religious Representations[52]

We recognise a religious representation from the fact that it corresponds to some degree to an attitude, or at least to a habitus, on the part of the individual towards a positive or negative rite; generally also, it corresponds to a myth.

Let us recall at this point that representations and rites must not be studied separately. The observer must never, not for one moment, confine himself to the abstract; he must always stay in contact with the rites. Thus some of the notions concerning substance are in fact notions concerning food; we have spoken earlier of rites concerning food.

In the societies pertaining to ethnography, religious representations correspond more or less to what for us are religious, magical or popular beliefs; they correspond also to what we call general ideas, and even sciences. The priest and magician are experts: *tohunga* in Maori, *kahuna* in Hawaii refer both to the priest and the expert. Among the Mandingo [of Mali], we find those who say sacred things and those who see secret things. These are men endowed with special competence. Let us not forget that it was Spinoza who really isolated thought from space; prior to Spinoza, matter was never regarded as something that was very material and the mind was never considered as something that was very immaterial.

One fundamental notion dominates all these tangled issues, namely the notion of symbol. If Durkheim exaggerated the role of the emblem in totemism, he nonetheless sensed the importance of this notion. People conceive of themselves symbolically. Even among us, it would be hard to find a concept that is not to some degree a symbol.

The study of symbolism proper should focus above all on graphic symbolisms, which can serve as a starting point for the enquiry. Behind graphic symbolisms lie all the geometrical symbolisms, and behind the latter all the figurative symbolisms, such as, for example, the language of flowers. The *ars plumaria*, both in North America and in South America, is wholly symbolic: there is not a single feather in the Sioux hairdo without its own meaning. Here is a world of notions that are at once homogeneous with ours and heterogeneous. Perhaps the distance is not so great as is generally believed – think of the importance of symbolism in linguistics. Religious representations enter into everything: the calendar, knowledge of the world, links between the notions of space and time ... Astronomical knowledge is nearly always religious at the same time as it is astronomical in the proper sense. Ornamentation is normally filled with religious meaning. Even notions such as that of orientation are in part religious ones: we orient ourselves with reference to a fixed North and an Equator. The whole of Asia, and especially Egypt, knew the gnomon. The astronomical knowledge of the Chukchi, a society regarded as primitive, is highly developed; this is related to the fact that the Chukchi live under the Polar night and can observe the stars.

The psychological study of mysticism will be carried out by describing precise cases of mysticism, with its revelations, trances and communications with the other world. Let us not forget that the same shamanic institutions extend from the depths of Lapland via the whole of North Asia and on into North America.[53] The Bori dance, studied by Tremearne,[54] is found in Morocco and also in Egypt, where it is still danced by Negroes.

For the classification of religious representations one can seek help from the one used in the *Année sociologique*: collective representations of natural beings and phenomena, representations of spiritual beings, and myths, legends and tales.

Representations of Natural Beings and Phenomena

Each object and each kind of object that has caught the attention of the natives is usually very well represented. Informants will speak at length about Air, Fire and Water. While it is true that religious representations often have a personal character, there are nonetheless also general notions. Observers have generally given too much attention to studying rites in themselves and neglected the representations to which the rites correspond. The correspondence is difficult to establish, but it is essential. In his studies on Vedic religion, Bergaigne[55] divides divinities into male and female; everything revolves around male and female, cow and bull, man and woman, heaven and earth, rain and sun. His work is far more convincing than Max Müller's attempts at personal interpretation.

Our way of conceptualising mythology, illustrated rather faithfully in [Offenbach's opera] *Orpheus in the Underworld*, is only one possible way; it is not the only way. The problem is to know how the natives think. Powell saw clearly the relations between religion and technology among the American Indians.[56]

An effort should therefore be made not to limit the study to the representations that form, for example, the list of categories considered in classes of philosophy. In addition to the questions we can pose, the natives can conceive of many others. The list of our categories – space, time, number ... – will not exhaust the list of categories of another society. The notion of food is one of the forms of the notion of substance. The question of space (*étendue*). The distinction of up and down, right and left, inversion, symmetry, sympathies, correspondences; everything that Lévy-Bruhl calls participation. A good list of omens, such as that in the *Grand Albert*,[57] will be most useful here.

The distinction between animate and inanimate is fundamental; it corresponds to the notion of element.[58] The notion of *mana* appears to be universal; it is often related to the notion of breath[59] or that of voice, or music.[60] The notion of quality can offer scope for all sorts of investigations: qualities, for example those of stone, are transmissible (facts observed in Polynesia, with identical ritual in India). What are the qualities of an amulet (to be observed at the time when it is conferred)? Notions of causality and purpose.

Finally, the notion of spirit, the notion of individual animism. In a great many cases, the spirits of the dead can possess everything, and they can reside everywhere: 'It is clear that generations and characters come from the dead' (Hippocrates). We eat dead things, thanks to which we procreate and live.

It is therefore necessary to study these notions, which for us are nameless, but give to societies different from our own that tint of the 'mystical', or of what we in our ignorance call 'mystical'. But we must not forget that our own notions, such as that of attraction, are not always clear to us.

Study also the notion of blessing; the notion of evil; and finally the notion of *mana* and that of the sacred. Let us recall the basic definition: everything religious is *mana*; everything that is *mana* is religious *and* sacred.

Durkheim studied the notion of genre and quality;[61] Lévy-Bruhl studied the notion of causality starting from human causation. It seems certain that if humanity had not believed that its magic would succeed, it would not have persevered with its techniques. One of the reasons why humankind had faith in itself was that it had other means at its disposal apart from its techniques. The essential task of the ethnographer will be to distinguish for each activity the contribution made by technology, religion and magic – everywhere, in each mind, at every moment. How do the natives imagine the world system; what is their *orbis pictus* [picture of the world]: this is the crucial question.

Representations of Spiritual Beings

On the basis of this set of general notions, one should study what is called mythology, that is to say individual beings. Firstly, the notion of spirits: spirits of the living, their 'souls'. In Catholicism, each individual still has his or her patron saint, guardian Angel, and soul. God protects the individual, and so do all the angels, while all the devils beset him. We still live surrounded by spirits which, in all their variety, are our doubles. In Rome, everyone had his Genius and her Juno, everyone had their Lar.[62] Soul double, external soul, protecting spirit, reincarnate spirit returning among the living, the spirit that procreates one's son – all this is very complicated.

Approach this study via the representation of the human soul. The notion of the soul proper is recent; it is attested for the first time in that great Greek marble, the Revelation of Psyche. By definition we believe the soul to be eternal; but eternal only in the future. Societies that believe in metempsychosis and reincarnation are more logical. Note the representations concerning the germination of humanity, animals and plants; how spirits get reincarnated, how they surround the dead, how they live among themselves; what are their relations with dreams and nightmares; sleep and ecstasy. Multiple souls are not necessarily contradictory; for the Chinese, souls are located in such and such places and correspond to such and such parts of the body – which renders acupuncture possible. Travels of the soul during sleep. Werewolves and vampires. The various parts of the body each have their soul: the soul of the head, of the brain, of the eyes, of the throat, of the liver. The links between life and the liver form the basis for a whole major theory of divination and augury. The question of breath and apertures of the body. The soul of the voice, the representation of breath.

As for the spirits themselves, what is the myth of the Land of the Dead, and the relation of this land with the Land of the Living? The travels of the soul to the Land of the Dead (major Polynesian myths). See the studies of shamanic representations carried out by the Russians in Siberia. The souls of animals, especially of bees. The souls of plants, the souls of metals and marriages between metals. The importance of the mythology of blacksmiths and smelters is huge;[63] in our countryside it was also the blacksmith who used to extract teeth (some good texts in *Don Quixote*). The relationship between souls and stars. Here is a series of rapprochements that we are not accustomed to making. Note with equal care the relationships that are familiar to us but unknown in the societies under study: spirits who have never been either men or gods; gods who have never been men or spirits, beings like [the Greek] Kronos.

All the gods and all the spirits should be studied one by one: spirits of men, women, animals and things. National and international gods, such as the little spirits of the crossroads. The major spirits of temples. Spirits of waters and mountains. Heroes. For each god, study his ritual and class; the place of his cult; his birth, death and deification, for the gods were deified – this is the theme of the whole *Golden Bough*. All this should be transcribed in the form of a narrative, reproducing everything that constitutes divine imagery. Do not forget colours, for the colour is as important as the drawing.

Once in possession of all these inventories, drawn up in all possible manners – only then can one write the mythology of each god.

Myths, Legends, and Tales

A myth is the story of a god; it is a fable with its invention and its moral. For each myth record who tells it, for whom and on what occasion. Myths confirm and contradict each other depending on points of view: my totem is very big, yours is quite small. The observer must be sensitive to these differences in viewpoint and record them. Usually, the god is represented as a man with a whole life story, having wives, having relations with animals, making alliances, and seeking protection: the god protects someone who has protected him (for example, the totem). The narratives are very often in verse, and can be found in the form of ballads or epics.[64]

A myth, *muthos* (= legend), is a myth about gods, a fable about gods, an apologia, the bearer of a moral. The whole range of religious literature includes myths, legends and tales, which we have already studied when dealing with literature, but which we must return to here. Originally, tragedy was the ode consecrated to the he-goat; the whole of the dramatic performance corresponds to the sacrifice of the goat whose throat is slit on the altar.

Myth proper is *a story in which people believe, which in principle implies rites.* Myth forms part of the obligatory system of religious representations; people are obliged to believe in the myth. In contrast to legends (it is incorrect to speak of the *Legend of the Saints*; if it is about a saint it is not a legend), myth is represented in eternity: a god is born, he was put to death, and he is born anew; all of this corresponds to a belief current at all periods. The Buddha was born in a precise era, but when one studies the holy books of Buddhism, one sees that he already belonged to eternity; he had been preceded by other Buddhas, and the world still awaits the future Buddha, confident of his coming. Likewise for Vishnu's avatars, and for the relations between Kronos and his son Jupiter [Zeus]. Myth unfolds in eternity, which does not mean it is not located in time and space. We know that Kronos gave birth to Jupiter, and that he was the first; but vis-à-vis mankind, the gods all live in eternity.

The legend[65] or saga ([etymologically] 'what people tell') is less believed in; more exactly, it is *believed in without necessarily having an effect.* Time is so to speak more localised: a saint's date of birth is known. Myth, even when it tells of precise events, is always located in a different era from that of humanity, while a legend always takes place in an era which is to some degree that of humanity. Myth can enter into legend. The gods intervene constantly in the *Rāmāyana* or in the *Mahābhārata*, in the *Iliad* or in the *Aeneid*; the relations they entertain with men lead to their taking part in the action. On the other hand, legend can scarcely enter into myth. But people believe in it; it is historical, no one doubts it; one knows the name of the man who fulfils such and such a deed, and he has a father, a mother and a whole epic.

People believe less in legend than they do in myth, and they believe even less in tales or fables than in legend. In Latin, *fabula* clearly refers to a little thing,[66] and the tale is simply possible. *The fable is the object of a belief that is altogether lukewarm.* It belongs to the realm of possibilities and of imagination; no one is forced to believe in it. The fable remains religious, but little believed in. Animal epics (in Africa for example) constitute jural precedents: it is good to be as clever as the hare, as sturdy as the tortoise, etc. All of this is expressed rather clearly by the position that gods, heroes and men occupy in dramatic art.[67]

Part of what we know about the religions of Antiquity is given us by this semi-profane literature. Of truly religious literature very little survives: the only prayers to have reached us are those of Orpheus. The longest Roman prayers are those from Carthage – simple incantations.

Such records need to be studied philologically. The great collections of legends, tales and myths are among the best documents we possess. Failure to collect them means mutilating the life of a particular religion or society.

For each hero the same observations should be made as for each god. Note the existence of cycles: some epics may be very long. But do not start off by studying particular themes, that is to say the elements of the narratives. One can limit oneself to the task of making a catalogue pure and simple: a catalogue by heroes (in [Kipling's] *Jungle Book*, Elephant stands for all elephants); by localities or by historical records – such and such a family is born of a man of this particular type, and of a woman of that different type – it is a myth, or a totemic myth, and that may also be a tale or a legend. But the narrative is always localised. Record all the historical legends: the Earth that is fished up, the town that is submerged, the birth of gods in some particular cave, the birth of the heroes and their ascent to heaven, their descent to underworlds or beneath the water, their life with the water nymphs ...

Do not be afraid of repeating themes, but mention the repetitions and number them. Never seek the original version, record all of them.

There are other ways of classifying: there is the whole set of foundation legends, the whole set of wars launched by the gods, the spirits, or the animals. The classifications mentioned here are working tools; their sole purpose is to allow the collection of documents in as complete a manner as possible. A general attempt to interpret myths and tales is not something to be undertaken while in the field.

Intended above all for amusement and instruction, the tale is more literary than the myth or legend. No doubt the epic of the gods, like the system of legends, contains a literary element, but this element takes on much larger dimensions in the tale.[68]

In a tale, distinguish the following: the themes (each theme); the interweaving of these themes; the location of the tale. Be aware that it is not only themes that travel, but the tale as a whole: there is not just one Sleeping Beauty, there are Beauties that have never been woken up, and Beauties that wake up by themselves ... While noting each theme an effort should be made to retain the specific meaning of the themes and their modes of interweaving.

Religious Organisation[69]

Every group of social phenomena always corresponds to a more or less permanent organisation, and religious phenomena always correspond to the 'Church', that is, to the religious society. No coherent system of beliefs lacks a relation to a coherent system of people. Even a tale is told during evening gatherings or in the public square.

Every social phenomenon, simply by virtue of being a social phenomenon, always has a moral aspect (*teinte*), an aesthetic aspect, and an aspect of faith.

Religious organisation is especially visible in the layout of festivals and also in the field of jurisprudence. We come across all these phenomena again, in an increasingly secular form, in the relations between the sexes and even more so in the relations between generations; apart from exceptional cases, women are more on the receiving end of religion than its agents.

Study in order the various religious units: age sets, castes, and in particular, priests: the elder, the clan headman, the magician are always more or less priests. Finally, the society of men will constantly turn up as a religious body in the societies that concern us. There is often an overlap between the temple and the men's house; for instance, in the *marae*, those large enclosures in Polynesia that were destroyed and only survive now in old engravings. Note the various classes of priests and their interrelations; the whole of African Guinea is familiar with 'convents of priestesses'; these women are in reality the gods' temple slaves. Study the hierarchy and specialisations of the priests of water and the priests of fire. A priest cannot offer just any old sacrifice; he is normally a specialist, specialising in his totem or at some particular sanctuary. Civic rank may coincide with religious rank, as is the case for example with priest-kings.[70] Study the special initiations; the life of the priest, his dwelling, his wives, his taboos, his relations with the gods, the way he is possessed, his visions, his revelations: he dreams at night, he issues prophecies, he prays. Prayer is a sign of the presence of the God: 'Eternal God, open my mouth and it will sing your praise'. It is Eternal God who opens the mouth of his priest.

Everything I have just said corresponds to the anatomical-physiological structure of religion. One must also observe the geographical structure of the religion's social morphology: the temples are located in sacred places, for precise reasons. Describe the temple; note the relative wealth of different temples and sacred places,[71] the number of worshippers who regularly visit each sanctuary. The respect felt towards a cairn is easy to establish: it is directly proportional to the cairn's dimensions. In America observers have seen the rise and fall of a whole religion that was a compromise between the cults of Sioux Indians and Christianity; the result was a Christian form of shamanism that lasted thirty years, spreading from the north to the south of the Rocky Mountains, and very far to the east and the south-east.[72] Only when such research has been completed, when one has observed as meticulously as possible how the religion functions – only then can one define the society in question from the point of view of its religion. The morality and religion of a country can only be evaluated by observing the functioning of its religion, and not *a priori*; France's morality is evaluated through its moral statistics and not vice versa. Estimate the importance of taboos and scruples (we have already done so), and of superstitions (we are about to do so); also the importance of initiations; the importance of the notion of sin, the number of expiations, the cures of illnesses caused by religious transgression. The relation between morality and law will provide useful information. War can be an entirely religious phenomenon: the military practices of the Romans were not very remote from those of the Hawaiians. The relation between religion and education, for example in those initiations of young Australian aborigines where the initiand must neither weep, nor laugh, nor cry out: his silence will prove that his soul is well pegged to his body.

Religious Phenomena in the Broad Sense

These cover mainly magic and divination, and in addition popular superstitions.

Magic[73]

Magic is a set of rites and beliefs often confused with religion; some people even confuse religion with magic, as do Malinowski and Frazer. In Melanesia, it is in fact fairly difficult to distinguish between religion and magic, a magician usually also being a priest or a high-ranking member of the secret society. Magic is an attempt at systematisation, or a set of recipes and secrets, that are generally more individual than religion. Certainly there do exist colleges of magicians, but the magicians do not all practise together; or if they practise together, it is in their capacity as priests, for instance to cast a spell on the enemy. Magic is linked to an important notion, namely that of symmetry and orthodoxy. Since a person has both a left and a right side, when two people confront each other, the right of the one necessarily corresponds to the left of the other. *My* magic is a religion for me and an evil spell for you; *your* religion for me is an evil spell and magic.[74] If the matter arises, I shall accuse you of deaths caused in my home, for it cannot be I who caused them. From my point of view, I am necessarily on the side of good, and you are necessarily on the side of evil. Magic can be distinguished from religion more clearly from a jural point of view. This is very clear throughout the Middle Ages.

Magic is usually theurgic, it dominates the spirits of the living and the spirits of the dead, both male and female; it also very often dominates the gods. The fullest texts of prayers to have come down to us from Greece and Rome are the tablets from Carthage, whose aim was to make racehorses stumble.

Magic is above all something that is relatively antinomian. It is constant, customary, exact, precise, and it has its personnel and traditions: nevertheless personnel and traditions remain somewhere on the margins of legality – marginal relative to the other party; while in an extreme case, I can be legally obliged to respect your god.

The notion of magic usually coincides with the notion of *mana*, but the magician will rarely use things that are properly speaking sacred; if he uses them for a magical aim, it is a sacrilege (e.g. the black mass).

Study the secretiveness of the magical tradition. The relations between magic and the techniques and crafts, relations which are usually much clearer than those between religion and techniques, and very down to earth (the sinister arts of medicine, poisoning, etc.).

The fieldworker will have to find the magicians, who are far less numerous than people say. In spite of their very frequently being accused of magic, women have few magical traditions; only in Paris are there more female magicians than male ones. Try and obtain from the magician his formulary, which is often of considerable size. Always include in the description of manual rites the oral formulas that accompany them. The magician is impotent if he cannot find a 'starter' such as nail clippings, a lock of hair, or the like. The formula will show the meaning of the constituents of the 'starter'. Without the formula you will not be able to go beyond Frazer's general idea of magic by contiguity, which is correct but inadequate.

Study those auxiliary spirits, those exaggerated forms of magic to which shamanism corresponds; the authority of the magician in the society of men; the conditions of ritual (negative and positive rites, as in religion). Describe all the gestures, and all the objects: Faust's arsenal is considerable.

Enquire next about everything bearing on belief in magic and on the effect it has on the person against whom it is used. Let us not forget that 'charm' comes from *carmen*, a poem endowed with efficacity. How does the magician incant, and what gestures accompany the recitation of the spell?

Elements of magic. The relations between magic and religion vary across societies. At the end of the study, one should be in a position to assess the degree of reliance on magic in the society being studied, just as one can assess its religiosity.

Divination[75]

Divination has unfortunately been very poorly studied. It can be defined as a system of representations concerning the future, determined as a function of the present and past. Divination proceeds on the basis of sympathies, correspondences, and *sui generis* forces. It looks at the past and the future in terms of the present, in a state of confusion that recalls that of dreams. Divination borrows from religion and magic all of its principles of reasoning.

A divination system can be studied by way of objects (the haruspex or extispex [who look at entrails]). The observer can take as models [Cicero's] *De fato* or *De divinatione*, in Latin. Above all, do not forget to mention points that remain unclear. Note the main religious notions: the notions of cause and person; the horoscope; omens; but above all, the entire system of divination, according to which such and such a thing is good for some particular use, but bad for another use, etc.; all this forming a set of recipes, which is often highly systematic, and transmitted as such. The systems best described are still the Polynesian and Malayan; the latter corresponds to a real cosmogony, in which Hindu and Malay-Polynesian elements combine with Muslim elements.[76]

If beliefs concerning divination vary greatly, the very scale of these beliefs and their wide distribution often remain unsuspected; thus the compass forms part of the cosmology of the tortoise. We more or less know about divination by questioning entrails: starting from a Chaldean source, it spread west as far as the Atlantic; to the east it reached the Timor Straits, which mark a very clear frontier for all divinatory phenomena. We should not forget that the Etruscan soothsayer used to draw the *mundus*, that is to say a square representing the world, inside which he located the person who was consulting him. We still ask people to 'tell us our fortune' (*la bonne aventure*).

The fieldworker should study the whole notion of signs and portents relating to distant events, questions about cosmological distribution, coincidences between time and space, the distribution of stars, of lunar quarters, of animal species, and of all conceivable events. Record all the scruples and all the divinatory rites, in which there is an inextricable mix of hours, numbers, lunar months, presages, magic and religion ... Every society has its own particular cosmology and its own system of classification. Of course, one should not imagine that everything holds together within it, in a sort of huge riddle built on signs and portents. But a classification dominates this whole, and correspondences interlink names, animal and plant species, dispositions (*états*), techniques and activities of all kinds.

Look also at the relations between divination and shamanism, and the relations between the diviner and the shaman; the diviner too may travel in the Other World.

Study finally the diviners and the fraternities of diviners, gathering their sayings, formulas, and so on.

Popular Superstitions

Around religion in the strict sense and around its two large satellites, magic and divination, there floats a huge shapeless mass, a nebula, namely the system of popular religion or popular superstitions. No more value should be attached to the word 'superstition' than to the word 'survival'; these popular beliefs are not necessarily much more ancient than the rest of the religion. Everything depends on the question of proportions; no society is without its religious superstitions or its popular traditions. The notions are very vague ones: about the value of such and such food taken at such and such a time; about the formulas that go with a sneeze ('God bless you') or with spitting. Alongside learned medicine, i.e. the medicine of the specialist, popular medicine always occupies a respectable place. A mass of things – a formless mass – here enters into religion. Women are usually at once more superstitious than men and less specialised in magic or divination. The fieldworker should note all the beliefs that bear on technical life, all those themes in tales where the spirits come to help a woman who is spinning, etc. In this context use only extremely broad divisions [of technology], so as to facilitate reading.

Notes

1. *Ils cherchent eux-mêmes sur eux-mêmes.*
2. See Dennett, R.E., *Notes on West African Categories*, London, 1911.
3. Radcliffe-Brown, A., *The Andaman Islanders*, Cambridge, 1922.

4. **Principal manuals**: Chantepie de la Saussaye, P.D., *Manuel d'histoire des religions*, trans. from German, 2nd ed. (eds H. Hubert and I. Lévy), Paris, 1904. Frazer, Sir J.G., *Le cycle du rameau d'or*, trans., 12 vols (after 3rd English ed.), Paris, 1921–35. *HERE*, 1908–26. Lowie, R.H., *Primitive Religion*, New York, 1924. Radin, P., *La religion primitive*, trans., Paris, 1940. Soustelle, J., 'Les phénomènes religieux', *Encyclopédie française VII: l'espèce humaine*, 16 and 18, Paris, 1936.

   Examples of major monographs on primitive religions: Boas, F., *The Eskimo of Baffin Land and Hudson Bay*, AMNH Bulletin 15, 1901 (1902). Bogoras, W., *The Chukchee, Vol. II., Religion*, Mem. AMNH (Jesup), 7/2, New York, 1907: 276–536. Callaway, H., *The Religious System of the Amazulu*, 2nd ed., London and New York, 1897. Caso, A., *La Religion de los Aztecas*, Mexico, 1936. Codrington, R.H., *The Melanesians: Studies in their Anthropology and Folklore*, Oxford, 1891. Crooke, W., *The Popular Religion and Folklore of Northern India*, 2 vols, Westminster, 1896. Dorsey, J.O., *A Study of Siouan Cults*, ARBAE 11 (1889–90), 1894. Haddon, A.C., *Reports ...* [Chapter 7, n. 19]. Jochelson, W., *The Koryak, Vol. I: Religion and Myths*, Mem. AMNH (Jesup), 6/1, New York, 1906. Junod, H.A., *Mœurs et coutumes des Bantous*, Paris, 1936. Koch-Grünberg, T., *Von Roroima zum Orinoco ...*, Berlin, 5 vols, 1917–28. Koppers, W. (with Gusinde M.), *Unter Feuerland-Indianern: eine Forschungsreise zu den südlichsten Bewohnern der Erde*, Stuttgart, 1924. Kruyt, A.C., 'De Toradjas van de Sa'dan, Masoepoe- en Mamasarivieren', *Tijdschrift voor Indische taal-, land- en volkenkunde van het Koninklijk Bataviaasch Genootschap van Kunsten en Wetenschappen* 23, 1923: 81–173; 1924: 259–401. Leenhardt, M., see esp. *Gens ...* [Chapter 2, n. 6] (New Caledonia). Lumholtz, C., *Unknown Mexico ...*, London, 1903. Preuss, K.Th., *Religion und Mythologie der Uitoto*, Göttingen and Leipzig, 1921 and 1924 (Colombia). Rivers, W.H.R., *The Todas*, London, 1906. Seligman, C.G., *The Melanesians of British New Guinea*, Cambridge, 1910. Seligman C.G. and Seligman, B.Z., *The Veddas*, Cambridge, 1911. Spencer, B., and Gillen, F., *The Northern Tribes of Central Australia*, London, 1904 (long review by Mauss M., *AS* 8, 1903–04: 242–252). Spieth, J., *Die Religion der Eweer im Süd-Togo*, Leipzig, 1911. Strehlow, C. and Leonhardi, M. von, *Die Aranda- und Loritja-Stämme in Zentral-Australien*, Veröffentlichungen des Frankfurter Museums für Völkerkunde, Frankfurt-am-Main, 1907–20. Swanton, J.R., *Social Condition, Beliefs and Linguistic Relationship of the Tlingit Indians*, ARBAE 26 (1904–05), 1908: 391–512. Thilenius, G., *Ergebnisse der Südsee-Expedition, 1908–1910*, ser. A, Melanesia, vols 2–3; ser. B, Micronesia, vols 4–11, Hamburg (from 1933).

5. Dapper, O., *Description de l'Afrique ...*, Amsterdam, 1686.

6. On the similarity between *mana* and *mens*, see Meillet, A., *De Indo-Europaea radice *MEN- 'Mente agitare'*, Paris, 1897.

7. Dubois, H.M., *Monographie des Betsileo*, Paris, 1938.

8. [The words of Jesus (Mat. 16.18) involve play on Greek *petra* 'a rock'.]

9. For examples of investigations conducted with the use of the philological method, see: Callaway, H., *... Amazulu* [n. 4]. Riggs, S.R., *Dakota Grammar, Texts and Ethnography*, Washington, 1893. Dorsey, J.O., *A Study ...* [n. 4]. Mooney, J., *The Cherokee Ball Play*, *Am. Anth.* 3/2, 1890: 105–132; *Myths of the Cherokee*, ARBAE 19 (1897–98), 1900. Grey, Sir G., *Polynesian Mythology and Ancient Traditional History of the New Zealand Race, as furnished by their priests and chiefs*, Auckland, 1885. Spieth, J., *Ewe-Stämme*, Berlin, 1906. Gaden, H., *Proverbes et maximes peuls et toucouleurs*, Paris, 1932. Strehlow, C. and Leonhardi, M. von, *Die Aranda ...* [n. 4].

10. See especially Preuss, K.Th., *Die Nayarit-Expedition, Textaufnahmen und Beobachtungen unter mexikanischen Indianern*, Leipzig, 1912; *Die Nayarit-Expedition: I. Die Religion der Cora Indianer*, Leipzig, 1912; *Die religiosen Gesänge und Mythen einiger Stämme der mexikanischen Sierra Madre*, Leipzig, 1908. Lumholtz, C., *Symbolism of the Huichol Indians*, New York, 1900.

11. [The description in fact comes in the eighteenth of the twenty-four books.]

12. La Flesche, F., several studies of the Osage Indians published by the BAE. See especially: *The Osage Tribe: Rite of the Chiefs: Sayings of the Ancient Men*, ARBAE 36 (1914–15), 1921. Hewitt, J.N.B., *Iroquoian Cosmology*, ARBAE 21 (1899–1900), 1903.

13. See Mooney, J., *The Ghost Dance Religion and the Sioux Outbreak of 1890*, ARBAE 14 (1892–93), 1896.

14. For example: Mooney, J., *Calendar History of the Kiowa Indians*, ARBAE 17 (1895–96), 1898. Seler, E., *Die bildlichen Darstellungen der mexikanischen Jahresfeste*, Berlin, 1899.

15. **For discussion of the topic**, see: Besson, M., *Le totémisme*, Paris, 1929. Durkheim, E., *Les formes élémentaires de la vie religieuse: le système totémique en Australie*, Paris, 2nd ed., 1925; 'Sur le totémisme', *AS* 5, 1900–01: 82–122. Frazer, Sir J.G., *Totemism and Exogamy*, London, 1911, 4 vols; *Totemica, a Supplement to Totemism and Exogamy*, London, 1937. Goldenweiser, A., 'Totemism, an Analytical Study', *J. Am. Folklore* 23/88, 1910: 179–293. Koppers, W., 'Der Totemismus als menschheitsgeschichtliches Problem', *Anthropos* 31, 1936: 159–176. Mauss, M., 'Note' in *AS* 8, 1903–04: 235–238. Gennep, A. van, *L'état actuel du problème totémique*, Paris, 1920.

  On totemic systems: Elkin, A.P., studies in *Oceania* since 1937. Gusinde, Father M., *Vierte Reise zum Feuerlandstamm der Ona*, 3 vols, Mödling-bei-Wien, 1931. Parkinson, R., *Dreissig Jahre in der Südsee* (Bismarck und Solomon), Stuttgart, 1907. Strehlow, C. and Leonhardi, M. von, *Die Aranda* ... [n. 4].

  Religious systems with advanced totemism: Boas, F., *Ethnology of the Kwakiutl* ... [Chapter 7, n. 19]. Fletcher, A.C. and La Flesche, F., *The Omaha Tribe*, ARBAE 27 (1905–06), 1911. Laval, P.H., *Mangareva: l'histoire ancienne d'un peuple polynésien*, Paris, Geuthner, 1938. Neuhauss, R., *Deutsch Neu-Guinea*, 3 vols, Berlin, 1911. Parsons, E.C., *American Indian Life*, New York, 1923. Radin, P., *The Winnebago Tribe*, ARBAE 37 (1915–16), 1923. Seligmann, C.G., *The Melanesians of British New Guinea*, Cambridge, 1910. Teit, J., *The Shuswap*, Mem. AMNH (Jesup, vols 2 and 7), New York, 1909. Thalbitzer, W., *The Ammassalik Eskimo*, Copenhagen, 1923.

16. This seems to me a purely dialectical issue. See Schmidt, W., *Origine et évolution de la religion*, trans. from German, Paris, 1931.

17. Trilles, R.P., *Les Pygmées de la forêt équatoriale*, Paris, 1933.

18. Moret, A., *La royauté dans l'Egypte primitive: totems et pharaons*, Paris, 1913.

19. See the studies by Strehlow, T.G.H. in the journal *Oceania*.

20. Radin, P., *The Winnebago Tribe* ... [n. 15].

21. See the above-mentioned studies by Strehlow, T.G.H. [n. 19].

22. See Hollis, A.C., *The Masai, their Language and Folklore*, Oxford, 1905.

23. Robertson Smith, W., *Lectures on the Religion of the Semites*, 3rd ed., London, 1927.

24. For examples of major tribal cults, see: Bogoras, W., *The Chukchee* ... [n. 4]. Dennett, R.E., *Nigerian Studies or the Religions and Political System of the Yoruba*, London, 1910. Driberg, J.H., *The Lango: a Nilotic Tribe of Uganda*, London, 1923. Jochelson, W., *The Koryak* ... [n. 4]. Mooney, J., *The Cheyenne Indians*, Mem. AAA 1, 1910: 357–478. Rattray, R.S., *Ashanti*, Oxford, 1923; *Religion and Art in Ashanti*, Oxford, 1927. Rivers, W.H.R., *The Todas* [n. 4]. Roscoe, J., *The Bakitara of Banyoro. The Banyankole. The Bagesu and Other Tribes of the Ugandan Protectorate*, 3 vols, Cambridge, 1923–24. Spieth, J., *Die Religion* ... [n. 4]. Talbot, P.A., *Life in Southern Nigeria*, London, 1923.

25. Deacon, A.B., *Malekula, a Vanishing People*, London, 1934.

26. Wirz, P., *Die Marind-anim von Holländisch-Süd-Neu-Guinea*, Hamburg, 1922.

27. See Frazer, Sir J.G., *Egypt and Negro Africa: a Study in Divine Kingship*, London, 1934.

28. Best, Elsdon [reference not given].

29. A very fine example of such a study is Leenhardt, M., *Gens* ... [Chapter 2, n. 6]; see also Crooke, W., *The Popular Religion* ... [n. 4].

30. Rivers, W.H.R., *The Todas* [n. 4].

31. See Oldenberg, H., *The Grhya Sūtras*, Sacred Books of the East 29–30, 1886–92.

32. See Granet, M., 'Le dépôt de l'enfant sur le sol', *Revue archéologique*, 1922.

33. On the notion of the person, see Mauss, M., 'Une catégorie de l'esprit humain: la notion de personne, celle de "moi"' (Huxley Memorial lecture, 1938), *JRAI*, 1938.

34. See Crawley, E., *The Mystic Rose: a Study of Primitive Marriage*, London, 1902. (See the review in *AS*, 1901–02.)

35. On death ceremonies, see notably Hertz, R., 'Contribution à une étude sur la representation collective de la mort', *AS* 10, 1905–06: 48–137.

36. See Steinmetz, S.R., 'Endokannibalismus', in *Gesammelte kleinere Schriften zur Ethnologie und Soziologie*, Groningen, 1928.

37. See Westermarck, E., *Survivances païennes dans la civilisation mahométane*, trans., Paris, Payot, 1935.

38. Major studies of rites: Dorsey, G.A., *The Cheyenne*, I, *Ceremonial Organisation*; II, *The Sundance*, Field Columbian Museum Publ., 99,103, Anthrop. Series (1905), vol. 9/1–2, Chicago, 1906. Fewkes, J.W., *Tusayan Snake Ceremonies*, ARBAE 16 (1894–95), 1897: 267–312; *Tusayan Katcinas*, ARBAE 15 (1893–94), 1897: 245–315; *The Alosaka Cult of the Hopi Indians*, Am. Anth, 1/1, 1899: 522–599. Lumholtz, C., *The Huichol Indians of Mexico*, AMNH Bulletin 10, 1898. Parsons, E. C., *The Scalp Ceremonies of Zuñi*, Mem. AAA 31, 1924. Teit, J., *The Thompson Indians of British Columbia*, Mem. AMNH (Jesup), vol. 1, Anthrop. ser. 3, 1900. Gennep, A. van, *Les rites de passage*, Paris, 1909. Voth, H.R., *Hopi Proper Names*, Field Columbian Museum, Anthrop. ser. 6/3, Chicago, 1905: 65–113; *Oraibi Natal Customs and Ceremonies*, ibid. 6/2, 1905: 47–61.
39. Frazer, Sir J.G., *Tabous et périls de l'âme*, trans., Paris, 1927 (2nd part of the cycle of the *Golden Bough*).
40. Fletcher, A.C., *The Hako: a Pawnee Ceremony*, ARBAE 22 (1900), 1904.
41. Hubert, H. and Mauss, M., 'Essai sur la nature et la fonction du sacrifice', *AS* 2, 1897–98: 29–138.
42. For example, Owen, M.A., *Folklore of the Musquakie Indians of North America and Catalogue of Musquakie Beadwork, etc.*, Folklore Society, London, 1904. Fewkes, J.W., *Hopi Katcinas*, ARBAE 21 (1899–1900), 1903.
43. See Fewkes, J.W., *The Tusayan Ritual: a Study of the Influence of Environment on Aboriginal Cults*, Smiths. Inst. Annual Report, 1895; 'A Few Summer Ceremonials at the Tusayan Pueblos', *J. Am. Ethnology and Archaeology* 2, 1892; 'The Sacrificial Element in Hopi Worship', *J. Am. Folklore* 10/38, 1897; 'The Winter Solstice Ceremony at Walpi', *Am. Anth.* 9, 1898.
44. Dennett, R.E., *At the back ...* [Chapter 7, n. 8] offers a good illustration.
45. Hubert, H., 'Etude sommaire de la représentation du temps dans la religion et la magie', *Annuaire de l'EPHE*, Paris, 1905.
46. On the fair, see Jullian, C., 'Feria' in C. Daremberg and E. Saglio, *Dictionnaire des antiquités grecques et latines*, Paris, 1877–1906.
47. See Hubert, H. and Mauss, M., 'Essai ...', [n. 41]. Preuss, K.Th., 'Der Ursprung der Menschenopfer in Mexico', *Globus* 86, 1904: 108 ff.
48. On prayer, see Mauss, M., *La Prière*, no date, no place of publ. [*Oeuvres*, vol. 1]. Sabatier, A., 'Prière', in *Dictionnaire protestant*. Maspero, G., *Les inscriptions des pyramides de Saqqarah*, Paris, 1894. Moret, A., *Le rituel du culte divin journalier en Egypte ...*, Paris, 1902.
49. Meillet, A., *Quelques hypothèses sur des interdictions de vocabulaire dans les langues indo-européennes*, Chartres, 1906.
50. Martrou, L., 'Les Eki des Fang', *Anthropos*, 1906: 745–761. Seidel, H., 'System der Fetischverbote in Togo', *Globus* 73/21, 1898: 340–344, and 73/22: 355–359.
51. See Hertz, R., 'Le péché et l'expiation dans les sociétés primitives', *RHR*, 1922. Standing, H.J. and Jully, F., 'Les Fady malgaches', *Bulletin trimestriel de l'Académie malgache* 3/2, 1904.
52. See especially: Bastian, A., *Die Heilige Sage der Polynesier, Kosmogonie und Theogonie*, Leipzig, 1881; *Zur Mythologie und Psychologie der Negritier in Guinea ...*, Berlin, 1894. Boas, F., *Tsimshian Mythology*, ARBAE 31 (1909–10), 1916. Bogoras, W., *The Chukchee ...* [n. 4]. Cushing, F.H., *Outlines of Zuñi Creation Myths*, ARBAE 13, 1891–92, 1896. Dennett, R.E., *At the Back ...* [Chapter 7, n. 8]. Granet, M., *La pensée chinoise*, Paris, 1934. Hentze, C., *Mythes et symboles lunaires*, Antwerp, 1932. Kroeber, A., *The Arapaho*, IV, 'Religion', AMNH Bulletin, New York, 1907: 267–465. Kruyt, A.C., *Het animisme in den Indischen Archipel*, The Hague, 1906. All the works of Lévy-Bruhl, L., especially *La mythologie primitive*, Paris, 1935. The Mem. AMNH, Anthrop., (Jesup) 2/2. Boas, F., *The Mythology of the Bella Coola Indians*, vol. 3/1. Lumholtz, C., *Symbolism ...* [n. 10]. Mooney, J., *Myths of the Cherokee*, ARBAE 19 (1897–98), 1900. Soustelle, J., *La Pensée cosmologique des anciens Mexicains*, Paris, 1940. Tylor, E.B., *Primitive Culture*, London, 1920 (6th ed.). Usener, H., 'Dreiheit', *Rheinisches Museum f. Philologie* n.F., 58, 1903.
53. On shamanism, see Nioradze, G., *Der Schamanismus bei den sibirischen Völkern*, Stuttgart, 1925.
54. Tremearne, A.J.N., *The Ban of the Bori*, London, 1914.
55. Bergaigne, A., *La religion védique*, Paris, 1878–83.
56. Powell, J.W., Prefaces to the first twenty volumes of the BAE. See also Darmesteter, A., *La vie des mots étudiés dans leur signification*, Paris, 1887.

57. [A compilation of magic and occult lore, first published in 1520, and widely distributed in the nineteenth century.]
58. See Diels, H., *Elementum*, Leipzig, 1899.
59. Preuss, K.Th., *Religion* ... [n. 4].
60. Hewitt, J.N.B., 'Orenda and a Definition of Religion', *Am. Anth.* 4, 1902.
61. See Durkheim, E. and Mauss, M., 'De quelques formes primitives de classification ...', *AS* 6, 1901–02: 1–72.
62. On the external soul, see Hartland, E.S., *The Legend of Perseus* ..., 3 vols, London, 1894–96.
63. See Granet, M., *Danses et légendes de la Chine ancienne*, Paris, 1926.
64. See Landtmann, G., *The Folk Tales of the Kiwai Papuan*, Helsinki, 1917. Boas, F., *Tsimshian Mythology* ... [n. 52]. Cushing, F.H., *Outlines* ... [n. 52]. Bülow, W. von, 'Die Geschichte des Stammvaters der Samoaner', *IAE* 11, 1898: 6–51.
65. Hartland, E.S., *The Legend* ... [n. 62]. Teit, J., *Traditions of the Thompson River Indians of British Columbia* ..., Mem. Amer. Folklore Society 6, 1898. Curtin, J., *Creation Myths of Primitive America in Relation to the Religious History of Mental Development in Mankind*, London, 1899.
66. [*Fabula* (from *fari* 'to say') is not in fact a diminutive.]
67. See H. Hubert's preface to Czarnowski, S., *Le culte des héros et ses conditions sociales: Saint Patrick, héros national de l'Irlande*, Paris, 1919.
68. On the science of tales, see Hartland, E.S., *The Science of Fairy Tales* ..., London, 1891. Cosquin, E., *Contes populaires de Lorraine* ..., Paris, 1886.
69. See Schurtz, H., *Altersklassen und Männerbunde*, Berlin, 1902. Crooke, W., *The Popular Religion* ... [n. 4]. Webster, H., *Primitive Secret Societies*, New York, 1908. Westermarck, E., *Survivances* ... [n. 37]; *Cérémonies du mariage au Maroc*, trans., Paris, 1921.
70. Seligmann, C., *Egypt and Negro Africa*, London, 1934. Frazer, Sir J.G., *Les origines magiques de la royauté*, trans., Paris, 1920. Bloch, M., *Les rois thaumaturges*, Strasbourg and Paris, 1924.
71. [Taking *dieux* as a misprint for *lieux*.]
72. See Mooney, J., *The Ghost Dance* ... [n. 13].
73. General works on magic: Hubert, H. and Mauss, M., 'Esquisse d'une théorie générale de la magie', *AS* 7, 1902–03: 108 ff. Marett, R.R., 'Magic', in *HERE*. Mauss, M., 'L'origine des pouvoirs magiques dans les sociétés australiennes', *Annuaire de l'EPHE, V^e section*, Paris, 1904, reprinted in Hubert, H. and Mauss, M., *Mélanges d'histoire des religions*, 2nd ed., Paris, 1929. Preuss, K.Th., 'Der Ursprung der Religion und der Kunst', *Globus* 86, 1904: 321–327, 355–363, 376–380, 389–393; *Globus* 87, 1905: 333–337, 347–351, 380–384, 394–400, 413–419. Rivers, W.H.R., *Medicine, Magic and Religion*, London, 1924. Vierkandt, A., 'Wechselwirkungen beim Ursprung von Zauberbräuchen', *Archiv f. die Gesamte Psychologie* 2, 1903: 81–93.
    Monographs on magic: Cuisinier, J., *Danses magiques de Kelantan*, Paris, 1936 (Malay peninsula). Doutté, E., *Magie et religion dans l'Afrique du Nord*, Algiers, 1909. Evans-Pritchard, E.E., *Witchcraft, Oracles and Magic among the Azande*, Oxford, 1937. Fortune, R., *Magicians of Dobu*, London, 1932 (Melanesia). Henry, V., *La magie dans l'Inde antique*, Paris, 1904. Malinowski, B., *Coral Gardens and their Magic*, London, 1935, 2 vols (Melanesia). Mooney, J., *Sacred Formulas of the Cherokees*, ARBAE 7 (1885–86), 1891 (Plains Indians). Seler, E., *Zauberei und Zauberer im alten Mexico*, Berlin, 1899. Skeat, W.W., *Malay Magic*, London, 1900. See also the October 1935 issue of *Africa*, which is devoted entirely to the study of magic in Black societies.
74. Cf. Huvelin, P., 'Magie et droit individuel', *AS* 10, 1905–06: 1–47.
75. See especially: Arnim, H.F.A. von, *Plutarch über Dämonen und Mantik*, Amsterdam, 1921. Bouché-Leclercq, A., *Histoire de la divination dans l'antiquité*, Paris, 1879–82. Contenau, G., *La divination chez les Assyriens et les Babyloniens*, Paris, Payot, 1940. Maupoil, B., *La géomancie à l'ancienne Côte des Esclaves*, Paris, 1943 (1945). Monteil, Ch., *La divination chez les Noirs de l'Afrique occidentale française*, Paris, 1932. Skeat, W.W., *Malay Magic* [n. 73].
76. Skeat, W.W., *Malay Magic* [n. 73]

Index

Peoples, Periods, Places, Languages
(Book titles have not been indexed.)

Individuals and Writers